KU-391-851

THE MINI ROUGH GUIDE TO

PARIS

Forthcoming travel guides include

The Algarve • The Bahamas • Cambodia
Caribbean Islands • Costa Brava • Zanzibar

Forthcoming reference guides include

Cult TV • Elvis • Weather

Rough Guides online

www.roughguides.com

Rough Guide Credits

Text editor: Ruth Blackmore
Series editor: Mark Ellingham
Proofreading: Gareth Nash
Typesetting: Katie Pringle
Cartography: Maxine Repath, Ed Wright
and Katie Lloyd-Jones

Publishing Information

This first edition published May 2001
by Rough Guides Ltd,
62–70 Shorts Gardens, London WC2H 9AH
Reprinted May 2002.

Distributed by the Penguin Group:

Penguin Books Ltd, 80 Strand, London WC2R ORL
Penguin Putnam, Inc. 375 Hudson Street, New York 10014, USA
Penguin Books Australia Ltd, 487 Maroondah Highway,
PO Box 257, Ringwood, Victoria 3134, Australia
Penguin Books Canada Ltd, 10 Alcorn Avenue,
Toronto, Ontario, Canada M4V 1E4
Penguin Books (NZ) Ltd,
182–190 Wairau Road, Auckland 10, New Zealand

Typeset in Bembo and Helvetica to an original design by Henry Iles.
Printed in Spain by Graphy Cems.

No part of this book may be reproduced in any form
without permission from the publisher except for the
quotation of brief passages in reviews.

© Rough Guides 2001. 400pp, includes index
A catalogue record for this book is available from the British Library.

ISBN 1-85828-679-4

The publishers and authors have done their best to ensure
the accuracy and currency of all the information in
The Rough Guide to Paris, however, they
can accept no responsibility for any loss, injury or
inconvenience sustained by any traveller as a result of
information or advice contained in the guide.

THE MINI ROUGH GUIDE TO

PARIS

by Rachel Kaberry
and Amy K. Brown

ROUGH
GUIDES

We set out to do something different when the first Rough Guide was published in 1982. Mark Ellingham, just out of university, was travelling in Greece. He brought along the popular guides of the day, but found they were all lacking in some way. They were either strong on ruins and museums but went on for pages without mentioning a beach or taverna. Or they were so conscious of the need to save money that they lost sight of Greece's cultural and historical significance. Also, none of the books told him anything about Greece's contemporary life – its politics, its culture, its people, and how they lived.

So with no job in prospect, Mark decided to write his own guidebook, one which aimed to provide practical information that was second to none, detailing the best beaches and the hottest clubs and restaurants, while also giving hard-hitting accounts of every sight, both famous and obscure, and providing up-to-the-minute information on contemporary culture. It was a guide that encouraged independent travellers to find the best of Greece, and was a great success, getting shortlisted for the Thomas Cook travel guide award, and encouraging Mark, along with three friends, to expand the series.

The Rough Guide list grew rapidly and the letters flooded in, indicating a much broader readership than had been anticipated, but one which uniformly appreciated the Rough Guide mix of practical detail and humour, irreverence and enthusiasm. Things haven't changed. The same four friends who began the series are still the caretakers of the Rough Guide mission today: to provide the most reliable, up-to-date and entertaining information to independent-minded travellers of all ages, on all budgets.

We now publish more than 150 titles and have offices in London and New York. The travel guides are written and researched by a dedicated team of more than 100 authors, based in Britain, Europe, the USA and Australia. We have also created a unique series of phrasebooks to accompany the travel series, along with an acclaimed series of music guides, and a best-selling pocket guide to the Internet and World Wide Web. We also publish comprehensive travel information on our Web site: www.roughguides.com

Help us update

We've gone to a lot of trouble to ensure that this Rough Guide is as up to date and accurate as possible. However, things do change and all suggestions, comments and corrections are much appreciated, and we'll send a copy of the next edition (or any other Rough Guide if you prefer) for the best letters.

Please mark letters "Rough Guide Paris Update" and send to:

Rough Guides, 62–70 Shorts Gardens, London WC2H 9AH, or Rough Guides, 4th Floor, 345 Hudson St, New York NY 10014.

Or send email to: mail@roughguides.co.uk
Online updates about this book can be found on Rough Guides' Web site (see opposite)

Acknowledgements

Amy would like to thank Edward Hillis, Elsa Hillis, Bill Brown and Grais Brown. At Rough Guides, the authors and editor are grateful to Katie Pringle for typesetting; Maxine Repath, Ed Wright and Katie Lloyd-Jones for maps; and Gareth Nash for proofreading.

CONTENTS

CONTENTS

MAP LIST

Introduction

t's little wonder that so many wistful songs have been penned over the years about France's capital, **Paris**. Few cities leave the visitor with such vivid impressions, whether it's the drifting cherry blossoms in the tranquil gardens of Notre-Dame, the riverside quais on a summer evening, the sound of blues in atmospheric cellar bars, or the ancient alleyways and cobbled lanes of the historic Latin Quarter and villagey Montmartre.

Paris has no problem living up to the painted images and movie myths with which we're all familiar. Indeed, the whole city is something of a work of art. Two thousand years of shaping and reshaping have resulted in monumental buildings, sweeping avenues, grand esplanades and celebrated bridges. Many of its older buildings have survived intact, having been spared the ravages of flood and fire and saved from Hitler's intended destruction. Moreover, they survive with a sense of continuity and homogeneity, as new sits comfortably against a backdrop of old – the glass Pyramid against the grand fortress of the Louvre, the Column of Liberty against the Opéra Bastille. Time has acted as judge, as buildings once surrounded in controversy – the Eiffel Tower, the Sacré-Cœur, the Pompidou Centre – have in their turn become well-known symbols of the city. Yet for all the tremendous pomp and magnificence of its monuments, the city operates on a very human scale, with exquisite, secretive little nooks tucked away off the Grands Boulevards and very definite little communities revolving around games of boules and the local boulangerie and café.

Architecturally, the **Cathédrale de Notre-Dame**, **Sainte-Chapelle** and the **Palais du Louvre**, in the city's centre, provide a constant reminder of Paris's religious and royal past. The backdrop of the streets is predominantly Neoclassical, the result of nineteenth-century development designed to reflect the power of the French state. Each period since, however, has added, more or less discreetly, novel examples of its own styles – with **Auguste Perret**, **Le Corbusier**, **Mallet-Stevens** and **Eiffel** among the early twentieth-century innovators. In recent decades, the architectural additions have been more dramatic in scale, producing new and major landmarks, and recasting down-at-heel districts into important centres of cultural and consumer life. New buildings such as **La Villette**, **La Grande Arche de la Défense**, the **Opéra Bastille**, the **Institut du Monde Arabe** and the **Bibliothèque Nationale** have expanded the dimensions of the city, pointing it determinedly towards the future.

Paris's **museums and galleries**, not least the mighty **Louvre**, number among the world's finest. The tradition of state cultural endowment is very much alive in the city and collections are exceedingly well displayed and cared for. Many are also housed in beautiful locations, such as old mansions and palaces, others in bold conversions, most famously the **Musée d'Orsay**, which occupies a former train station. The Impressionists here and at the **Musée Marmottan**, the moderns at the **Palais de Tokyo**, the smaller **Picasso** and **Rodin** museums – all repay a visit. In addition, the contemporary scene is well represented in the **commercial galleries** that fill the Marais, St-Germain, the Bastille and the area around the Champs-Élysées, and there's an ever-expanding range of museums devoted to other areas of human endeavour – science, history, decoration, fashion and performance art.

Few cities can compete with the thousand-and-one **cafés**, **bars** and **restaurants** that line every Parisian street and boulevard. The variety of style and décor, cuisine and price is hard to beat too. Traditional French food has become increasingly innovative and the many ethnic origins represented among the city's millions have opened eateries providing a range of gastronomic options for every palate and pocket.

The city entertains best at night, with a deserved reputation for outstanding **film** and **music**. Paris's cinematic prowess is marked by annual film festivals, with a refreshing emphasis on art, independent and international films. Music is equally revered, with nightly offerings of excellent jazz, top-quality classical, avant-garde experimental, international rock, West African *soukous* and French–Caribbean *zouk*, Algerian *raï*, and traditional *chansons*.

If you've time, you should certainly venture out of the city to one of the worthy attractions detailed in Chapter 13 of the *Guide*. The region surrounding the capital – the Île de France – is dotted with cathedrals and châteaux as stunning and steeped in history as the city itself – **Chartres**, **Versailles** and **Fontainebleau**, for example. An equally accessible excursion from the capital is that most un-French of attractions, **Disneyland Paris**, covered in Chapter 21.

When to go

The best time to visit Paris is largely a question of personal taste. The city has a more reliable **climate** than Britain, with uninterrupted stretches of sun (or rain) year-round.

However, while it maintains a vaguely southern feel for anyone crossing the English Channel, Mediterranean it is not. Winter temperatures drop well below freezing, with sometimes biting winds. If you're lucky, spring and autumn will be mild and sunny; in summer it can reach the 30s°C (80s°F).

In terms of pure aesthetics, winter sun is the city's most flattering light, when the pale shades of the older buildings become luminescent and long shadows criss-cross the parks. By contrast, Paris in high summer can be unpleasant, with the fumes of congested traffic becoming trapped within the high narrow streets, and the reflected light in the city's open spaces too blinding to enjoy.

One of the quietest times of year to visit is during the **French summer holidays** from July 15 to the end of August, when large numbers of Parisians flee the city for the coast or mountains. However, a lot of Paris's shops and restaurants will be closed during this period. There is, too, the **commercial calendar** to consider – fashion shows, trade fairs and the like. Paris hoteliers warn against visiting during the months of September and October, and **finding a room** even at the best of times can be problematic. Early spring, autumn if you book ahead, or the midwinter months will be most rewarding.

Paris's climate

	F°		C°		RAINFALL	
	AVERAGE DAILY		AVERAGE DAILY		AVERAGE MONTHLY	
	MAX	MIN	MAX	MIN	IN	MM
Jan	43	34	6	1	2.2	56
Feb	45	34	7	1	1.8	46
March	54	39	12	4	1.4	35
April	60	43	16	6	1.7	42
May	68	49	20	10	2.2	57
June	73	55	23	13	2.1	54
July	76	58	25	15	2.3	59
Aug	75	58	24	14	2.5	64
Sept	70	53	21	12	2.2	55
Oct	60	46	16	8	2.0	50
Nov	50	40	10	5	2.0	51
Dec	44	36	7	2	2.0	50

THE GUIDE

Introducing the city

Geography and history have combined to give Paris a remarkably coherent and intelligible structure. The city lies in a basin surrounded by hills. It is very nearly circular, confined within the limits of the the ring road, the boulevard périphérique, which follows the line of the city's nineteenth-century fortifications. The capital's raison d'être and its lifeline, the **River Seine**, flows east to west, carving the city in two. Anchored at the hub of the circle, in the middle of the river, is the island from which the rest of Paris grew: the **Île de la Cité**, home of the capital's oldest religious and secular institutions – Notre Dame cathedral and the Palais de Justice.

The north or **Right Bank** (*rive droite*) of the Seine is characterized by imposing government buildings, sweeping vistas and elegant boulevards. The longest and grandest thoroughfare is the so-called **Voie Triomphale**, which runs from the Louvre to the Grande Arche de la Défense in the northwest, taking in the Tuileries gardens, Champs-Élysées and Arc de Triomphe, each monument an expression of royal or state power across the centuries. To the immediate north and east of the Voie Triomphale spread the commercial and financial quarters, site of the stock exchange, the refurbished nineteenth-century *passages* and Les Halles shopping centre. Just to the east of Les Halles lie the **Marais** and **Bastille** quarters, two of the city's liveliest and most happening areas.

The south bank of the river, or **Left Bank** (*rive gauche*), owes its existence to the cathedral school of Notre-Dame, which spilled over from the Île de la Cité and became the university of the Sorbonne, attracting scholars and students from all over the medieval world. Ever since, it has been the traditional domain of academics, writers and artists.

The city is divided into twenty **arrondissements**, whose spiral arrangement provides a fairly accurate guide to its historical growth. Centred on the Louvre, they wind outwards in a clockwise direction. The inner hub of the city comprises arrondissements 1er to 6e, and it's here that most of the major sights and museums are to be found. The outer or higher-number arrondissements were mostly incorporated into the city in the nineteenth century – some, such as

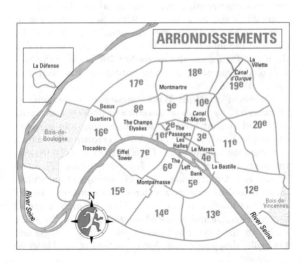

Montmartre, **Belleville** and **Passy**, have succeeded in retaining something of their separate village identity. Historically, the districts to the west attracted the aristocracy and the newly rich, while those to the east accommodated mainly the poor and the working class, distinctions which largely hold true to this day, though much of the east is gradually being gentrified.

Paris is not particularly well endowed with parks. The largest, the **Bois de Boulogne** and the **Bois de Vincennes**, at the western and eastern limits of the city respectively, do possess small pockets of interest, but are largely anonymous sprawls. For a break from the bustle of the city, it is best to try an out-of-town excursion, to the gardens of **Giverny**, for example, or the forest of **Fontainebleau**.

Arrival

Whatever your point of arrival, it's fairly easy to get into central Paris. The city's **airports** are well served by trains, buses and taxis. Paris's **train stations** are all very central with direct access to the métro and RER network, while the main **bus station**, just outside the city proper, is close to a métro station.

BY AIR

The two main Paris airports dealing with international flights are Roissy Charles de Gaulle and Orly, known collectively as the *Aéroports de Paris*. Both have bureaux de change and information desks providing free maps and accommodation listings.

ARRIVAL

Roissy Charles de Gaulle Airport

Some 23km to the northeast of the city, **Roissy–Charles de Gaulle Airport** (24hr information in English ☎01.48.62.22.80), often referred to simply as Charles de Gaulle and abbreviated to CDG or Paris CDG, has two main terminals – CDG1 and CDG2. The quickest way into the centre is the express **Roissyrail** link (every 15min 5am till midnight), which runs on line B of the RER, the suburban train network (see p.14). There is direct access from CDG2 to the station, while CDG1 is connected to the RER by a free shuttle. It takes thirty minutes to get to Gare du Nord and goes on to stop at Châtelet-les-Halles, St-Michel and Denfert-Rochereau, all with connections to the métro. Tickets cost 49F/€7.47. When it comes to **leaving Paris**, all but the first train of the day depart from platform 43 of Gare du Nord, where there is an English-speaking information desk (daily 8am–8pm). Ordinary commuter trains also run on this line, but make more stops and have fewer facilities for luggage storage.

You've also got the choice of three **bus** services operated by Air France (information in English ☎01.41.56.89.00). The green-coded line 2 (60F/€9.15 one-way, 105F/€16 return) leaves from CDG2 every twelve minutes from 5.40am to 11pm, terminating at Porte Maillot métro station on the northwest edge of the city, and going via avenue Carnot, outside Charles-de-Gaulle-Étoile RER/métro between the Arc de Triomphe and rue Tilsitt. The yellow-coded line 4 (70F/€10.67 one-way, 120F/€18.29 return) departs from both CDG1 and CDG2 every thirty minutes from 7am to 9pm, terminating near Gare Montparnasse and stopping off en route at Gare de Lyon; journey times vary from 25 minutes to over an hour in rush hour. On the way back, the green-coded line 2 (for CDG2) departs from avenue Carnot, right outside the RER exit of Charles-de-

BY AIR

Gaulle-Étoile, and from Porte Maillot. The yellow-coded line 4 (for both CDG1 and CDG2) leaves from 2bis boulevard Diderot outside Gare de Lyon and near Gare Montparnasse at rue du Commandant-René-Mouchotte in front of the *Méridien Hotel*.

A cheaper bus option is the **Roissybus** (48F/€7.32), which connects CDG2 with the Opéra-Garnier (corner of rues Auber and Scribe; RER Auber/Métro Opéra). It runs every fifteen minutes from 5.45am to 11pm and takes around 45 minutes.

Highly convenient is the **Airport Shuttle**, a minibus door-to-door airport service, with no extra charge for luggage (89F/€13.57 per head if there are more than two people, 120F/€18.29 for a single person; advance bookings – English-speaking – on ℡01.45.38.55.72, ℻01.43.21 .35.67, ⓦ*www.airportshuttle.fr*). Alternatively, **taxis** into central Paris from CDG cost 205F/€31.25 minimum, plus a small luggage supplement (6F/€1 per piece of luggage), and should take between fifty minutes and an hour.

**Information on Paris's airports is
available online at *www.adp.fr***

Orly Airport

Orly Airport, 14km south of Paris, has three connections to RER lines and a choice of buses. The quickest option is the **Orlyval** (every 5–7min Mon–Sat 6am–10.30pm, Sun and Hols 7am–11pm; 57F/€8.69), a fast train shuttle to RER station Anthony where you can continue on to central Paris via RER line B, with métro connections at Denfert-Rochereau, St-Michel, Châtelet-les-Halles and Gare du Nord. It takes around thirty minutes to reach the centre. Also fairly swift is the **Orlybus** to Denfert-

BY AIR

Rochereau RER/métro station in the 14e (every 15–20 min 6am–11.30pm); journey time is thirty minutes and tickets cost 35F/€5.34. Going the other direction, the bus departs from place Denfert-Rochereau (every 15–20min 5.45am–11pm).

Slightly longer, but cheaper, **Orlyrail** is a bus–rail link to central Paris; a shuttle bus goes to RER station Pont de Rungis (line C), from where the Orlyrail train leaves every fifteen minutes from 5.45am to 9pm, half-hourly thereafter until 11pm, for the Gare d'Austerlitz and other métro connections (30F/€4.57; total journey around 50min).

Air France buses (information in English ☎01.41.56.89.00) connect Orly with the Invalides Air France terminus via Montparnasse (also stopping at Porte d'Orléans and Duroc if requested in advance). The 35-minute service leaves every 12 minutes from 6am to 11.30pm, and costs 45F/€6.86 one-way, 75F/€11.43 return. **On the way back**, the bus can be caught from the Invalides Air France Terminal and from Montparnasse on rue du Commandant-René-Mouchotte in front of the *Méridien Hotel*: departures are every 12 minutes from 5.45am to 11pm. Alternatively, **Jetbus** runs to Villejuif-Louis Aragon métro, the terminus of line 7, every 12 to 15 minutes from 6am to 10.15pm. It takes 15 minutes and costs 24F/€3.66 (you will then need a métro ticket to get into the centre).

A **taxi** will take around 35 minutes to the centre of Paris and cost at least 130F/€19.82. The **Airport Shuttle** door-to-door minibus service (see p.7) is also offered to and from Orly.

Disneyland Paris is linked by bus from both Charles de Gaulle and Orly airports; for details of these services, plus train links from the centre to the purpose-built Marne-La-Vallée TGV, see p.306.

BY TRAIN AND BUS

Eurostar trains (℡08.36.35.35.39, ⓦ*www.eurostar.com*) from Britain terminate at **Gare du Nord**, rue Dunkerque, 10ᵉ. From here there are connections to the métro and RER. Arriving by train from somewhere in France or neighbouring countries, you'll come into one of Paris's numerous mainline stations, all of which are connected to the métro.

Eurolines (℡01.49.72.51.51, ⓦ*www.eurolines.fr*) and almost all **buses** coming into Paris – whether international or domestic – use the **main gare routière** on the eastern edge of the city at 28 avenue du Général-du-Gaulle, Bagnolet. The métro station here (Mᵒ Galliéni), the terminus of line 3, provides a link to the centre.

BY CAR

If you're **driving** into Paris, don't try to go straight across the city to your destination. Use the ring road – the **boulevard périphérique** – to get to the *porte* nearest to your destination: it's much quicker, except at rush hour, and easier to find your way at any time. Once ensconced at your accommodation, you'd be well advised to park the car at your hotel and use public transport, as **parking** is a major problem in the city centre.

Information

The **main tourist office** is at 127 avenue des Champs-Élysées, 8ᵉ (April–Sept Mon–Sat 9am–8pm, Sun 11am–7pm, closed May 1; Oct–March Mon–Sat 9am–8pm, Sun 11am–6pm; ℡08.36.68.31.12, ℻01.49.52.53.00,

PARIS ON THE INTERNET

Though we list relevant **websites** throughout the guide, below are some general sites on Paris. For information on internet access while travelling, check the "Directory" section of this guide (p.315).

Ⓦ *www.insee.fr* Website of the National Institute of Statistics and Economical Studies – France in facts and figures.

Ⓦ *www.pagesjaunes.fr* French yellow pages on-line.

Ⓦ *www.paris-france.org* Paris mairie's website for information on the day-to-day running of the city, events and visiting Paris.

Ⓦ *www.parisbalades.com* Well-orchestrated site that zooms in on Parisian localities with in-depth historical and architectural detail.

Ⓦ *www.zinqueures.com* All you need to know about Parisian bistrot life, with concerts, exhibitions and show listings.

Ⓦ *www.parissi.com* A listings website with up-to-date information on events and nightlife.

Ⓦ *www.culture.fr* A Ministry of Culture and Communication's site with press releases and links to cultural organizations throughout France.

Ⓦ *www.jazzfrance.com* Brilliant bilingual site with everything from concerts, venues and music store links.

Ⓦ *www.pariscope.fr* Mostly in French with a bit of English, this is a rendering of the popular weekly Parisian listings mag online.

Ⓦ *www.paris-touristoffice.com* The website of the Paris Tourist Office with impressive detail and useful links, though not as up-to-date as one would hope.

Ⓦ *tout.lemonde.fr* In French only; a version of the highbrow daily newspaper.

Ⓦ *www.webbar.fr* The website of Paris's best cybercafé (see p.203).

Ⓦ*www.paris-touristoffice.com*; M° Charles-de-Gaulle–Étoile). There is a **branch offices** at Gare de Lyon (Mon–Sat 8am–8pm; Ⓣ01.43.43.33.24) and also at the Eiffel Tower (April–Sept daily 11am–6pm; Ⓣ01.45.51.22.15). Each gives away plenty of brochures and leaflets, as well as maps.

For recorded **tourist information in English**, phone Ⓣ01.49.52.53.56. Alternative sources of information are the Hôtel de Ville information office, **Bureau d'Accueil**, at 29 rue de Rivoli, 4ᵉ (Mon–Sat 9am–6pm; Ⓣ01.42.76.43.43; M° Hôtel de Ville), and electronic billboards dotted around town. Within the new Carrousel du Louvre, 99 rue de Rivoli, 1ᵉʳ, below the triumphal arch at the east end of the Tuileries, you'll find the **Espace du Tourisme d'Île de France** (10am–7pm; closed Tues; Ⓣ01.44.50.19.98), with stylishly presented information on attractions and activities in Paris and the surrounding area.

For **what's on** information, one of the best sources is the free monthly, *Paris Le Journal*, published by the mairie and available at the Bureau d'Accueil (see above), as well as in museums and shops. Also good for museum and other cultural information are Paris's two listings magazines, *Pariscope* (with a small section in English) and *L'Officiel des Spectacles*, available at *tabacs* and métro stations.

Getting around

Finding your way around Paris is remarkably easy, as the city proper, stripped of its suburbs, is compact and relatively small, with an integrated public transport system – the **RATP** (Régie Autonome des Transports Parisiens). The system is cheap, fast and meticulously signposted, comprising buses, underground métro and suburban express trains, known as RER (Réseau Express Régional) trains. The whole network is divided into five **zones**, though the entire métro system fits into zones 1 and 2. Information is available online at Ⓦ *www.ratp.fr.*

At its widest point, Paris is only about 12km across, which, at a brisk pace, is not much more than a pleasant two hours' walk.

FARES AND PASSES

Tickets can be bought in **carnets** of ten from any station or *tabac* showing a green métro ticket sign; the cost is 55F/€8.38, as opposed to 8F/€1.23 for a single ticket. Only one 8F/€1.23 *billet* is ever needed per journey on the métro system. It's also valid for any journey within zones 1 and 2 on the RER or by bus, but you cannot switch between buses or between bus and métro/RER on the same ticket. Night buses require separate tickets costing 15F/€2.29 each, unless you have a weekly or monthly travel pass (see below). For RER journeys beyond zones 1 and 2, you must buy an RER ticket; visitors often get caught out, for instance, when they take the RER instead of the métro to La Défense. **Children** under four travel free and from four to ten at half price.

Be sure to keep your ticket until the end of your journey: you'll be charged a stiff fine on the spot if you can't produce one.

If you've arrived early in the week and are staying three days or more, it may be more economical to obtain a photocard, the **Carte Orange** (you'll need a passport photo –

available from the booths in the main stations), with a weekly travelcard, known as a *coupon hebdomadaire*; you'll probably want one for zones 1 and 2 to cover the city and inner suburbs. Costing 82F/€12.50, the zone 1 and 2 version is valid for an unlimited number of journeys from Monday morning to Sunday evening, and is on sale at all métro stations and *tabacs*. You can only buy a travelcard for the current week until Wednesday; from Thursday you buy a *coupon* to begin the following Monday. You need to write your *Carte Orange* number on the travelcard. There's also a monthly pass (*mensuel*), costing 279F/€42.53, for zones 1 and 2. A word of warning: the *Carte Orange* is technically for Île de France residents only, though most clerks will sell you one as a visitor.

Other options include the **Paris Visites**, 1-, 2-, 3- and 5-day visitors' passes at 50F/€7.62, 80F/€12.20, 120F/€18.29 and 170F/€25.91 for Paris and inner suburbs, or 100F/€15.24, 175F/€26.68, 245F/€37.34 and 300F/€45.73 to include the airports, Versailles and Disneyland Paris (make sure you buy this one when you arrive at Roissy Charles de Gaulle or Orly to get maximum value). A children's version is available at half price for 1, 2 or 3 days. The main advantage of *Paris Visites* passes is that, unlike the *coupon hebdomadaire*, whose validity runs unalterably from Monday to Sunday, they can begin on any day. They also allow you discounts at certain monuments, museums, shops and restaurants.

Both the *Carte Orange* and the *Paris Visites* entitle you to **unlimited travel** (in the zones you have chosen) on bus, métro, RER, SNCF and the Montmartre funicular. On the métro you put the *coupon* through the turnstile slot, but make sure you return it to its plastic folder. On the bus you show the whole *carte* to the driver as you board – you don't put it into the punching machine.

A *mobilis* **day pass** is also available, taking in all forms of RATP transport (from 30F/€4.57 for the city, 70F/€10.67 to include the outer suburbs and airports).

FARES AND PASSES

THE MÉTRO AND RER

The **métro** (M°) runs from 5.30am to 12.30am, the RER from 5am to midnight. Stations are far more frequent than on most underground systems, though many entrances are a long way from the platforms and most interchanges involve long walks and lots of stairs. A choice of three free **maps** is available at most stations: the *Grand Plan de Paris* for the whole RATP system, which also usefully overlays the métro system onto a map of Paris's streets; the more at-a-glance *Petit Plan de Paris*; or the pocket-sized *Paris Plan de Poche*. In addition, every station has a big map posted.

**A colour map of the Paris métro can be
found at the back of the *Guide*.**

The métro lines are colour-coded and numbered 1 to 14; the RER lines are designated by the letters A, B, C or D. Within the system, you find your way around by following signs bearing the name of the station at the end of the line in the direction in which you are travelling: *Direction Porte Dauphine*, *Direction Gallieni* and so on. The numerous inter-changes, or **correspondances** (look for the orange signs), make it possible to travel anywhere in the city in a more or less straight line.

For RER journeys beyond the city, make sure that the station you want is illuminated on the platform display board.

BUSES

Free **bus route maps** are available at métro stations, bus terminals and the tourist office; the best is the *Grand Plan de Paris*. Every bus stop displays the numbers of the buses that stop there, a map showing all the stops on the route, and the times of the first and last buses. Only the #20 bus is designed to be easily accessible for wheelchairs and prams. Generally speaking, buses run from around 6.30am to 8.30pm, with some services continuing to 12.30am. Many lines do not operate on Sundays and holidays, or run a reduced service.

From mid-April to mid-September, a special **Balabus** service passes all the major tourist sights between La Défense Grande Arche and Gare de Lyon, on Sundays and holidays between noon and 9pm; the entire route takes about fifty minutes. Bus stops are marked "Balabus"; standard bus fares apply.

Night buses (Noctambus) ply eighteen routes every hour from 1am to 5.30am, linking place du Châtelet, near the Hôtel de Ville, with the suburbs. Again, there is a reduced service on Sunday.

TAXIS

Taxi charges are fairly reasonable – between 40F/€6.10 and 70F/€10.67 for a central daytime journey, though considerably more if you call one out. There are three different fare rates: indicator lights on the roof of the taxi tell you which fare is being applied. "A" indicates the daytime rate (7am–7pm; around 3.45F/€0.53/km) for Paris and the boulevard périphérique; "B" is the rate for Paris at night (7pm–7am), on Sundays and on public holidays, and for the suburbs during the day (around 5.45F/€0.83/km); "C" is the night rate for the suburbs (around 7F/€1.07/km). When you get into the taxi, check that the meter shows the appropriate fare rate. In addition, there's a pick-up charge of around 13F/€1.98 and a time charge (around 120F/€18.29/hr) for when the car is stationary, an additional 5F/€0.76 charge if you're picked up from a mainline train station, and a 6F/€0.95 charge per piece of luggage.

Taxis will often refuse to take more than three people (they don't like you to sit in the front seat); if they do take you, they'll charge extra for the fourth person (about 9F/€1.37). **Tipping** is not mandatory, but ten percent will be expected. Finding one of Paris's 470 taxi ranks (*arrêt taxi*) is usually better than trying to hail one down in the street. The large white light means the taxi is free; the orange light below means it's engaged.

BOATS

A passenger boat, known as the **Batobus**, operates from May to September, stopping at six points along the Seine in this order: port de la Bourdonnais (Eiffel Tower–Trocadéro), quai de Solférino (Musée d'Orsay), quai Malaquais (Saint Germain-des-Prés), quai de Montebello (Notre-Dame), quai de l'Hôtel de Ville (Hôtel-de-Ville–Pompidou Centre) and quai du Louvre (Musée du Louvre). Boats run every thirty minutes or so from 10am to 7pm: total journey time is twenty minutes, and tickets cost 20F/€3.05 for the first stop, 10F/€1.52 for subsequent stops, or 60F/€9.15 for a day pass.

Museums and monuments

If you're planning to visit a number of museums in a short time, it's worth buying the **Carte Musées et Monuments** (1-day 80F/€12.20, 3-day 160F/€24.39, 5-day 240F/€36.59), available from the tourist office, métro stations, museums, and the Eurostar terminal at London

Waterloo. Valid for seventy museums and monuments in and around Paris, the pass allows you to bypass ticket queues (though it doesn't provide entry to special exhibitions and you will still need to queue up for security checks). **Reduced admission** is often available for those over 60 and under 18, for which you'll need your passport as proof of age, and for students under 26, for which you'll need an ISIC (International Student Identity Card). Many museums and monuments are free for children under twelve, and nearly always for kids under four. Under-26s can also get a free Youth Card, *Carte Jeune*, available in France from youth travel agencies like USIT and from main tourist offices (120F/€18.29, valid one year), which entitles you to reductions throughout Europe. Some museums have free or half-price admission on Sunday; many are closed on Monday and Tuesday.

The Islands

Elegant and calm, the two river islands at the heart of the city, the **Île de la Cité** and the **Île St-Louis**, comprise one of the most walkable, enjoyable and romantic sections of Paris.

ÎLE DE LA CITÉ

Map 2, G8. Mº Cité & Mº/RER St-Michel.

The **Île de la Cité** is where Paris began. The earliest settlement of any size was the small Gallic town of Lutetia, overrun by Julius Caesar's troops in 52BC. The Romans garrisoned it and laid out one of their standard military town plans. The town gradually established itself as an administrative centre, becoming the seat of the Merovingian kings in 508 AD, then of the counts of Paris, who in 987 AD became kings of France.

A thriving community grew up on the island and it became the city's centre of religious and political power. In the mid-nineteenth century, however, much of the medieval character of the island was erased by Baron Haussmann, Napoleon III's somewhat overzealous town planner. He demolished the homes of around 25,000 people, as well as churches, shops and lanes, in order to make way for several buildings in bland Baronial-

Bureaucratik style and to clear the space in front of the cathedral of **Notre-Dame** — the result is the large windswept square you see today.

Aside from the cathedral, the island's main sights are the **Palais de Justice**, formerly the residence of the Capetian kings; the remains of the medieval **Conciergerie**; and the Gothic **Sainte-Chapelle**. The enormous Préfecture de Police looms nearby, as does the Hôtel-Dieu, a hospital, begun under the auspices of Notre-Dame and now administered by the state. Among the island's most charming areas are the leafy **square du Vert-Galant**, the serene **place Dauphine** and the quais at its tail end.

Pont-Neuf and the quais

Map 2, F7. M° Pont-Neuf.

The best way to approach the island is via the graceful, arched **Pont-Neuf**, which despite its name is the city's oldest bridge and the first to be constructed without the traditional complement of medieval houses on it. Built in 1607 by Henri IV, whose statue stands at the end of the bridge, the Pont-Neuf is a curious mix of finely detailed carvings and eclectic styles, the result of centuries of alteration and repair.

A flight of steps leads down from the bridge to the **quais** and the **square du Vert-Galant**, a small tree-lined oasis of shade trees and sunny patches of grass tucked into the triangular stern of the island. The name *Vert-Galant*, meaning "green" or "lusty" gentleman, allegedly celebrates Henri IV's success with women. Not surprisingly, the square is popular with lovers, who make for the extreme point to enjoy the view of the city, the Seine and the sunsets. Less romantic, the north quay is the dock for the tourist river boats, the Bateaux-Vedettes du Pont-Neuf.

ÎLE DE LA CITÉ

19

For details of the Bateaux-Vedettes du Pont-Neuf
and other river boats, see p.312.

Place Dauphine and the Palais de Justice

Map 2, F7. Mº Cité.

On the eastern side of the bridge, across the street from the statue of Henri IV, seventeenth-century houses flank the entrance to the sanded, chestnut-shaded **place Dauphine**, one of the city's most secluded and exclusive squares. The far end of the square is blocked by the dull mass of the **Palais de Justice**, formerly the palace lived in by the French kings until Étienne Marcel's bloody revolt in 1358 frightened them off to the greater security of the Louvre.

Sainte-Chapelle

Map 2, F7. Daily: April–Sept 9.30am–6.30pm; Oct–March 10am–5pm; 32F/€4.88, combined ticket with Conciergerie 50F/€7.62. Mº Cité.

Within the Palais de Justice, the only part of the older complex that remains in its entirety is Louis IX's chapel, the **Sainte-Chapelle**, built to house a collection of holy relics which Louis had bought for extortionate rates from the bankrupt empire of Byzantium. During the Revolution, the chapel became an easy target for angry mobs who damaged the building and looted some of its treasures; those since salvaged are now in the treasury of Notre-Dame and the Bibliothèque Nationale.

Though much restored, the two-level chapel, consecrated in 1248, remains one of the finest achievements of French High Gothic. Very tall in relation to its length, it looks like a cathedral choir lopped off and transformed into an independent building. Its most radical feature is the exquisite **stained glass** in the upper chapel, reached by a narrow spiral staircase. The windows tell the stories of the Bible, beginning with the *Book of Genesis* (on the left), followed by the *Book of Kings*, along with the history of the relics (on the right) and ending with the *Book of Revelation* illustrated in the rose window. The seemingly pencil-thin supports, made possible by the minimal use of structural masonry, coupled with the sheer vastness of the windows, combine to create what appears to be a huge uninterrupted expanse of glowing jewel-like blues, reds and grass-green. For the most enjoyable visit, arrive early, as it becomes very busy later in the day.

The Conciergerie

Map 2, G7. Daily: April–Sept 9.30am–6.30pm; Oct–March 10am–5pm; 32F/€4.88, combined ticket with Ste-Chapelle 50F/€7.62. M° Cité.

Around the corner from the Sainte-Chapelle is the medieval **Conciergerie**, formerly the oldest prison in Paris. It's entered from quai de l'Horloge, where you'll see Paris's first public clock, built in 1370 and now fully restored. The Conciergerie was where Marie-Antoinette and, in their turn, the leading figures of the Revolution were incarcerated before execution; her cell and various macabre mementos of the guillotine's victims are really the most exciting things here. The other main point of interest is the enormous vaulted late-Gothic **Salle des Gens d'Armes**, canteen and recreation room of the royal household staff. It's amazingly well preserved, though there is little to look at beyond the impressive architecture.

The Cathédrale de Notre-Dame

Map 2, H8. Mon–Fri & Sun 8am–7pm, Sat 8am–12.30pm & 2–7pm

ÎLE DE LA CITÉ

(free); the towers are open daily April–Sept 9.30am–7.30pm; Oct–March 10am–5pm; admission to towers 32F/€4.88. M° Cité & M°/RER St-Michel.

The **Cathédrale de Notre-Dame** itself is so much photographed, painted and sketched that, seeing it even for the first time, the edge of your response may be somewhat dulled by familiarity. In recent years, however, workers have painstakingly removed decades of dirt, grime, pollution and pigeon droppings, and the results are almost startling. Now a gleaming alabaster, it is truly impressive. The great H-shaped west front, with its strong vertical divisions, is counterbalanced by the horizontal emphasis of gallery and frieze, all centred on the rose window – a solid, no-nonsense design that confesses its Romanesque ancestry. For a more fantastical kind of Gothic, look rather at the **north transept façade**, with its crocketed gables and huge fretted window-space.

Notre-Dame was begun in 1160 under the auspices of Bishop de Sully and completed around 1345. In the nineteenth century, Viollet-le-Duc carried out extensive renovation work. He added the steeple and baleful-looking gargoyles, which you can see close up if you brave the ascent of the towers, and he remade most of the statuary – the entire frieze of Old Testament kings had been damaged during the Revolution by enthusiasts who took them for the kings of France.

The cathedral's original statues are in the
Musée National du Moyen Âge, p.73.

Inside, the immediately striking feature is the dramatic contrast between the darkness of the nave and the light falling on the first great clustered pillars of the choir. It's the end walls of the transepts that admit all this light, nearly two-thirds glass, including two magnificent rose windows

coloured in imperial purple. These, the vaulting and the
soaring shafts reaching to the springs of the vaults are all
definite Gothic features, yet, inside as out, there remains a
strong Romanesque element in the stout round pillars of
the nave and the general sense of four-squareness. Free
guided tours (1hr–1hr 30min) take place in French every
weekday at noon and Saturday at 2pm, and in English on
Wednesday at noon. There are free organ recitals every
Sunday at 5 or 5.30pm, plus four Masses on Sunday morning and one at 6.30pm. The **trésor** (daily 9.30am–6pm;
15F/€2.29) is not really worth the entry fee.

The crypte archéologique
Daily: April–Sept 10am–6pm; Oct–March 10am–4.30pm; 32F/€4.88,
or 50F/€7.62 combined admission with the cathedral towers.
In the square out in front of the cathedral is what appears to
be (and smells like) the entrance to an underground toilet.
It leads, in fact, to the cathedral's crypt, which houses a
very well put together and interesting museum, the **crypte
archéologique**, revealing remains of the church that pre-
dated the cathedral, as well as streets and houses of the Cité
dating as far back as the Roman era.

> On the pavement by the west door of the cathedral is a spot
> known as **kilomètre zéro**, the symbolic heart of the country,
> from which all main road distances in France are calculated.

The Mémorial de la Déportation

Map 2, H9. Daily 10am–noon & 2–5pm; free. Mº Cité
At the eastern tip of the island is the **Mémorial de la
Déportation**, the symbolic tomb of the 200,000 French
who died in Nazi concentration camps during World War
II – Resistance fighters, Jews and forced labourers. Their

ÎLE DE LA CITÉ

moving memorial, barely visible above ground, is a kind of bunker-crypt studded with thousands of points of light representing the dead. Above the exit are the words "Forgive. Do not forget . . .".

THE ÎLE ST-LOUIS

Map 2, I8 & I9. Mº Pont-Marie & Mº Sully-Morland.

Often considered the most romantic part of Paris, the peaceful **Île St-Louis** is prime strolling territory. Unlike its larger neighbour, the Île de la Cité, it has no monuments or métro stations, and only a single, small **museum** at 6 quai d'Orléans, devoted to the Romantic Polish poet **Adam Mickiewicz** (Thurs 2–6pm or by appointment on ☎01.43.54.35.61; free). You'll find high houses on single-lane streets, tree-lined quais, a school, a church, assorted restaurants and cafés, and interesting little shops.

For centuries, Île-St-Louis was nothing but swampy pastureland, owned by Notre-Dame, until along came the seventeenth-century version of a real-estate developer, Christophe Marie, who had the bright idea of filling it with elegant mansions, so that by 1660 the island was transformed. In the 1840s, the island became a popular Bohemian hang-out. The Club des Hachichins, whose members included Baudelaire, Dumas, Delacroix and Daumier, met every month and got high on hashish at the **Hôtel Lauzun**, 17 quai d'Anjou. Baudelaire in fact lived for a while in the attic and wrote *Les Fleurs du Mal* here. The hôtel, built in 1657, has an intact interior, complete with splendid trompe l'oeil decorations; prearranged group visits are possible (☎01.42.76.57.99).

Nowadays, the island is the most covetable of the city's addresses – you only get to have your home here if you're the Aga Khan, the Pretender to the French throne, or an ex-grand duke of Russia.

A visit to the Île-St-Louis wouldn't be complete for most people without a visit to M. Berthillon at 31 rue St-Louis-en-l'Île (see p.189), makers of exceptional fruit sorbets.

The island is particularly atmospheric in the evening, and dinner here (see p.194 for restaurant recommendations), followed by an arm–in–arm wander along the quais, is a must in any lovers' itinerary.

The Louvre

Paris's largest monument is the **Louvre**, for centuries the site of the French court, and renowned today as one of the world's greatest art galleries. It began life as a fortress, built by Philippe-Auguste in 1200 as a place to store his scrolls, jewels and swords. Charles V was the first French king to actually live there, but it wasn't until the reign of François I, in the mid-sixteenth century, that the foundations of the palace were laid and the fortress demolished. From then on, almost every sovereign added to it. Twice, it came very close to being demolished. The first occasion was under Louis XIV, when Bernini was very nearly hired to redesign the palace. His proposal was to raze it to the ground and start from scratch, but fortunately, he lost the commission. The palace's other close shave came in the mid-eighteenth century, when the Louvre was taken over by artists and squatters; over a hundred different families lived around the cour Carrée. Louis XV's response was to call for its immediate destruction, but he was eventually dissuaded by his officials.

Every alteration and addition up to 1988 created a surprisingly homogeneous building, with a grandeur, symmetry and Frenchness entirely suited to this most historic of Parisian edifices. Then came the most recent addition, made by President Mitterrand as part of his Grand Louvre

THE LOUVRE

0 100 m

▶ = Entrances

Palais Royal

RUE ST-HONORÉ

RUE DE RIVOLI

Louvre-Rivoli Ⓜ

PONT DES ARTS

Cour Carrée

S U L L Y

Pavillon de l'Horloge

Ⓜ Palais Royal/ Musée du Louvre

PASSAGE RICHELIEU

Pyramid & Main Entrance

River Seine

PLACE DU PALAIS ROYAL

Cour Napoléon

D E N O N

QUAI DU LOUVRE

PONT DU CARROUSEL

RUE DE RIVOLI

R I C H E L I E U

PLACE DU CARROUSEL

AV DE L'OPERA

Comédie Française

PLACE ANDRÉ-MALRAUX

Musée de la Mode et du Textile, Musée des Arts Décoratifs & Musée de la Publicité

Arc du Carrousel

Porte des Lions

D E N O N

RUE ST-HONORÉ

Pavillon de Marsan

Jardin des Tuileries

Pavillon de Flore

QUAI DES TUILERIES

PT ROYAL

N

THE LOUVRE

●

27

renovation project – a huge glass pyramid, set bang in the centre of the cour Napoléon. It was an extraordinary leap of daring and imagination. Conceived by the Chinese-born architect Ieoh Ming Pei, it has no connection to its surroundings, save as a symbol of symmetry. Mitterrand also managed to persuade the Finance Ministry to move out of the northern Richelieu wing. Its two courtyards were roofed over in glass and now house the museum's French sculpture and the Objets d'Art collections. A public passageway, the **passage Richelieu**, linking the cour Napoléon with rue de Rivoli, allows you to look down into these courtyards.

Mitterrand's project also dramatically extended the Louvre underground, with the entrance hall, the **Hall Napoléon**, beneath the Pyramid, leading into a series of galleries known as the **Carrousel du Louvre**. Smart shops, restaurants, exhibition and conference spaces fill the vast spaces, and an inverted glass pyramid lets in light from place du Carrousel.

Napoleon's pink marble **Arc du Carrousel**, just east of place du Carrousel, which originally formed a gateway for the former Palais des Tuileries, has always looked a bit out of place; now it is definitively and forlornly upstaged by the Pyramid.

The **Palais du Louvre** itself houses **four museums**: the Musée du Louvre; the Musée de la Mode et du Textile; the Musée des Arts Décoratifs; and the Musée de la Publicité. Each has been revamped under the Grand Louvre project, and each is an important collection in its own right, but the most renowned by far – and *the* reason to come to Paris for many of its visitors – is the mighty **Musée du Louvre**.

THE LOUVRE

THE MUSÉE DU LOUVRE

Map 2, C5–E5. Daily except Tues 9am–6pm, late opening till 9.45pm on Mon (selected rooms only) & Wed; 46F/€7.01, after 3pm & Sun 30F/€4.57, free first Sun of the month unless public holiday; same-day readmission allowed; Ⓦ *www.louvre.fr* M° Palais-Royal-Musée-du-Louvre.

The **Musée du Louvre**, hung with the private collections of monarchs and their ministers, was first opened to the public in 1793, during the Revolution. Within a decade, Napoleon had expanded it with takings from his empire and made it the largest art collection on earth.

Until recently, it required heroic willpower and stamina to navigate your way around the thousands of works on display. The Grand Louvre project, however, has breathed new life into the building: exhibition floor-space has almost doubled, necessitating a complete reorganization in order to display the thousands of works of art previously kept in the reserves. As a result of the improvements brought about by the Mitterrand's project, the number of visitors has increased significantly and there are nearly always long queues to get into the building. One way of avoiding the queues is to buy tickets in advance: these are available from branches of FNAC (see pp.283 & 291), Virgin Megastore in the Carrousel du Louvre and other big department stores.

Finding your way around the museum

There are two **entrances** to the museum where you can buy **tickets**. The main entrance, with a bookshop, café and information desk, is the Hall Napoléon, reached via the Pyramid or the underground Carrousel du Louvre. The **Carrousel du Louvre** can be accessed directly from the métro, on either side of the Arc du Carrousel and at 99 rue de Rivoli. The other entrance, the Porte des Lions, at the

Tuileries end of the Denon wing, gives direct access to the arts of Africa, Asia, Oceania and the Americas. For those who already have a ticket, the entrance in the passage Richelieu (between place du Palais-Royal and cour Napoléon) avoids the queue for the Pyramid.

Lifts and escalators lead from the Hall Napoléon to each of the three wings of the four-floor building. The wings are **Sully**, around the cour Carrée; **Denon**, the south wing; and **Richelieu**, the north wing. At first overwhelming and seemingly nonsensical, the layout of the museum is a delight to unravel. The indispensable **floor-plan**, available free from the information desk in the Hall Napoléon, highlights some of the more renowned masterpieces, such as the *Mona Lisa*, for those wishing to do a whistle-stop tour, although don't expect to be able to contemplate them peacefully.

The museum's collections are divided into **seven main categories**: Painting; Prints and Drawings; Oriental Antiquities and Islamic Arts; Egyptian Antiquities; Greek, Etruscan and Roman Antiquities; Objets d'Art; and Sculpture. Each category spreads over more than one wing and several floors. There is also an exhibition on the history of the Louvre, called the **Medieval Louvre** in which you can visit the foundations of Philippe-Auguste's fortress and Charles V's fourteenth-century palace conversion via the moats under the cour Carrée on the *entresol* (lower-ground level) of the Sully wing. A new, though probably temporary, collection, made up of 120 works of art from **Africa, Asia, Oceania and the Americas** (nearest entrance Porte des Lions), opened in 2000. It is likely that the collection will be moved to the new museum at the quai Branly (see p.88) in the near future.

The collections

By far the largest of the museum's collections is its **paintings**, covering French works from the year dot to the mid-nineteenth century, along with Italian, Dutch, German, Flemish and Spanish art. The early **Italians** (Denon, first floor, 1–6) are perhaps the most interesting part of the collection. Among them is one of the most recognizable paintings in the history of the genre, Leonardo da Vinci's **Mona Lisa** (*La Joconde*, 1503–1505). The secretive smile of the subject has captured the imagination of centuries of beholders. If you want to get near her, it's best to go first or last thing in the day. Other highlights of the Italian collection include two complete Botticelli frescoes; Giotto's *Stigmatization of St Francis of Assisi*, demonstrating a revolutionary use of space; and Fra Angelico's *Coronation of the Virgin*, displaying a new awareness of perspective. Fifteenth- to seventeenth-century paintings line the length of the Grande Galerie (rooms 5, 8 and 12), which was built by Catherine de Médicis to link the Louvre and now-destroyed Palais des Tuileries. Outstanding works here are da Vinci's *Virgin and child with St Anne* and *Virgin of the Rocks*, plus several Raphael masterpieces. You can also admire the geometrical precision of Mantegna's *Crucifixion*.

In the Dutch and Spanish collections, works worth lingering over are Rembrandt's superb *Supper at Emmaus*, with its dramatic use of chiaroscuro, Murillo's tender *Beggar Boy*, and the Goya portraits.

The **French collection** is so vast that a selective approach is necessary unless you intend to spend at least a couple of days devoted to the subject. A good place to start is with the master of French classicism, Poussin; his profound themes, taken from antiquity, the Bible and mythology, together with his harmonious painting style, were to influence generations of artists to come. Large-scale nineteenth-century French works are displayed in rooms 75 and 77, among them the huge epic painting *The Coronation of Napoleon I*, by David, and Ingres' languorous nude, *La Grande Odalisque*. Leading Romantic painters Delacroix and Géricault dominate in rooms 61 and 77. One of the latter's best known works on display is his dramatic *Raft of the Medusa*, depicting the extremes of emotion felt by survivors of a shipwreck. The final part of the collection takes in Corot and the Barbizon school, the precursors of Impressionism.

The Louvre's collection of French painting stops at 1848, a date picked up by the Musée d'Orsay (see p.92).

Interspersed throughout the painting section are rooms dedicated to the Louvre's impressive collection of **prints and drawings**, including prized sketches and preliminary drawings by Ingres and Rubens and some attributed to Leonardo. Because of their susceptibility to the light, however, they are exhibited by rotation.

The **Oriental Antiquities and Islamic Arts** category covers the Mesopotamian, Sumerian, Babylonian, Assyrian and Phoenician civilizations, and the art of ancient Persia, India and Spain. One of the collection's most important exhibits is the *Code of Hammurabi*, a basalt stele covered in Akkadian script setting down King Hammurabi's rules of conduct for his subjects.

The **Egyptian Antiquities** collection starts with the atmospheric crypt of the Sphinx (room 1). Everyday life is illustrated through cooking accessories, jewellery, the principles of hieroglyphics, musical instruments, sarcophagi and a host of mummified cats. The collection continues upstairs, with the development of Egyptian art. Highlights include the expressive *Seated Scribe* (c.2500 BC) and the huge bust of Amenophis IV (1365–1349 BC).

The biggest crowd-pullers in the museum after the Mona Lisa are found in the **Greek and Roman Antiquities**: the dramatic *Winged Victory of Samothrace* (Denon first floor, at the top of the great staircase), believed to have been created in commemoration of a Rhodian naval battle, and the late-

THE MUSÉE DU LOUVRE

second-century BC *Venus de Milo* (Sully, ground floor, 12), striking a classic model's pose. Her antecedents are all on display, too, from the graceful marble head of the *Cycladic Idol* and the delightful *Dame d'Auxerre* (seventh century BC) to the classical perfection of the *Athlete of Benevento*. In the Roman section are some attractive mosaics from Asia Minor and luminous frescoes from Pompeii and Herculaneum, which seem to foreshadow the decorative lightness of touch of a Botticelli still more than a thousand years away.

The **Objets d'Art** collection is heavily weighted on the side of imperial opulence with finely crafted tapestries, ceramics, jewellery and furniture. The exception is the more austere Middle Ages section, which features carved Parisian and Byzantine ivories and Limoges enamels, depicting saints and biblical scenes. The exhibition is partly housed in the former Minister of State's apartments, which have been open to the public since the Finance Ministry was ousted in the 1980s, and are full of plush upholstery, immense chandeliers, gilded putti and caryatids, and dramatic ceiling frescoes in true Second-Empire style.

The **Sculpture section** covers the entire development of the art in France from the Romanesque to Rodin, all in the Richelieu wing, and Italian and northern European sculpture in the Denon wing, including Michelangelo's *Slaves*, designed for the tomb of Pope Julius II (Denon, ground floor, 4). The huge glass-covered courtyards of the Richelieu wing – the cour Marly with the Marly Horses, which once graced place de la Concorde, and the cour Puget with Puget's *Milon de Crotone* as the centrepiece – are very impressive, if a bit overwhelming.

THE OTHER PALAIS DU LOUVRE MUSEUMS

Map 2, D4. 107 rue de Rivoli. Mº Palais-Royal-Musée-du-Louvre.

The Rohan wing of the Louvre houses three other

museums: the Musée de la Mode et du Textile, Musée des
Arts Décoratifs and Musée de la Publicité. The entrance is
at 107 rue de Rivoli. One ticket gives access to all three of
the collections, though the Musée des Arts Décoratifs was
undergoing major reorganization at the time of research, so
access may be limited.

The Musée de la Mode et du Textile, Musée des Arts
Décoratifs and Musée de la Publicité are open
Tues–Fri 11am–6pm, Wed until 9pm, Sat & Sun
10am–6pm; admission to all three is 35F/€5.34.

Musée de la Mode et du Textile

The **Musée de la Mode et du Textile**, on the first and
second floors of the Rohan wing, houses an exquisite collection of fashion, too large to be shown all at once – and
in any case, individual items are too fragile to be exposed
for long periods. The result is a yearly rotation of garments
and textiles based on changing themes.

Musée des Arts Décoratifs

The collection of religious artefacts and bourgeois *objets* in
the **Musée des Arts Décoratifs** seems rather humble in
comparison with the high art next door in the Musée du
Louvre. The craftsmanship is nonetheless apparent, and the
thematic arrangement with two period mock-ups – a late-
fourteenth-century castle bedroom and a fifteenth-century
reception room – contextualizes the objects. The museum
starts on the third floor with a section devoted to the
period from the Middle Ages to the Renaissance; the rest of
the permanent collection comprises furnishings, fittings and
everyday components of French interiors up to the present

THE OTHER PALAIS DU LOUVRE MUSUEMS

day, with works by French, Italian and Japanese designers. The twentieth-century collection was closed at the time of research, but when it reopens it promises to be fascinating – a bedroom by Guimard, Jeanne Lanvin's Art Deco apartments, and a salon created by Georges Hoentschel for the 1900 Exposition Universelle.

Musée de la Publicité

On the fourth floor, the **Musée de la Publicité** celebrates the art of advertising from nineteenth-century poster art to contemporary electronic publicity. Comprising multimedia and temporary exhibitions, and with free access to a wealth of computerized archives, the museum creates a neutral space in which to contemplate the inspiration and influence of the persuasive art.

The Tuileries and Champs-Élysées

The **avenue des Champs-Élysées** is part of Paris's monumental axis, La Voie Triomphale, which runs in a dead-straight line from the Louvre (see Chapter 3) along the central alley of the **Tuileries** gardens, across place de la Concorde and through the **Arc de Triomphe**, finally ending up at La Défense (see Chapter 12). Its nine-kilometre length is punctuated by grandiose constructions erected over the centuries by kings and emperors, presidents and corporations, each a monumental gesture aimed at promoting French power and prestige.

THE TUILERIES

Map 2, B4. Mº Tuileries & Mº Concorde.

Stretching from the Louvre to the place de la Concorde, the **Tuileries gardens** (Jardins des Tuileries) have long been popular with bourgeois Parisian families taking their Sunday promenade, though nowadays, the chairs placed around the water-features are often occupied by tourists resting after a tour of the Louvre or one of the smaller galleries in the gardens, the **Jeu de Paume** and **Orangerie**.

Named after the medieval warren of tilemakers (*tuileries*) that once occupied the site, the Tuileries gardens are all that survive of the palace and grounds commissioned by Catherine des Médicis in the mid-sixteenth century. The palace was burnt down during the Paris Commune in 1871. Catherine took great interest in her garden and had a maze, a chequerboard of flowerbeds and formal vegetable gardens laid out, to be admired by guests at her sumptuous parties. A hundred years later, Le Nôtre, who landscaped the grounds at Versailles, created the current schema of the gardens, installing a central axis, *terrasses*, and round and octagonal pools. Later, sculptures were brought here from Versailles and Marly, including Coysevox's rearing horses *Fama* and *Mercury*. The originals are now housed in the Richelieu wing of the Louvre and have been replaced by copies.

During the eighteenth century, fashionable Parisians came to the gardens to preen and party, and in 1783, the Montgolfier brothers, Joseph and Étienne, launched the first successful hot-air balloon here. The first serious replanting was carried out after the Revolution, and in the nineteenth century, rare species were added to the garden, by this time dominated by chestnut trees. Unfortunately, the December 1999 storms which ravaged northern France, stripped the Tuileries gardens of some of its oldest trees: the centennial chestnuts around the two central oval ponds are now the most senior. Le Nôtre's original design, however, remains little changed. In recent years, some **modern sculptures** have been placed around the gardens, mostly works by Giacometti, Ernst, Moore, Raymond Mason and a couple of colourful Roy Lichtensteins. Another new feature is the award-winning **Solférino footbridge**, which was opened in 1999 and links the Tuileries with the Musée d'Orsay (see p.92) on the Left Bank.

Between the Tuileries and the Louvre lies the
labyrinthine **Jardin du Carrousel**, its hedges
interspersed with statues of rotund female nudes
by the French-Catalan sculptor, Maillol.

The Orangerie

Map 2, A4. M° Concorde.

Situated at the west end of the Tuileries gardens is the
Orangerie, at present undergoing major reorganization
and due to reopen at the end of 2001. It houses several of
Monet's *Water Lilies*, as well as a private art collection,
weighted heavily in favour of the Impressionists and including works by Matisse, Cézanne, Utrillo, Modigliani,
Renoir, Soutine and Sisley. The current work involves
restructuring the building and replacing many of the existing exterior walls with glass, in line with the building's
original function as an orangery. After all the upheaval,
much of the Orangerie's collection will be rearranged, and
with any luck, extra room will be created for paintings from
the museum's reserves.

Jeu de Paume

Map 2, A3. Tues noon–9.30pm, Wed–Fri noon–7pm, Sat & Sun
10am–7pm; 38F/€5.79. M° Concorde.

Opposite the Orangerie, the **Jeu de Paume** was formerly
home to the state's Impressionist collection before its
relocation to the Musée d'Orsay. It is now used for temporary shows of contemporary art, usually major retrospectives
of established artists, but also, every autumn, more cutting-
edge stuff by artists invited for the **Festival d'Automne**
(see p.271).

PLACE DE LA CONCORDE

Map 2, A3. Mº Concorde.

Marking the beginning of the Champs-Élysées' graceful gradients, the **place de la Concorde** is much less peaceful than its name suggests. Between 1793 and 1795, some 1300 people died here beneath the Revolutionary guillotine: Louis XVI, Marie-Antoinette, Danton and Robespierre among them. Today, the centrepiece of the *place*, an obelisk from the temple of Ramses at Luxor, offered as a favour-currying gesture by the viceroy of Egypt in 1829, is surrounded by a constant sea of traffic. The obelisk serves as a pivotal point for more geometry: the alignment of the French parliament, the Assemblée Nationale, on the far side of the Seine, with the church of the Madeleine (see p.48), at the end of rue Royale, to the north. The Neoclassical *Hôtel Crillon* – the ultimate luxury address for visitors to Paris – and its twin, the *Hôtel de la Marine*, housing the Ministry of the Navy, flank the entrance to rue Royale.

THE CHAMPS-ÉLYSÉES

Map 7, E2–L5.

Stretching from the place de la Concorde to the Arc de Triomphe, the **Champs-Élysées** has long been associated with Parisian glitz and glamour. A victim of its own success, nowadays the Champs-Élysées is less attractive, dominated as it is by airline offices, car showrooms, fast-food outlets and shopping arcades. However, the glamour has not completely disappeared: there's still the Lido cabaret, *Le Fouquet's* high-class bar and restaurant, which hosts the César film awards each year, as well as plenty of cinemas and expensive cafés. At no. 68, the perfumier Guerlain occupies an exquisite 1913 building; the belle-époque façade of the former *Claridge Hotel*, at no. 74, has been given a facelift; and the *Travellers Club* still glories in the mid-nineteenth-century opulence of the *Hôtel de la Païva*, at no. 25. Newer arrivals, mostly transatlantic, continue the avenue's connection with the entertainment industries: Virgin Megastore, a Disney shop and the *Planet Hollywood* restaurant. At the Renault showrooms (nos. 49–53) is a free display of cars, bikes and vans from the earliest days.

The less commercial stretch of the Champs-Élysées, between place de la Concorde and the Rond-Point round-about, is bordered by chestnut trees and municipal flowerbeds, pleasant enough to stroll among, but not sufficiently dense to muffle the squeal of accelerating tyres. On the north side stand the guarded walls of the presidential **Élysée Palace**. The gigantic building with grandiose Neoclassical exteriors, glass roofs and exuberant flying statuary rising above the greenery to the south, is the Grand Palais, created with its neighbour, the Petit Palais, for the 1900 Exposition Universelle. Today, both the Grand Palais and Petit Palais contain permanent museums, as well as hosting good temporary exhibitions.

Petit Palais

Map 7, K5. Mº Champs-Élysées-Clemenceau.
The **Petit Palais** is currently closed until sometime in 2003 for renovation, but is normally the site of major, changing exhibitions and also houses the Musée des Beaux-Arts, which at first sight seems to be a collection of leftovers, from every period from the Renaissance to the 1920s, after the other main galleries have taken their pick. It does, however, hold some real gems: Monet's *Sunset at Lavacourt* and Boudin's *Gust of Wind at Le Havre* stand out against some rather uninspiring Renoirs, Morisots, Cézannes and Manets. The rest of the collection ventures into several different areas: jewellery of the Art Nouveau period, effete eighteenth-cen-

tury furniture, and plaster models designed for the Madeleine church (see p.48) in the early nineteenth century.

The Grand Palais

Map 7, J5. Opening times and prices vary. M° Champs-Élysées-Clemenceau.

The 144-foot-high dome of the **Grand Palais** can be seen from most of the city's viewpoints. The western part of the building houses the Galeries Nationales, a space devoted to major exhibitions, the best of which draw queues that stretch down avenue Churchill.

Pariscope (see p.239) will have
details of exhibitions at the Grand Palais, and you'll
probably see plenty of posters around.

The eastern wing houses the **Palais de la Découverte** (Tues–Sat 9.30am–6pm, Sun 10am–7pm; 30F/€4.57, 45F/€6.86 with planetarium), the old science museum, which has been brightened up considerably since the Cité des Sciences (see p.123) came on the scene. Although it can't really compete, it does have plenty of interactive exhibits, some very good temporary shows and an excellent **planetarium**.

THE ARC DE TRIOMPHE

Map 7, E2. Daily: April–Sept 9.30am–11pm; Oct–March 10am–10.30pm; 40F/€6.10. M° Charles-de-Gaulle-Étoile.

The best views of the Champs-Élysées are to be had from the terrace at the top of the **Arc de Triomphe**, Napoleon's homage both to the armies of France and to himself. Construction of the arch began in 1806, but was interrupted in 1814 with the demise of Napoleon I and finished in 1836. The emperor and his two royal successors spent ten million francs between them on this edifice, which victorious foreign armies would later use to humiliate the French. After the Prussians' triumphal march in 1871, the Parisians lit bonfires beneath the arch and down the Champs-Élysées to eradicate the "stain" of German boots. These days, the Bastille Day procession, composed of the president and an entourage of tanks, guns and flags, sets off from here and continues down the Champs-Élysées. A more poignant ceremony is conducted every evening at 6.30pm, when the continually burning flame on the tomb of an unknown soldier, killed in the Great War, is stoked up by war veterans. A small collection of prints and photos depicting illustrious scenes from the history of the arch is on show on the way up to the terrace, as well as drawings for the glorious friezes and sculptures that adorn the pillars. The Champs-Élysées side in particular boasts a fine high-relief sculpture: *the Marseillaise* by François Rude.

Access to the Arc de Triomphe is gained from stairs on the north corner of the Champs-Élysées. From the top of the arch, your attention is most likely to be caught, not by the view, but by the mesmerizing traffic movements below in place Charles-de-Gaulle, the world's first organized roundabout.

ÉTOILE AND AROUND

Map 7, E2. Mᵒ Charles-de-Gaulle-Étoile.

Twelve avenues make up the star of the **Étoile**, or place Charles-de-Gaulle, with the Arc de Triomphe at its centre. The avenues stretching into the northern 16ᵉ and eastern 17ᵉ arrondissements are for the most part cold and soulless, and the huge fortified apartments here are empty much of the time, as their owners – royal, exiled royal, ex-royal or just extremely rich – move between their other residences dotted about the globe. The 8ᵉ arrondissement, north of the Champs-Élysées, however, has more to offer commercially and culturally, with some of the *hôtels particuliers* (mansions) housing select museums.

The superb classical Hôtel Salomon de Rothschild at 9–11 rue Berryer is where the **Centre National de Photographie** (map 7, G2; daily except Tues noon–7pm; 30F/€4.57) hosts excellent temporary photographic exhibitions. At 63 rue de Monceau, the **Musée Nissim de Camondo** (map 7, H1; Wed–Sun 10am–5pm; 30F/€4.57), comprising a collection of late-eighteenth-century French aristocratic furnishings, is housed in a residence in the style of the Petit Trianon at Versailles. The Hausmannian Hôtel André, at 158 boulevard Haussmann, offers the highlight of the area, the magnificent art collection of the **Musée Jacquemart-André** (map 7, I1; daily 10am–6pm; 49F/€7.47), accumulated on the travels of the art-lover Édouard André and his wife, former society portraitist Nélie Jacquemart. They loved Italian art above all, and a stunning collection of fifteenth- and sixteenth-century Italian genius, including the works of Tiepolo, Botticelli, Donatello, Mantegna and Uccello, forms the core of their collection. Almost as compelling as the splendid interior and art collection is the insight gleaned into an extraordinary marriage and grand nineteenth-century lifestyle.

The Musée Jacquemart-André has a fabulously elegant *salon de thé.*. See p.195.

ÉTOILE AND AROUND

43

The Grands Boulevards and around

The term "Grands Boulevards" describes the long, broad thoroughfare that stretches from the Madeleine to République then down to the Bastille. The area is home to grandiose financial, cultural and state institutions and is associated with established commerce such as the rag trade and newspapers, plus well-heeled shopping. Many of the area's chic boutiques are to be found in the attractive nineteenth-century shopping arcades or **passages**, just off the boulevards. Characteristic of a later generation of indoor shopping, major department stores such as Galeries Lafayette congregate nearby in the 9e arrondissement, just north of the **Palais Garnier** opera house. Catering to the seriously rich, the boutiques at the western end of the 1er, around the church of the **Madeleine**, and the streets to either side of the Champs-Élysées display the wares of every top couturier, jeweller, art dealer and furnisher. More run-of-the-mill high-street shops can be found around **Les Halles**, once the site of the city's food market, now an underground RER/métro station and shopping centre.

THE GRANDS BOULEVARDS

Running from the Madeleine to the Bastille, the **Grands Boulevards** comprise boulevards de la Madeleine, des Capucines, des Italiens, Montmartre, Poissonnière, Bonne-Nouvelle, St-Denis, St-Martin, du Temple, des Filles du Calvaire and Beaumarchais. The western section, from the Madeleine to Porte St-Denis, follows the old defensive rampart built by Charles V. When its purpose became redundant with the aggressive foreign policy of Louis XIV, the walls were pulled down and the ditches filled in, leaving a wide promenade. This was given the name *boulevard* after the military term for the level part of a rampart. In the mid-eighteenth century, the boulevard became a fashionable place to be seen on horseback or in one's carriage, and gradually a desirable thoroughfare on which to reside.

The western end attracted a more bourgeois habitué, while the eastern end, known as the *boulevard du Crime*, developed a more colourful reputation, with street theatre, mime, juggling, puppets, waxworks and cafés of ill repute. By the early half of the nineteenth century, the Grands Boulevards had been cobbled and Paris's first horse-drawn omnibus rattled from the Bastille to the Madeleine. The *petit peuple* from the east rubbed shoulders with the bourgeois intellectuals from the west, and the café clientele of the **boulevard des Italiens** set the trend for all of Paris, in terms of manners, dress and topics of conversation. In the latter half of the nineteenth century, however, the *boulevard du Crime* was largely erased by Baron Haussmann and replaced by a huge crossroads, the place de la République.

Today, dotted among the burger bars, there are still remnants of the fun-loving times – theatres and cinemas, including the splendid early twentieth-century Max Linder and Rex cinemas (see p.260), and numerous brasseries and cafés, which, though not the city's hippest or most innovative, still belong to the tradition of the Grands Boulevards, immortalized in the film *Les Enfants du Paradis*. Another leftover from these days is the waxworks museum, the **Musée Grévin** (map 3, H8; daily: April–Aug 1–7pm, school hols 10am–7pm; Sept–March 1.30–6.30pm, school hols 10am–6.30pm; 58F/€8.84), on boulevard Montmartre, though its replicas of famous people and scenes from French history are unlikely to enthral a modern audience. Children, however, might enjoy the light and mirrors show in the "Palais des Mirages".

Boulevard des Capucines is associated with two notable historical firsts. At no. 14, in 1895, the first film (or animated photography, as the Lumière brothers' invention was called) was shown. Some years earlier, another artistic revolution had taken place at no. 35, the studio of the photographer Nadar: this was the venue for the first ever Impressionist exhibition, which was greeted with outrage by the art world. As one critic said of Monet's *Impression: Soleil Levant*, "It was worse than anyone had hitherto dared to paint."

THE OPÉRA (PALAIS GARNIER)

Map 3, E8. Mº Opéra.
Set back from the boulevard des Capucines is the dazzling Opéra de Paris – now commonly referred to as the **Palais Garnier** to distinguish it from the new opera house at the Bastille. It crowns the avenue de l'Opéra, which was deliberately kept free of trees in order to allow uninterrupted views of the building. Its imposing façade bristles with columns

and sculptures, including a copy of Carpeaux's sculpture *The Dance*, on the right-hand side. The Opéra's architect, Charles Garnier, pulled out all the stops to provide a building splendid enough for the tastes of aristocratic Second-Empire opera-goers: you can just imagine the carriages drawing up outside and the women in their crinolines sweeping up the spectacularly embellished main staircase.

**The original of Carpeaux's *The Dance* is
kept in the Musée d'Orsay; see p.92.**

By day, you can visit the sumptuous gilded **interior** (daily 10am–5pm; 30F/€4.57), including the auditorium, as long as there are no rehearsals; your best chance of seeing the auditorium is between 1 and 2pm. The ceiling, depicting opera and ballet scenes, is the work of **Chagall**. The entry ticket includes a visit to the **Bibliothèque-Musée de l'Opéra**, containing model sets, dreadful nineteenth-century paintings, and rather better temporary exhibitions on operatic themes. The classic horror movie *The Phantom of the Opera* was set, though never filmed, here; a real underground stream lends credence to the tale.

PARIS-STORY

Map 3, D8. Daily with shows on the hour every hour: Nov–March 9am–6pm; April–Oct 9am–8pm; 50F/€7.62. M° Opéra, M° Chaussée-d'Antin-La-Fayette & RER Auber.

For an overview of the myths, history and styles that have created Paris today you could do worse than visit **Paris-Story**, west of the Opéra, at 11bis rue Scribe. A 45-minute sound-and-vision show depicts Paris from its Roman beginnings as Lutetia through to the present, and provides an informative, albeit romantic, introduction to the make-up of the city.

PARIS-STORY

PRINTEMPS AND GALERIES LAFAYETTE

Map 3, C7–E7. M° Havre-Caumartin, M° Chaussée-d'Antin-La-Fayette & RER Auber.

To the north of the Opéra, on the treeless boulevard Haussmann, you'll find two of the city's biggest department stores: **Printemps** and **Galeries Lafayette**, opposite the largest Paris branch of Marks & Spencer. Though they still possess their proud, fin-de-siècle glass domes, much of the beauty of their interiors has been hacked away. For reviews of Printemps and Galeries Lafayette, see p.286.

See p.283 for listings of the best shops in Paris.

MADELEINE

Map 3, B9–C9. M° Madeleine.

A popular place for society weddings, the church of the **Madeleine**, southwest of the Opéra, is an obese structure on the classical temple model. It was originally intended to be yet another monument to the glory of Napoleon's army. With France's defeat in Russia, however, the construction of the Madeleine was interrupted, only to be taken up again by Louis XVIII, who retained the original design of the classical temple, but decided to convert it into a Catholic church. The single wide nave is decorated with Ionic columns and surmounted with three huge domes – the only source of natural light inside.

On the east side of the church in **place de la Madeleine**, a flower market sets up every day except Monday, and there's a luxurious Art-Nouveau loo by the métro at the junction of place and boulevard de la Madeleine. However, it is for rich gourmands that the *place* holds the most appeal. In the northeast corner, the upmaket delicatessen Fauchon tempts you in with its displays of wines, chocolates, *marrons glacés* and other luxurious foods; down the west side, you'll find the smaller Hédiard's, selling similar treats, as well as caviar, truffles and spirits.

For listings of specialist food shops
and delicatessens, see p.287.

THE PASSAGES

Designed by town planners in the nineteenth century to give pedestrians protection from mud and horse-drawn vehicles, the **passages** (shopping arcades), between the Grands Boulevards and the Louvre, are enjoying a new lease of life as havens from today's far busier traffic. For decades they were left to crumble and decay, but many have now been renovated, their tiled floors and glass roofs restored. Their entrances, however, remain easy to miss, and where you emerge at the other end can be quite a surprise. Many are closed at night and on Sundays.

Between rue Croix-des-Petits-Champs and rue Jean-Jacques Rousseau, **Galerie Véro-Dodat** (map 2, E4), is the most homogeneous and aristocratic of the *passages*, with painted ceilings and panelled shop fronts divided by black marble columns. It's named after the two pork butchers who set it up in 1824. Although the *galerie* is a little dilapidated, with peeling paint on many of the shop fronts, fashionable new shops have begun to open up in place of the older businesses. Retaining the old style at no. 26, Monsieur Capia still keeps a collection of antique dolls in a shop piled high with miscellaneous curios.

The beautifully lit **Galerie Colbert** (map 2, E2), one of two very upmarket *passages* linking rue Vivienne with rue des Petits-Champs, contains an expensive 1830s-style brasserie, *Le Grand Colbert*, to which senior librarians and rich academics from the nearby Richelieu site of the Bibliothèque Nationale retire for lunch. The flamboyant decor of Grecian and marine motifs in the larger **Galerie Vivienne** (map 2, E2) establishes the perfect ambience in which to buy Jean-Paul Gaultier gear, or you can browse in the antiquarian bookshop, Librairie Jousseaume, which dates back to the *passage's* earliest days.

For restaurants, cafés and bars in
the *passages* area, see p.197.

Three blocks west of the Bibliothèque Nationale is a totally different style of *passage*. Just like a regular high street, the **passage Choiseul** (map 2, D2), between rue des Petits-Champs and rue St-Augustin, has takeaway food, cheap clothes shops, stationers and bars, plus a few arty outlets along its two-hundred-metre tiled length. It was here that the author Louis-Ferdinand Céline lived as a boy, a period and location vividly recounted in his novel *Death on Credit* (see "Books" on p.355).

For a combination of old-fashioned chic and workaday you need to explore the **passage des Panoramas** (map 3, H8), the grid of arcades north of the Bibliothèque Nationale, beyond rue St-Marc, though they're still in need of a little repair and don't have the fancy mosaics of the other arcades. Most of the eateries here make no pretence at style, but one old brasserie, *L'Arbre à Cannelle* (see review on p.197), has fantastic carved wood panelling, and there are still bric-a-brac shops, stamp dealers and an upper-crust print shop with its original 1867 fittings. It was around the Panoramas, in 1817, that the first Parisian gas lamps were tried out.

In **passage Jouffroy** (map 3, H8), across boulevard Montmartre, a M. Segas sells walking canes and theatrical antiques opposite a shop displaying every conceivable fitting and furnishing for dolls' houses. Near the romantic *Hôtel Chopin*, Paul Vulin sets out his secondhand books along the passageway, and Ciné-Doc caters to cinephiles. Crossing rue de la Grange-Batelière, you enter **passage Verdeau** (map 3, H7), where a few of the old postcard and camera dealers still trade alongside new art galleries and a designer Italian delicatessen.

At the top of rue Richelieu, the tiny **passage des Princes** (map 3, G8), with its beautiful glass ceiling, stained-glass decoration and twirly lamps, has finally been restored, but unfortunately lies empty – high rents have chased out the shops that were here. Its erstwhile neighbour, the passage de l'Opéra, described in surreal detail by Louis Aragon in *Paris Peasant*, was eaten up with the completion of Haussmann's boulevards – a project that demolished scores of old *passages*.

Back in the 2ᵉ arrondissement, close to Mᵒ Étienne-Marcel, the three-storey **passage du Grand-Cerf** (map 2, H3), between rue St-Denis and rue Dessoubs, is stylistically the best of all the *passages*. The wrought-iron work, glass roof and plain-wood shop fronts have all been cleaned, attracting stylish arts, crafts and antique shops.

THE PALAIS ROYAL

Map 2, E3–E4. Mᵒ Palais-Royal-Musée-du-Louvre.

Bang in the centre of the 1ᵉʳ arrondissement lies **place du Palais-Royal**, a favourite haunt of pavement artists, performers and rollerbladers. On the north side of the *place* stands the **Palais Royal**, built for Cardinal Richelieu in 1629. Much altered since then, it now houses various government and constitutional bodies, as well as the **Comédie Française** where the classics of French theatre are performed (see p.262 for more details).

The palace **gardens** to the north were once the gastronomic, gambling and entertainment hotspot of Paris. Amusements included a *café mécanique*, where you sat at a table, sent your order down one of its legs, and were served via the other. The prohibition on public gambling in 1838 put an end to the fun, but the flats above the empty cafés remained desirable lodgings, counting among its residents Cocteau and Colette, who died here in 1954.

The three arcades running along the sides of the Palais Royal gardens have hardly changed since they were built in 1784. At 153 Galerie de Valois you'll find one of the arcade's oldest art-and-antique dealers, **Guillaumot**, founded in 1785. Further down, at no. 142, Les Salons du Palais Royal Shiseido *parfumerie* conceals an exquisite interior done out with purple panelling.

LES HALLES

Map 2, F4–G5. Mº Les-Halles & RER Châtelet-les-Halles.

Les Halles was until recently a largely working-class district and the site of a large food market, dating back around 800 years. In 1969, however, the whole area was redeveloped and the main body of the market was moved out to the suburbs. Despite widespread opposition, the market's nineteenth-century pavilions were cleared to make way for a major RER/métro interchange and commercial centre, the **Forum des Halles**, much of it extending underground. Nowadays, rents in the quartier rival the 16e, and all-night restaurants and bars proliferate.

From RER Châtelet-les-halles, you surface only after ascending from levels -4 to 0 of the Forum des Halles centre, whose shops and leisure amenities stretch underground from the Bourse du Commerce rotunda to rue Pierre-Lescot. Gardens have been planted above the subterranean leisure area and transport interchange, except for the northeastern corner where the shops surface in a curved mirrored-glass structure topped by an exhibition space, the **Pavillon des Arts** (Tues–Sun 11.30am–6.30pm; 30F/€4.57), and poetry and craft centres.

On the north side of the gardens stands the high Gothic and Renaissance church of **St-Eustache**. Molière was baptized here; and in the Chapelle St-Joseph, a Raymond Mason relief, entitled *The Departure of Fruit and Vegetables from the Heart of Paris, 28 February 1969*, depicts the area's more recent history.

Note that pickpocketing and sexual harassment are something of a problem around Les Halles. Police are often in evidence, and at night it can be quite tense.

RUE ST-DENIS AND PLACE DU CHÂTELET

Map 2, H4–G6. M° Châtelet & RER Châtelet-les-Halles.

The streets on the eastern side of Les Halles have plenty of cafés where you can take a break from the shoving crowds, and are traversed by the long **Rue St-Denis**, which has been the red-light district of Paris for centuries. Attempts by the local mairie to rid the street of its pimps and prostitutes have been to no avail; despite the fact that the area between rues Étienne-Marcel and Réaumur has been pedestrianized to stop kerb-crawling and cafés like the English *Frog and Rosbif* have been encouraged to set up among the porn outlets, weary women still wait in doorways between peepshows, striptease joints and sex-video shops.

Listings for jazz venues are given on p.248.

The area south of here towards **place du Châtelet** teems with jazz bars, nightclubs and restaurants, and is far more crowded at 2am than 2pm.

The Quartier Beaubourg, the Marais and Bastille

A few blocks away from Les Halles across boulevard Sébastopol lies the **Pompidou Centre** (Centre Georges Pompidou) – or Beaubourg as it's known locally. Hailed as a radical architectural breakthrough for its daring and unusual design when it first opened in the 1970s, the Centre was recently renovated to the tune of £69m and reopened amid the fanfare and fireworks of Paris's Millennium celebration. By all accounts, the results were worth waiting for and the centre remains a popular focus for the bustling **quartier Beaubourg**, with its art galleries and cafés.

East of the quartier Beaubourg, rampant gentrification has erased many of the vestiges of the **Marais'** more recent history of poverty and neglect. The once delapidated mansions have been done up, and many now house museums and expensive galleries. With its medieval lanes and colourful Jewish quarter, plus a plethora of small, appealing restaurants, shops, funky cafés and gay bars, this is a great place to hang out during the day or night.

Further east, the **Bastille** quartier used to belong in spirit and in style to the working-class districts of eastern Paris, but since the construction of the new Bastille opera house in 1989, it has become a magnet for artists and young people. Bursting with small shops, ethnic restaurants, trendy bars and energetic nightclubs, this area has rapidly become one of central Paris's hotspots.

THE POMPIDOU CENTRE

Map 2, H5. Daily except Tues 11am–9pm; 30F/€4.57, includes entry to the Atelier Brancusi but not special exhibitions; Ⓦ *www .centrepompidou.fr* M° Rambuteau & M° Hôtel-de-Ville.

When it opened in 1977, the **Pompidou Centre** caused a sensation on account of its radical design. In order to maximize indoor gallery space, architects Renzo Piano and Richard Rogers had placed all infrastructure, including utility pipes and escalator tubes, on the exterior, giving the building its bizarre inside-out look. The Centre's closure in 1997 for extensive renovation led sceptics to grumble that the young architects had been overly ambitious, but the structure has weathered two years of internal renovations with aplomb. Newly outfitted with slick lighting, gleaming polished concrete floors, a stylish café and an expensive rooftop restaurant, the Centre shines after its much needed update. Sadly, the escalator rides, complete with fabulous views of the city, are no longer free; access to them now requires purchasing a ticket to the Musée (see overleaf).

A good place from which to admire the exterior of the Pompidou Centre is the *Café Beaubourg* (see p.202).

THE POMPIDOU CENTRE

Musée National d'Art Moderne

The **Musée National d'Art Moderne** occupies the fourth and fifth floors of the Pompidou Centre. With around 40,000 pieces, the museum offers a near-complete visual essay on the history of contemporary art. The layout of the collection is chronological, starting on the fifth floor and continuing below on the fourth.

Henri Matisse features prominently among the early artists on the **fifth floor**. In rooms 9, 30 and 41, you can chart the painter's journey from the previously unexplored frontiers of space and colour of **Fauvism** to the more introspective focus of a dawning **Expressionism**. Early works include a fascination with the nude, as in *Luxury I* (1907); among highlights from his later period are the swirling *Decorative Figure on an Ornamental Background* (1925–26) and the shockingly colourful *Large Red Interior* (1948). In the far reaches of rooms 31 and 32, paintings such as Picasso's *The Guitar Player* (1910) and Braque's *The Table (Still Life with Violin)* (1911) prefigure **Cubism**. Marcel Duchamp mocked the art establishment with his ready-made *Porte-bouteilles* (*The Bottle Rack*, 1914; near room 7), a bottle rack on display as art. Further along in rooms 10 and 11, abstract artist **Wassily Kandinsky**'s series the *Impressions* and the *Improvisations* mark a shift away from an obsession with subject and towards a passion for process. In room 19, the distorted and menacing *Ubu Imperator* (1927) by the German-born Max Ernst, a leading figure of the **Surrealist movement** of the interwar period, is said to symbolize the perversion of male authority. In room 39 hang Jackson Pollack's splattery *No 26A, Black and white* (1948) and Joan Miró's series, *Three Blues*, the bright lapis and azure made more intense by watery red dabs and dots of opaque jet black. Giacometti's impossibly thin and wonderfully graceful *Standing Woman* (1964) stands guard at the end of the long hallway and, in room 34, Jean Dubuffet's *Hotel in Shades of Apricot* (1947) is a choppy portrait of a dishevelled head whose slightly crossed eyes suggest more than a hint of madness.

The **fourth floor** picks up where the fifth left off, namely with **Pop Art** (room 3). Easily recognizable is Andy Warhol's piece *Ten Lizes* (1963), which features the actress Elizabeth Taylor sporting a Mona Lisa-like smile. In room 4, the **New Realists** put a disturbing spin on everyday objects, though Yves Klein's *The Tree, Large Blue Sponge* (1962), with its large sponge soaked in plaster, synthetic resin and blue pigment, is oddly serene. In the airy main hall, Claes Oldenburg's *Giant Ice Bag* sits "melting", while buried away in room 15, Joseph Beuys' hot, stale and utterly claustrophobic *Plight* (1985) features a forlorn piano surrounded by burlap. One of the most unsettling pieces in this section is Wendy Jacob's *The Somnambulist (Blue) A* (1993), made up of blankets which heave up and down as if covering a sleeping person. Further on, things become increasingly disturbing: Marie-Ange Guilleminot's sculpture *The Rotator* (1995) is a rotating object resembling a dismembered dressmaker's dummy, attempting a gymnastic routine on uneven bars.

The first three levels of the Pompidou Centre are devoted to a public library, the Bibliothèque Publique d'Information, boasting an impressive collection of periodicals, CDs and documentary films.

Atelier Brancusi

Daily except Tues 11am–9pm; admission 20F/€3.05, 30F/€4.57 combined entry with the Musée.

On the northern edge of the Pompidou Centre, down

THE POMPIDOU CENTRE

some steps off the piazza, in a small, separate building, is the **Atelier Brancusi**, the reconstructed studio of the sculptor **Constantin Brancusi**, who, when he died in 1956, bequeathed the contents of his *atelier* to the state, on condition that the rooms be arranged exactly as he left them. Studios one and two are crowded with fluid sculptures of highly polished brass and marble, his trademark abstract bird and column shapes, and stylized busts. Perhaps more satisfying are studios three and four, his private quarters, where you really get an idea of how the artist lived and worked.

QUARTIER BEAUBOURG

Map 2, H5. Mº Rambuteau & Mº Hôtel-de-Ville.

The cluster of streets surrounding the Pompidou Centre constitutes the **Quartier Beaubourg**. Beside the Pompidou Centre is place Igor Stravinsky with its **Stravinsky fountain** made up of colourful moving sculptures and squirting fountains designed by Jean Tinguely and Niki de St-Phalle. Beneath it lies **IRCAM** (Institut de la Recherche et de la Coordination Acoustique/Musique), a research centre for contemporary music founded by the composer and conductor Pierre Boulez. Its overground extension is by Renzo Piano, one of the architects of the Pompidou Centre.

IRCAM's activities are described on p.256.

North of rue Aubry-le-Boucher on the narrow, picturesque rue Quincampoix is a concentration of small **commercial art galleries**, where you can browse to your heart's content for free.

Just north of the Pompidou Centre, an impressive collection of dolls is displayed at the **Musée de la Poupée** (Tues–Sun 10am–6pm; 30F/€4.57; Mº Rambuteau),

THE HÔTEL DE VILLE

South of the Pompidou Centre, rue Renard runs down a large *place* dominated by the huge, gleaming **Hôtel de Ville**, the seat of the city's local government. Those opposed to the establishments of kings and emperors created their alternative municipal governments in this building in 1789, 1848 and 1870. The poet Lamartine proclaimed the Second Republic here during the working-class revolt of 1848, and Gambetta the Third in 1870. But, with the defeat of the Commune in 1871, the conservatives, in control once again, concluded that the Parisian municipal authority had to go, if order, property, morality and the suppression of the working class were to be maintained. For the next hundred years, Paris was ruled directly by the national government.

The city once again broke away from national control when **Jacques Chirac** became mayor in 1977 and ran Paris as his own fiefdom. He even retained the mayorship while he was prime minister – a power grab unequalled in French politics – and when he became president in 1995, he more or less nominated his successor, current mayor at the time of writing, Jean Tiberi. Both Chirac's and Tiberi's terms in office as mayor, however, have been tainted by allegations of corruption, and Chirac is currently coming under fierce pressure to explain himself to the French people.

hidden on impasse Berthaud, running off rue Beaubourg. Children especially will love the finely detailed tiny irons, sewing machines and other minuscule accessories.

THE MARAIS

Having largely escaped the depredations of modern development, as well as the heavy-handed attentions of

THE MARAIS

Baron Haussmann, the **Marais**, comprising most of the 3^e and 4^e arrondissements, remains one of the most seductive districts of Paris – old, secluded, as lively and lighthearted by night as it is by day. Through the middle, dividing it in two, roughly north and south, runs the lengthy **rue de Rivoli** and its continuation rue St-Antoine, which leads to the Bastille. South of this line is the quartier St-Paul-St-Gervais, the riverside, the Arsenal, and the Île St-Louis (see p.24). In the more heterogeneous and eclectic north are most of the Marais' shops and museums, the elegant place des Vosges, Jewish quarter, quartier du Temple, and **rue des Francs-Bourgeois**, the main lateral street of the northern part of the Marais, which also forms the boundary between the 3^e and 4^e arrondissements.

**For eating and drinking options
in the Marais, see pp.201–206.**

Originally, the area was little more than a riverside swamp (*marais*). However, in the thirteenth century, the Knights Templar settled in its northern section, now known as the **quartier du Temple**, and began to drain the land. It became a magnet for the aristocracy in the early 1600s after the construction of the **place des Vosges** – or place Royale, as it was then known – by Henri IV in 1605. This golden era was relatively short-lived, however, as the aristocracy began to move away after the king took his court to Versailles in the latter part of the seventeenth century, leaving their mansions to the trading classes, who were in turn displaced during the Revolution. Thereafter, the masses moved in, the mansions were transformed into decaying multi-occupied slum tenements and the streets degenerated into unserviced squalor – and stayed that way until the 1960s.

Since then, gentrification has proceeded apace, and the quartier is now known for its exclusivity, sophistication, and artsy leanings. It's also the neighbourhood of choice for gay Parisians, who are to be credited with bringing both business and style to the area. Renovated mansions, their intimate cobbled courtyards hidden behind magnificent *portes cochères* (huge double carriage gates), have become museums, libraries, offices and chic flats, flanked by chichi boutiques, ethnic grocers, and crowded cafés, bars and restaurants.

Maison Européenne de la Photographie

Map 4, B11. 4 rue de Fourcy. Wed–Sun 11am–8pm; 30F/€4.57, free Wed after 5pm. M° St-Paul & M° Pont-Marie.

The **Maison Européenne de la Photographie** occupies a gorgeous Marais mansion, the early eighteenth-century Hôtel Hénault de Cantobre. It's a vast and serene space dedicated to the art of contemporary photography. Temporary shows combine with a revolving exhibition of the Maison's permanent collection, featuring young photographers, news photographers and multimedia artists. A library and vidéothèque can be freely consulted, and there's a stylish café designed by architect Nestor Perkal.

Musée Carnavalet

Map 4, C10. Entrance off rue des Francs-Bourgeois at 23 rue de Sévigné. Tues–Sun 10am–5.40pm; 27F/€4.12, 35F/€5.34 with special exhibitions. M° St-Paul.

The **Musée Carnavalet** traces the history of Paris from its origins until the belle époque. The museum's extensive and beautifully presented collection fills two adjoining converted Renaissance mansions. Paris's history is presented as viewed and lived by its people: working class, bourgeoisie, aristocrats and royalty.

THE MARAIS

Note that not all the rooms are open at the same time: the Second Empire to the twentieth century section is only open from 10 to 11.50am, and the section on the sixteenth to the eighteenth century from 1.10 to 5.40pm, so to see everything you should arrive early. The ticket lasts all day so you can take a break and return later. After a trawl of the collection, you can rest in the peaceful, formally laid-out garden courtyards.

The **collection** begins with finely detailed nineteenth- and early twentieth-century shop and inn signs and fascinating models of Paris through the ages, along with maps and plans. Decorative arts feature strongly, with numerous re-created salons and boudoirs dating from the reigns of Louis XII to Louis XVI and salvaged from buildings destroyed to make way for Haussmann's boulevards. The second floor hosts mementos of the French Revolution: models of the Bastille, original *Declarations of the Rights of Man and the Citizen*, tricolours and liberty caps, sculpted allegories of Reason, crockery with Revolutionary slogans, models of the guillotine and execution orders to make you shed a tear for the royalists as well. In addition, selections from the museum's impressive collection of photographs by Brassaï, Atget and Doisneau are periodically exhibited.

Musée de l'Histoire de France

Map 4, B9. 60 rue des Francs-Bourgeois. Mon & Wed–Fri noon–5.45pm, Sat & Sun 1.45–5.45pm; closed Tues and hols; 20F/€3.05. Mº St-Paul & Mº Rambuteau.

The **Musée de l'Histoire de France** displays documents from the Archives Nationales de France. Highlights include a medieval English monarch's challenge to his French counterpart to stake his kingdom on a duel and written materials from Joan of Arc's trial proceedings, with a doodled impression of her in the margin. For most visitors, however, the museum is simply an opportunity to enter the Palais Soubise, perhaps the Marais' most splendid mansion, with some fine Rococo interiors, and paintings by the likes of Boucher.

Musée Cognacq-Jay

Map 4, C10. 8 rue Elzévir. Tues–Sun 10am–5.40pm; 22F/€3.35. M° St-Paul & M° Chemin-Vert.

The **Musée Cognacq-Jay** houses art works collected by the family who built up the Samaritaine department store – you can see a history of the family and their charitable works in a series of dioramas on the tenth-floor terrace of the store (see p.286 of "Shopping"). As well as being noted philanthropists, the Cognacq-Jays were lovers of European art. Their collection of eighteenth-century pieces on show includes works by Canaletto, Fragonard, Greuze, Tiepolo and Rembrandt, displayed in beautifully carved wood-panelled rooms.

Musée Picasso

Map 4, C9. Daily except Tues 9.30am–6pm, Thurs till 8pm; March & April till 5.30pm; 38F/€5.79, on Sun 28F/€4.27; ⓦ *www.rmn.fr* M° Chemin Vert & M° St-Paul.

Opened in 1986, the **Musée Picasso** occupies a magnificent classical seventeenth-century mansion, Hôtel Salé, at 5 rue Thorigny and houses the largest collection of Picasso's work anywhere. The paintings, however, are not the artist's most impressive – the museums of the Côte d'Azur and the Picasso gallery in Barcelona are more exciting. Nor are they even the most recognizable – the museum relies on temporary exhibitions to cover the periods least represented: the Pink Period, Cubism, the immediate post-war period and the 1950s and 1960s. However, they are the most personal,

THE MARAIS

as the collection is made up of works Picasso chose to keep. The numerous sketches, studies, paintings, scultpures and drawings supply what many art-lovers yearn for: an unedited body of work providing a sense of the artist's growth and insight into the person behind the myth. The paintings of his wives, lovers and families – the portraits of Marie-Thérèse, Claude Dessinant Françoise and Paloma, for example – are some of the gentlest and most endearing. The portrait of Dora Maar, like that of Marie-Thérèse, was painted in 1937, during the Spanish Civil War when Picasso was going through his worst personal and political crises, a period when heightened emotion and passion produced some of his most inspired work.

The museum also displays numerous paintings that the artist bought or was given by his contemporaries, as well as African masks and sculptures, photographs, letters and other personal memorabilia – items that were in the possession of the Spanish-born, Paris-based artist at the time of his death in 1973 and seized by the state in lieu of taxes owed. There are also a cinema, reference library and pleasant outdoor café.

Musée d'Art et d'Histoire du Judaisme

Map 4, A8. Mon–Fri 11am–6pm, Sun 10am–6pm; 35F/€5.34. M°
Hôtel-de-Ville.

The Hôtel de Saint-Aignan, at 71 rue du Temple, is the new home of the **Musée d'Art et d'Histoire du Judaisme**. Opened in 1998, the museum owns the Dreyfus archives, the collections of the now closed Musée d'Art Juif in Montmartre and also pieces collected by Isaac Strauss, composer and former conductor of the Paris Opera orchestra.

The museum's collection illustrates the culture, history, religion and artistic endeavours of the Jewish people in all parts of Europe and North Africa from the Middle Ages to the twentieth century. Among the **highlights** is a gilded Italian circumcision chair, one of only three surviving chairs of its kind from the early eighteenth century; an unbelievably well-preserved and completely intact nineteenth-century Austrian *Sukkah*, a makeshift hut erected for the Feast of the Tabernacles; and a Torah case from Shanghai. Throughout the museum are vast collections of prayer books, Hannukkah lamps, wedding garments, rings, and gorgeous, almost whimsical, spice containers, plus paintings by Marc Chagall, among others, which are as valuable for their subject matter – daily Jewish life – as for their artistic merits. The collection comes to a rather abrupt end with a tribute by Christian Boltanski to the hôtel's former inhabitants, Jewish artisans, who lost their lives to the Nazis in the 1930s and 1940s. Their names, dates, and birthplaces inscribed on paper rectangles, approximately the size of bricks, are posted on the walls of a tiny courtyard, echoing the death announcements posted on the walls of towns in Eastern Europe.

Place des Vosges

Map 4, D11. Mº Chemin-Vert, Mº St-Paul & Mº Bastille.

At the western end of rue des Francs-Bourgeois you can't miss the **place des Vosges**, a masterpiece of aristocratic elegance and the first example of planned development in the history of Paris. Begun in 1605 under **Henri IV** and inaugurated in 1612 for the wedding of Louis XIII and Anne of Austria, it's a vast square of symmetrical brick and stone mansions built over arcades. These days, expensive restaurants spread their tables under the arcades, the shaded benches are a favourite spot with octogenarians, buskers fill the air with classical music and toddlers and schoolchildren giggle and play in the gardens. This is the only green space of any size in the locality and, unusually for Paris, you're actually allowed to sprawl on the grass.

Through all the vicissitudes of history, the *place* has never lost its cachet as a smart address. Among the many celebrities who made their homes here was Victor Hugo; his house, at no. 6, where he wrote much of his novel *Les Misérables*, is now a museum, the **Maison de Victor Hugo** (Tues–Sun 10am–5.40pm; closed hols; 27F/€4.12). Though the extraordinary Japanese dining room he put together holds some interest, the usual portraits, manuscripts and memorabilia shed sparse light on the man and his work, particularly if you don't read French.

From the southwest corner of the *place*, a door leads through to the formal château garden, *orangerie* and exquisite Renaissance façade of the **Hôtel de Sully**. The garden, with its park benches, makes for a peaceful rest-stop, or you can pass through the building, nodding at the sphinxes on the stairs, as a pleasing shortcut to rue St-Antoine. Temporary photographic exhibitions, usually with social, historical or anthropological themes, are mounted in the hôtel by the **Mission du Patrimoine Photographique** (Tues–Sun 10am–6.30pm; 25F/€3.81), and there's a good history-focused bookshop (Tues–Sun 10am–7pm).

The Jewish Quarter

Map 4, B10. Mº St-Paul.

As the tide of gentrification sweeps remorselessly through the Marais, the only remaining islet of genuine local, community life is in the city's main Jewish quarter, still centred around **rue des Rosiers**, just as it was in the twelfth century. Though many of the little grocers, bakers, bookshops and original cafés are under pressure to sell out to more upmarket enterprises (for a long time local flats were kept empty, not for property speculation, but to try to stem the middle-class invasion), the area manages to retain its Jewish identity. There's also a distinctly Mediterranean flavour to the quartier, testimony to the influence of the **North African Sephardim**, who, since the end of World War II, have sought refuge here from the uncertainties of life in the French ex-colonies. They have replenished Paris's Jewish population, depleted when its Ashkenazim, having escaped the pogroms of Eastern Europe, were rounded up by the Nazis and the French police and transported back east to concentration camps.

Don't leave the area without wandering around the clutch of surrounding streets which best represent the evolving identity of the quartier: rue du Roi-de-Sicile, with its unpretentious eateries, the minute place Bourg-Tibourg off rue de Rivoli; the intimate rue des Écouffes; rue Ste-Croix-de-la-Bretonnerie, with its lively gay bars; rue Vieille-du-Temple, full of contemporary art galleries; and rue des Archives, where a medieval cloister, the Cloître des Billettes, at nos. 22–26, hosts free exhibitions of art and crafts (daily 10am–8pm). On the other side of rue de Rivoli, at 17 rue Geoffroy l'Asnier, the **Centre de Documentation Juive Contemporaine** mounts exhibitions concerned with genocide and oppression of peoples, and guards the sombre **Mémorial du Martyr Juif Inconnu** (Memorial to the Unknown Jewish Martyr).

THE BASTILLE

Map 4, E12. Mº Bastille.

The landmark column topped with the gilded "Spirit of Liberty" on **place de la Bastille** was erected not to commemorate the surrender in 1789 of the notorious prison, but the July Revolution of 1830 that replaced the autocratic Charles X with the "Citizen King" Louis-Philippe. When Louis-Philippe fled in the more significant 1848

Revolution, his throne was burnt beside the column and a new inscription added. Four months later, the workers again took to the streets. All of eastern Paris was barricaded, with the fiercest fighting on rue du Faubourg-St-Antoine. The rebellion was quelled with the usual massacres and deportation of survivors, and it is of course the 1789 Bastille Day, symbol of the end of feudalism in Europe, that France celebrates every year on July 14.

The Bicentennial of the Revolution in 1989 was marked by the inauguration of the **Opéra-Bastille** (see p.255), Mitterrand's pet project and subject of the most virulent sequence of rows and resignations. Filling almost the entire block between rues de Lyon, Charenton and Moreau, it has shifted the focus of place de la Bastille, so that the column is no longer the pivotal point; in fact, it's easy to miss it altogether when dazzled by the night-time glare of lights emanating from this "hippopotamus in a bathtub", as one critic dubbed it.

**For details of performances given
at the Opéra Bastille, see p.255.**

The Opéra's construction destroyed no small amount of low-rent housing, but, as with most speculative developments, the pace of change has been uneven: cobblers and ironmongers still survive alongside cocktail haunts and sushi bars that make up the simultaneously trendy and gritty **quartier de la Bastille**. **Place and rue d'Aligre** still have their raucous daily market and, on **rue de Lappe**, *Balajo* (see p.246) is one remnant of a very Parisian tradition: the *bals musettes*, or music halls of 1930s *"gai Paris"*, frequented between the wars by Edith Piaf, Jean Gabin and Rita Hayworth. It was founded by one Jo de France, who introduced glitter and spectacle into what were then seedy gangster dives, and brought Parisians from the other side of the city to the rue de Lappe lowlife. Nowadays the street is full of fun, trendy bars, full to bursting at the weekend. You'll find art galleries clustered around **rue Keller** and the adjoining stretch of **rue de Charonne**; and indie music shops and gay, lesbian and hippy outfits on rues Keller and **des Taillandiers**.

The Left Bank

The **Left Bank** (*rive gauche*) is synonymous with all things Bohemian, dissident and intellectual. In the first half of the twentieth century, the area's reputation for alternative thought and innovation attracted painters and writers like Picasso, Apollinaire, Breton, Henry Miller, Anaïs Nin and Hemingway, and later, the Existentialist philosophers Camus and Sartre. The quartier was the scene of violent student demonstrations in 1968, leading to widespread unrest and the near-overthrow of the de Gaulle government. Ironically, the very streets from which such revolution sprang are currently home to expensive flats, art galleries, and mod fashion boutiques, and the cafés once frequented by the penniless intellectuals are now filled with the well-educated bourgeois. Over the years, those who question authority and the status quo have decamped to other parts of the city and their place has been filled by the myth-makers of the image industry: designers, politicians, fashion photographers, journalists.

The heart of the Left Bank is the warren of medieval lanes around the **boulevards St-Michel** and **St-Germain**, known as the **Quartier Latin** because, until the Revolution, Latin was the language spoken at the quartier's prestigious university, the **Sorbonne**.

THE QUARTIER LATIN

The pivotal point of the **Quartier Latin** is the buzzing
place St-Michel, with its fountain, a favourite meeting
point. Leading off from here is the wide tree-lined boulevard St-Michel, with its endless cafés and bookshops, and
Rue de la Huchette, given over mainly to Greek restaurants of indifferent quality and inflated prices. In the post-
World War II years, it was the mecca of beats and bums,
and its Théâtre de la Huchette is still showing Ionesco's
Cantatrice Chauve ("The Bald Prima Donna") more than
fifty years on. Connecting rue de la Huchette to the riverside is the city's narrowest street, **rue du Chat-qui-Pêche**,
giving some idea of what Paris must once have looked like
before Haussmann set to work. One word of warning:
you'll need to watch your wallet, as the area is known for its
pickpockets and petty thieves.

Eating and drinking options in the
Quartier Latin are listed on pp.211–215.

The riverbank

M° St-Michel & RER St-Michel/Notre-Dame.
Across rue Lagrange from the square Viviani, rue de la
Bûcherie is the home of the American-run English-language bookshop **Shakespeare and Co** (see p.284), haunt-
ed by the shades of James Joyce and other great expat
literati, though only by proxy – the American Sylvia Beach,
publisher in 1922 of Joyce's *Ulysses*, had her original
Shakespeare and Co bookshop on rue de l'Odéon.

More books, postcards, prints, sheet music, records and
assorted goods are on sale from the **bouquinistes**, who display their wares in green, padlocked boxes hooked onto the

parapet of the **riverside quais** – which, in spite of their romantic associations, are not much fun to walk along because of the ceaseless traffic and the hopelessly crowded sidewalks. Better to press on as far as the tip of the Île St-Louis and the **Pont de Sully**, from which there's a dramatic view of the apse and steeple of Notre-Dame, and the beginning of a sunny riverside garden dotted with pieces of modern sculpture, known as the **Musée de Sculpture en Plein Air** (map 4, B14; Tues–Sun 10am–5pm; free).

Institut du Monde Arabe

Map 2, I10. Tues–Sun 10am–6pm; museum entry 25F/€3.81, special exhibitions extra; Ⓦ *www.imarabe.org* Mº Jussieu & Mº Cardinal-Lemoine.

At the end of the Pont de Sully, shaming the factory-like buildings of the Paris-VI university next door, stands the sleek and modern **Institut du Monde Arabe**, a cultural centre whose aim is to further national understanding of the Arab world. It opened in 1987, another of Mitterand's *Grands Projets* and a collaborative effort between France and nineteen Arab countries. Designed principally by Jean Nouvel, also behind the Fondation Cartier building (see p.101), its most stunning feature is the broad southern façade, comprising thousands of tiny and astounding light-sensitive shutters reminiscent of a *moucharabiyah* – the traditional Arab latticework balcony.

The Institute's impressive **museum** is spread over seven spacious floors and has a serene and rarefied atmosphere, not unlike that of a mosque. Exhibits such as weights and measures, celestial globes, astrolabes, compasses and sundials, along with the grinding and mixing implements for medicines, illustrate Arab scientific research between 750 and 1258 AD. There are coins from an even earlier era and beautiful illuminated manuscripts, as well as some exquisite silk carpets. Ceramics and the tools of calligraphy and cookery are also represented.

The ground floor displays **contemporary paintings and sculpture** from the Arab world, many of which have an emotional urgency that is absent in most Western art of the same period. The boldness of colour denoting sea, sand and city in Saliba Douaihy's *Beirut-Mediterranean* is made more intense by its political context, the Civil War in Beirut. Striking a more universal chord, Sami Mohamed Al-Saleh's bronze sculpture *Sabra and Chatila* represents profound agony in any context.

Located in the basement is the **Espace Image et Son** (Tues–Sat 10am–6pm; free), an archive of thousands of slides, photographs, films and recordings, which you can access yourself. There is also a specialist library (Tues–Sat 1–8pm; free).

The expensive Franco–Arab eats at *Ziryab* on the ninth floor of the Institut du Monde Arabe come with a commanding view over the Seine. Alternatively, mint tea and snacks are available in the café downstairs.

The Musée National du Moyen Âge (Thermes-de-Cluny)

Map 2, F9. Daily except Tues 9.15am– 5.45pm; 30F/€4.57, 20F/€3.05 on Sun, guided tours 35F/€5.34. Mº Cluny-La-Sorbonne & Mº St-Michel.

The **Hôtel de Cluny**, at the foot of the Montagne Ste-Geneviève, the hill on which the Panthéon stands, is a sixteenth-century mansion resembling an Oxford or Cambridge college. It was built on the site of ruined **Gallo–Roman baths** by the abbots of the powerful Cluny monastery as their Parisian pied-à-terre. It now houses the

THE QUARTIER LATIN

very beautiful **Musée National du Moyen Âge** (entrance at 6 place Paul-Painlevé), a treasure house of medieval art and tapestries.

The tapestries

The **tapestry rooms**, mainly rooms 2–4 and 12–14, contain numerous beauties, such as a marvellous depiction of the grape harvest, crafted in the Flemish city of Tournai at the end of the fifteenth century (room 2). A Resurrection scene, embroidered in gold and silver thread, stands out in room 3, along with a fourteenth-century embroidery of two leopards in red and gold and some surprisingly bright Coptic textile fragments, woven around the fourth to the sixth centuries. The sixteenth-century Dutch tapestries in room 4 depict scenes of genteel manorial life, such as flowers, birds, a woman spinning thread, a lover making advances and a hunting party leaving for the chase.

The greatest wonder of all, however, is the exquisitely executed series of tapestries, the **Lady with the Unicorn**, displayed in a special round room (room 13) on the first floor: it's simply the most stunning piece of tapestry you are ever likely to see. Dating from the late fifteenth century, the series was perhaps made in Brussels for the Le Viste family, merchants from Lyon. Their family coat of arms – three crescents on a diagonal blue stripe – is shown on flags in various scenes.

The series consists of six richly coloured and detailed allegorical scenes, each featuring a beautiful though rather sorrowful-looking young woman flanked by a lion and a unicorn. Five of the tapestries relate to the senses. The maiden is variously shown perched on a green island, playing a portable organ (hearing); taking a sweet from a proffered box (taste); making a necklace of fragrant carnations (smell); holding a mirror up to the unicorn who whimsically admires his reflection (sight); and stroking the unicorn's horn with one hand (touch). The final panel, entitled *A Mon Seul Désir* ("To My Only Desire"), depicts the ambiguous scene of the woman putting away her necklace into a jewellery box held out by her servant. Two popular interpretations are that it represents the rejection of sensual pleasure or the doctrine of free choice.

Other highlights

Scattered throughout the museum are architectural fragments and bits of sculpture from churches which provide a close-up of details usually too distant to view. The badly eroded twenty-one heads of the thirteenth-century **Kings of Judea** (room 8) from the cathedral of Notre-Dame were lopped off during the French Revolution, though only discovered in a 1977 excavation near the Palais Garnier. Room 5 holds wood and alabaster altarpiece carvings produced in England by the **Nottingham workshops**, which found homes in churches all over Europe. Room 6 is full of stained-glass panels from the **Sainte-Chapelle** (see p.20), removed here during the chapel's mid-nineteenth-century renovation.

In room 18 are fifteenth-century church stalls, and pages from various **Books of Hours**, complete with zodiac signs – these are behind glass but you can mechanically turn the pages.

Further architectural remnants from various French churches and Romanesque sculpture are displayed in the remains of the original **Gallo-Roman baths** that stood on the site. Three chambers have survived: the frigidarium (cold-bath room), caldarium (hot-bath room) and tepidarium (tepid-bath room).

The museum also has a fine collection of jewellery and metalwork, the most precious item of which is the delicate, long-stemmed **Golden Rose of Basel**, dating from 1330, in room 16.

THE QUARTIER LATIN

Regular concerts of medieval music are held
in the Roman baths. Concert tickets (around 60F/€9.15)
also provide after-hours access to the museum.
Information on ☏ 01.53.73.78.00.

The Sorbonne and around

Map 2, F10–F11. M°Cluny-La-Sorbonne.
The grim-looking buildings to the south of rue des Écoles
are the **Sorbonne**, the **Collège de France** – where
Michel Foucault taught – and the **Lycée Louis-le-Grand**,
which numbers Molière, Robespierre, Pompidou and
Victor Hugo among its graduates, and Sartre among its
teachers. All these institutions are major constituents of the
brilliant and mandarin world of French intellectual activity.

You can have a look around the **Sorbonne** courtyard
without anyone objecting. The **Richelieu chapel**, dominating the uphill end and containing the tomb of the great
cardinal, was the first Roman-influenced building in seventeenth-century Paris and set the trend for subsequent developments.

The Panthéon

Map 2, G11. Daily: April–Sept 9.30am–6.30pm; Oct–March
10am–6.15pm; closed hols; 32F/€4.88. RER Luxembourg & M°
Cardinal-Lemoine.
The broad rue Soufflot provides a grand perspective on
the domed and porticoed **Panthéon**, Louis XV's thank-
you to Sainte Geneviève, patron saint of Paris, for curing
him of illness. It was transformed during the Revolution
into a mausoleum for the great, and the ashes of Voltaire,

Rousseau, Hugo and Zola, among others, were transferred here and laid to rest in the vast barrel-vaulted crypt
below. If you've ever read Umberto Eco, you might be
interested to see a working model of Foucault's Pendulum
swinging at the site of the French physicist's 1851 experiment. A video with headphones in English tells the whole
story.

Rue Mouffetard

Map 2, H12–H14. Mº Cardinal-Lemoine.

Beginning just off tiny place de la Contrescarpe, medieval
rue Mouffetard has slightly tacky tourist leanings, but
nevertheless offers some authentic local ambience. It's lined
with numerous clothes, shoe, secondhand record and CD
shops and unpretentious cafés. The lower half of the street
is taken over by a lively market on Tuesday and Sunday
mornings.

The Paris mosque

Map 5, G3. Tours daily except Fri & Muslim hols 9am–noon &
2–6pm; 15F/€2.29. Mº Censier-Daubenton.

A little further east of rue Mouffetard, across rue Monge
and down rue Daubenton, are the crenellated walls of the
Paris mosque. You can visit the sunken garden and
patios with their polychrome tiles and carved ceilings on a
guided tour, but not the prayer room, unless you're wor-
shipping, of course. There's also a **hammam**, open to all,
though with different days for the two sexes; see p.315 for
details. The **tearoom** and restaurant (see p.211) are a
haven of calm, and a shop sells clothes, birdcages and sou-
venirs.

THE QUARTIER LATIN

Jardin des Plantes and Muséum National d'Histoire Naturelle

Map 5, I2–H3. Mº Censier-Daubenton & Mº Monge.

Opposite the mosque are the magnificent, varied floral beds of the **Jardin des Plantes**, which was founded as a medicinal herb garden in 1626 and gradually evolved into Paris's botanical gardens, with hothouses, shady avenues of trees, lawns, a brace of museums and a zoo. There are entrances at the corner of rues Geoffroy-St-Hilaire and Buffon, further north on the corner with rue Cuvier, the main gate on rue Cuvier itself, and on quai St-Bernard.

Within the Jardin des Plantes stands the **Muséum National d'Histoire Naturelle** (Wed–Mon 10am–6pm, Thurs till 10pm; 30F/€4.57; Ⓦ *www.mnhn.fr*), made up of several buildings, housing musty old collections of paleontology, mineralogy, entomology and paleobotany, all upstaged by the Grande Galerie de l'Évolution.

Grande Galerie de l'Évolution

Wed–Mon 10am–6pm, Thurs till 10pm; 40F/€6.10. Mº Censier-Daubenton & Mº Monge.

The impressive **Grande Galerie de l'Évolution** (entrance off rue Buffon) opened in 1994. It occupies the former Galerie de Zoologie, built in the nineteenth century and dramatically transformed. Behind the scrubbed stone façade, you'll be wowed by the sheer scale of the magnificent interior, supported by iron columns and roofed with glass. The museum tells the story of evolution and the relations between human beings and nature with the aid of a cast of life-like stuffed animals, a combination of clever lighting effects, ambient music and birdsong, videos and touch-screen monitors. On the lower level, submarine light suffuses the space where deep-ocean creatures are displayed. Above, glass lifts rise silently from the "savannah" – where a closely packed line of huge African animals look as if they are stepping onto Noah's ark. It's all great fun for children, and there's even a small interactive centre for kids on the first floor (see "Kids' Paris", p.300).

Ménagerie

Summer Mon–Sat 9am–6pm, Sun till 6.30pm; winter Mon–Sat 9am–5pm, Sun till 6.30pm; 30F/€4.57. M° Monge & M° Jussieu.

Located in the northeast corner of the park near rue Cuvier, the **Ménagerie** is France's oldest zoo, dating back to the Revolution. It houses an impressive assortment of creatures, from big cats to snakes, but they're kept in unacceptably cramped conditions.

The gardens

Daily: summer 7.30am–7.45pm; winter 8am–dusk. M° Austerlitz, M° Jussieu & M° Monge.

The **gardens** make a pleasant place to while away the middle of a day. Near the rue Cuvier entrance stands a fine Cedar of Lebanon, planted in 1734 and raised from seed sent over from the Botanical Gardens in Oxford. There's also a slice of an American sequoia more than 2000 years old, with the birth of Christ and other historical events marked on its rings. On a cold day there's no better place to warm up than the hot and humid winter garden, a greenhouse filled with palms, cacti and chattering birds. In the nearby physics labs, Henri Becquerel discovered radioactivity in 1896, and two years later the Curies discovered radium.

Arènes de Lutèce

Map 5, G2. M° Jussieu.

Northwest of the Jardins des Plantes, between rue Linné and rue Monge, lies the **Arènes de Lutèce**, a partly restored amphitheatre, the only other Roman remain in

THE QUARTIER LATIN

Paris besides the Gallo-Roman baths (see p.75). It's an unexpected and peaceful backwater hidden from the street and has a boules pitch in the centre, benches, gardens and a kids' playground behind.

ST-GERMAIN

The northern half of the 6ᵉ arrondissement, **St-Germain**, centred on place St-Germain-des-Prés, is the most picturesque and animated square kilometre in the entire city. It's got money, elegance and sophistication, but also an easy-going tolerance and simplicity that comes from a long association with mould-breakers and trend-setters in the arts, philosophy, politics and sciences. However, increasingly the fashion business is taking over from the literary world, with many names more associated with the Right Bank opening up shop here, pushing out booksellers and the like who cannot afford the spiralling rents.

The most dramatic approach to St-Germain is via the **Pont des Arts** footbridge, across the river from the Louvre, giving you a classic upstream view of the Île de la Cité.

Historical associations in the area are legion. Picasso painted *Guernica* in rue des Grands-Augustins. Molière started his career in rue Mazarine. Robespierre et al. split ideological hairs at *Le Procope* – Paris's first coffeehouse, opened in 1686 – in rue de l'Ancienne-Comédie. In rue Visconti, Racine died, Delacroix painted, and Balzac's printing business went bust. In the parallel rue des Beaux-Arts, Oscar Wilde died, Corot and Ampère – father of amps – lived, and crazy poet Gérard de Nerval walked a lobster on a lead.

South along rue Bonaparte, the tranquil church of **St-Sulpice** is the focal point of stylish place St-Sulpice. Further along, the Jardins surrounding the **Palais du**

Luxembourg bustle with activity, particularly on afternoons and weekends.

See pp.215–219 for eating and drinking
options in St-Germain.

Musée Delacroix

Map 2, D8. 6 rue de Furstenberg. Daily except Tues 9.30am–5.30pm; 30F/€4.57, 23F/€3.55 on Sun. Mº St-Germain-des-Prés.

The **Musée Delacroix** is where the artist lived and worked from 1857 until his death in 1863. The renovated and enlarged museum holds changing temporary exhibitions of Delacroix's work (consult *Pariscope* for details). Displayed here permanently in the painter's old apartment and studio are a few of his watercolours, a self-portrait of him dressed as Hamlet and some graphic paintings of a lion hunt. Delacroix's major work is exhibited permanently at the Louvre and the Musée d'Orsay (see pp.31 and 94), and you can see the murals he painted at nearby St-Sulpice church (see p.82).

Place St-Germain-des-Prés

Map 2, D8. Mº St-Germain-des-Prés.

Place St-Germain-des-Prés, the hub of the quartier St-Germain, is only a two-minute walk from the Musée Delacroix, with *Les Deux Magots* café (see p.215) on the corner, and *Flore* (see p.216), just down the street. Both cafés are renowned for the number of philosophico-politico-poetico-literary backsides that have shined their seats, as is the snootier *Brasserie Lipp* (see p.217), across the boulevard. All these establishments are expensive and extremely crowded in summer, but you can always eat elsewhere and just have a drink here.

ST-GERMAIN

**The riverside part of the quartier is cut
lengthways by rue St-André-des-Arts and rue Jacob,
and is full of bookshops, commercial art galleries,
antique shops, cafés and restaurants.**

The tower opposite *Les Deux Magots* belongs to the church of St-Germain, all that remains of a once-enormous Benedictine monastery. There has been a church on the site since the sixth century. Inside, the pure Romanesque lines are still clear beneath the deforming paint of nineteenth-century frescoes, while in the corner of the churchyard by rue Bonaparte, a little Picasso head of a woman is dedicated to the memory of the poet Apollinaire.

St-Sulpice

Map 2, D9. Daily 7.30am–7.30pm. M° St-Sulpice.

The enormous church of **St-Sulpice**, south of St-Germain, was erected around the turn of the eighteenth century. It's an austerely classical edifice, with a Doric colonnade surmounted by an Ionic one, and Corinthian pilasters in the towers, all unfinished apart from one, which serves as a nesting site for kestrels. The severity of the façade is somewhat softened by the chestnut trees and fountain of the square, and the ensemble is peaceful and harmonious. The best thing about the gloomy interior are the three **Delacroix murals**, including one of St-Michael slaying a dragon, found in the first chapel on the right.

Around St-Sulpice

Map 2, D8–D9. M° Mabillon.

The streets around the church of St-Sulpice are calm and classy. **Rue Mabillon**, in particular, is pretty, with a row of old houses set back below the level of the modern street. Among its two or three restaurants is the old-fashioned *Aux Charpentiers*, property of the Guild of Carpenters, decorated with models of rafters and roof-trees.

Aux Charpentiers is reviewed on p.217, along with other local eating and drinking options.

On the sunny north side of the **place St-Sulpice** stand the fashion boutiques, like Agnès B and Christian Lacroix, and the elegant **Yves Saint Laurent Rive Gauche** on the corner of the ancient **rue des Canettes**. Rues Bonaparte, Madame, de Sèvres, de Grenelle, du Four, and des Saints-Pères are lined with more of the same.

The Village Voice, a small, friendly and well-stocked American bookshop on rue Princesse, stocks the latest literature and journals.

The Palais and Jardin du Luxembourg and around

Map 2, D11–E13. Mº Odéon & RER Luxembourg.

The **Palais** and **Jardin du Luxembourg** were built by Marie de Médicis, Henri IV's widow, to remind her of the Palazzo Pitti and Giardino di Boboli of her native Florence. The palace is now the seat of the French Senate. Opposite the gates, scarcely noticeable on the end wall of the colonnade of no. 36 rue de Vaugirard, is a metre rule, set up during the Revolution to guide the people in the introduction of the new metric system.

The **gardens** are the chief lung and recreation ground of the Left Bank, with tennis courts, pony rides, a children's playground, boules pitch, yachts to rent on the pond and,

ST-GERMAIN

in the wilder southeast corner, a miniature orchard of elaborately espaliered pear trees. It has a distinctly Mediterranean air on summer days. Strollers and sunbathers vie for their own metal chair or space on a bench, while the most contested spot for lovers is the shady, seventeenth-century **Fontaine de Médicis**, in the northeast corner. There are many other sculptural works in the park, including an 1890 monument to the painter Delacroix by Jules Dalou.

In the last week of September, an "Expo-Automne" takes place in the **Orangerie** (entrance from 19 rue de Vaugirard, opposite rue Férou), where fruits – including the Luxembourg's own wonderful pears – and floral decorations are sold.

Trocadéro, the Eiffel Tower and Les Invalides

When it comes to town planning on a grand scale there is little to rival the area west of St-Germain-des-Prés, stretching from the 7e into the 16e arrondissement across the river. The sweeping vista from the terrace of the Palais de Chaillot on **place du Trocadéro** across the river to the **Eiffel Tower** and École Militaire, no doubt familiar to many visitors from countless images and photos, is truly impressive. Equally magnificent is the view from the ornate Pont Alexandre III along the grassy Esplanade to the colossus that is the **Hôtel des Invalides**. The 7e arrondissement is home to the Assemblée Nationale and has the greatest concentration of ministries, embassies and official residences in Paris. The area's main art gallery, the **Musée d'Orsay**, is also housed in an impressive and unusual building, a cavernous, decommissioned railway station.

PALAIS DE CHAILLOT

Map 7, B7–C6. M° Trocadéro.

The Trocadéro area, made up of the place du Trocadéro and terraced gardens, is dominated by the **Palais de Chaillot**. Built in 1937 for the Exposition Universelle, it's a rather ugly building, in sober Neoclassical style. The central terrace between its two wings has been kept clear, forming a perfect frame for the Eiffel Tower beyond. The vast building houses the radical Théâtre National de Chaillot (see p.264) and four museums, only two of which are currently visitable – the **Musée de l'Homme** and the **Musée de la Marine**. Damage from a fire in 1996 closed the **Musée du Cinéma Henri-Langlois**, for which a permanent home has still to be found. The **Musée des Monuments Français** has been closed for renovation and will form part of a planned "Cité de l'Architecture et du Patrimoine", a vast architectural information resource centre, due to open in 2003.

Musée de l'Homme

Daily except Tues 9.45am–5.15pm; 30F/€4.57.

The **Musée de l'Homme** examines the origins, cultures, languages and genetics of humans, from "Lucy", the *Australopithecus afarensis* who roamed Ethiopia roughly 3.2 million years ago, to the present day. In 2002, however, a large section of the museum's collection will be uprooted and transferred to a brand-new museum on quai Branly, the other side of the river (see p.88).

Musée de la Marine

Daily except Tues 10am–6pm; 38F/€5.79.

Sharing the southern wing of the Musée de l'Homme, the

Musée de la Marine displays beautiful models of French ships, ancient and modern, warring and commercial.

EAST OF TROCADÉRO

As you head east and downhill from Trocadéro, you'll find a handful of museums all within a stone's throw of each other. The first, on place d'Iéna, is the **Musée National des Arts Asiatiques – Guimet** (map 7, D5), currently closed for renovation, but due to reopen at the beginning of 2001. It features a huge and exquisite collection of art from China, India, Japan, Tibet and Southeast Asia, and much more of the collection will be on display when the museum reopens. The original core of the collection, which the art collector, Émile Guimet, brought back from his travels in Asia in 1876, is exhibited nearby in the small and attractive **Musée du Panthéon Bouddhique** (map 7, D5; daily except Tues 9.45am–5.45pm; 16F/€2.44), at 19 avenue d'Iéna. At the back of the museum is a small Japanese garden, complete with bamboo, pussywillow and water.

The **Palais de Tokyo** (map 7, E6), a contemporary of the Palais de Chaillot and no less hideous, is a short way east of the Panthéon Bouddhique, its entrance on avenue du Président Wilson. The east wing houses the **Musée d'Art Moderne de la Ville de Paris** (Tues–Fri 10am–5.30pm, Sat & Sun 10am–6.45pm; 30F/€4.57), whose outstanding permanent collection of twentieth-century art includes Dufy's enormous mural *La Fée Électricité* (*The Electricity Fairy*), the pale leaping figures of Matisse's *The Dance* and Robert and Sonia Delaunay's huge whirling wheels and cogs of rainbow colour. The west wing of the Palais de Tokyo is due to open at the end of 2001 as the **Site de Création Contemporaine**, a space devoted to the promotion of contemporary art which promises interesting temporary exhibitions.

Opposite the Palais de Tokyo, set in small gardens at 10 avenue Pierre 1er de Serbie, stands the grandiose Palais Galliera (map 7, E5), home to the **Musée de la Mode et du Costume** (open during exhibitions only, Tues–Sun 10am–6pm; 30F/€4.57). The museum's collection of clothes and fashion accessories from the eighteenth century to the present day is exhibited in temporary, themed shows. There are two or three per year – during changeovers the museum is closed.

Across the Seine from the Palais de Tokyo, on quai Branly, the temporary structures of the Espace Eiffel-Branly (map 7, E7), host to international trade fairs, occupy a space which is to be transformed under Jean Nouvel, architect of the Institut du Monde Arabe, into a purpose-built museum housing the collections from the Musée de l'Homme's ethnography department and the Musée des Arts d'Afrique et d'Océanie. The new museum is due to open in 2004. In the meantime, a showcase for the museum has been put together and is being exhibited in the Louvre in the pavillon des Sessions.

**For progress on the Musée du quai Branly,
check the website Ⓦ www.quaibranly.fr**

THE EIFFEL TOWER

Map 7, D8. Daily: Sept–May 9.30am–11pm (access to stairs closes at 6.30pm); June–Aug 9am–midnight. M° Bir-Hakeim/Trocadéro, RER Champ-de-Mars-Tour-Eiffel.

On its completion in 1889 for the Exposition Universelle, the **Eiffel Tower** was, at 300m, the tallest building in the world. At the time, it provoked some violent reactions and was described as "useless" and "monstrous" by leading critics of the day. Eiffel himself thought it was beautiful. "The first principle of architectural aesthetics," he said, "prescribes that the basic lines of a structure must correspond precisely to its specified use . . . To a certain extent the tower was formed by the wind itself."

Lit from within by a complex system of illumination, the Tower looks at its magical best after dark, as light and fanciful as a filigree minaret. By day, it's only really worth the expense of going to the top if the weather is absolutely clear. **Tickets** cost 62F/€9.45 to the top by lift or 36F/€5.49 if you take the stairs up the first two levels and the lift up to the final level. You can also go part-way: 22F/€3.35 for the lift to the first level, 44F/€6.71 to the second, and 18F/€2.74 (both levels) if you take the stairs. All tickets allow free entry to the audiovisual show about the Tower on the first level.

LES INVALIDES

Map 7, J9. Mº Invalides, Mº Latour-Maubourg & Mº Varenne.

The **Esplanade des Invalides** strikes due south from **Pont Alexandre III** and provides a functional 500m of grassy area, intersected by roads and edged by trees and *boules* terrain. The wide façade of the **Hôtel des Invalides**, topped by its distinctive dome, resplendent with gilding, fills the whole of the further end of the Esplanade. It was built on the orders of Louis XIV as a home for wounded soldiers, and part of the building is still used for this. Under the dome are two churches: one for the soldiers, the other intended as a mausoleum for the king, but now containing the mortal remains of Napoleon.

Both churches are cold and dreary inside. The **Église du Dôme**, in particular, is a supreme example of architectural pomposity. Corinthian columns and pilasters abound. The inside of the dome is covered with paintings and flanked by four round chapels containing the tombs of various luminaries such as Marshal Foch and Joseph, Napoleon's older

LES INVALIDES

brother. Napoleon's sarcophagus, of smooth, red porphyry, is sunk into the floor and enclosed within a gallery. Friezes on the walls depict Napoleon sporting a laurel wreath and toga and addressing his subjects. The captions display awesome conceit: "Co-operate with the plans I have laid for the welfare of peoples"; "By its simplicity my code of law has done more good in France than all the laws which have preceded me"; "Wherever the shadow of my rule has fallen, it has left lasting traces of its value."

The Hôtel also houses a couple of museums, the larger of which is the **Musée de l'Armée**, France's vast national war museum (daily: April–Sept 10am–6pm; Oct–March 10am–5pm; 37F/€5.64, ticket includes entry to Napoleon's tomb and Musée des Plans-reliefs). The exhibition, displayed over several floors and wings, starts with ancient weapons and armoury, including François I's suit of armour and some beautifully decorated oriental war outfits. In the east wing, the history of the French armed forces is documented via its uniforms and weaponry, while in the south-westerly wing, a new three-floor section on World War II has recently opened. Battle tactics, the resistance and liberation are documented through the usual maps and displays, but it's the reels of contemporary footage (English translation available) that are the most stirring.

The Hôtel des Invalides also houses the **Musée des Plans-reliefs** (daily: April–Sept 10am–6pm; Oct–March 10am–5pm; entry included in the ticket for the Musée de l'Armée), an important and historic collection of models of strategic and fortified towns, formerly indispensable for military reconnaissance and planning manoeuvres.

AROUND LES INVALIDES

Just beyond the southeastern corner of Les Invalides, and perfectly in line with the view east from Trocadéro, stands the **École Militaire** (map 6, B7–C5), founded in 1751 by Louis XV for the training of aristocratic army officers – no prizes for guessing who the most famous graduate was. Taking avenue Bosquet from the École Militaire brings you down to the quai d'Orsay and the entrance to the **Musée des Égouts** (map 6, A1; Mon–Wed, Sat & Sun: May–Oct 11am–5pm; Nov–April 11am–4pm; 25F/€3.81), a visitable part of the city's sewer system. The underground visit is fairly disappointing, though, taking you through a few large tunnels filled with a small amount of smelly water and finishing with a rather dull video on how the sewers are maintained.

East of Les Invalides runs rue de Varenne, lined with aristocratic mansions, including the **Hôtel Matignon**, the prime minister's residence, and a museum devoted to one of France's great sculptor's, Rodin.

Musée Rodin

Map 6, E4. 77 rue de Varenne. Tues–Sun: April–Sept 9.30am–5.45pm; Oct–March 9.30am–4.45pm; the garden closes at 7pm; 28F/€4.27, on Sun 18F/€2.74, garden only 5F/€0.76; Ⓦ *www.musee-rodin.fr* M° Varenne.

The **Musée Rodin** is housed in a beautiful eighteenth-century mansion, which the sculptor leased from the state in return for the gift of all his work at his death. In the garden you'll find major works like *The Burghers of Calais*, *Balzac*, *The Thinker* and the unfinished *Gates to Hell*, inspired by Dante's vision of hell in his *Divine Comedy*. Indoors are studies and smaller works like *The Kiss*: the two lovers were originally meant to represent Paolo and Francesca and intended to feature in the *Gates to Hell* piece. Other notable works can be found inside, including *The Hand of God* (or *The Creation*), seemingly in the process of taking shape, studies for his larger works and a whole room

AROUND LES INVALIDES

devoted to Camille Claudel, Rodin's pupil, model and lover. Among her pieces is a bust of Rodin himself. Claudel's perception of her teacher was so akin to Rodin's own that he regarded it as a self-portrait.

Musée Maillol

Map 6, H5. 61 rue de Grenelle. Daily except Tues 11am–6pm; 40F/€6.10. Mº Varenne.

An elegant eighteenth-century house houses the **Musée Maillol**. The exhibits inside belong to Dina Vierny, former model and inspiration to the sculptor Aristide Maillol, whose work adorns the Jardin du Carrousel by the Louvre. The carefully studied curves of the female form are rendered in an abundance of paintings, drawings and sculptures; his most famous work, the seated *Mediterranean*, an allegory for his artistic inspiration and heritage, can be found on the first floor at the top of the stairs.

THE MUSÉE D'ORSAY

Map 6, H2. 1 rue de Solférino. Oct–June 20 Tues, Wed, Fri, & Sat 10am–6pm, Thurs 10am–9.45pm, Sun 9am–6pm; June 21–Sept Tues–Sun 9am–6pm, Thurs till 9.45pm; 40F/€6.10; Ⓦ *www.musee-orsay.fr* Mº Solférino & RER Musée-d'Orsay.

The heavy-set, stone **Musée d'Orsay**, in a converted railway station, located on the riverfront, contains three floors of painting and sculpture from 1848 to 1914, including the electrifying **Impressionists** and their successors, the **Post-Impressionists**.

The building itself was originally inaugurated as a railway station in 1900, continuing to serve the stations of southwest France until 1939. After that, the theatre troupe Renaud-Barrault staged several productions here, Orson Welles filmed his version of Kafka's *The Trial* here and De

Gaulle used it to announce his coup d'état of May 19, 1958. Notwithstanding this illustrious history, it was only spared a hotel developer's bulldozer by a colossal wave of public indignation and remorse on the part of the city authorities at the destruction of Les Halles (see p.52).

The job of redesigning the interior as a museum was given, in 1986, to fashionable Milanese architect Gae Aulenti. The results are, without doubt, ingenious, a combination of well-laid out galleries, ample lighting, fine presentation and an invigorating pulse reminiscent of its days as a train station. Critics complain that the space is overdesigned and the collection overwhelmingly large, but don't be put off: the collection is unsurpassed in quality, as well as quantity. It's well worth taking half a day, if not a whole one, to meander through it.

The collection

The **collection** is arranged in a cavernous central space and on three storeys either side. The **general layout** follows a loose chronological thread, beginning on the ground floor, continuing on the top floor and finishing on the middle level. Each room is numbered, a fact generally ignored by most visitors, and seeing them in order is highly advisable.

Romantic and Neoclassical artists are exhibited on the ground floor, including, in the central aisle, the **mid–nineteenth–century** sculptors Carpeaux, whose titillating piece *The Dance* (1863–1869) shocked contemporary audiences, and Barye, whose bronze cast of *The Seated Lion* (1847) was more warmly received. The galleries in the far left corner of the building display **furniture** and **architectural models** spanning Viollet-le-Duc to Frank Lloyd Wright, and offer unobstructed views of Sacré-Cœur. The far end of the ground floor features models and drawings of the **Opéra Garnier**, completed in 1875.

THE MUSÉE D'ORSAY

To the right of the central aisle, rooms dedicated to Ingres and Delacroix highlight the colourful and dramatically emotional **Romanticism** of the early nineteenth century. Puvis de Chavannes, Gustave Moreau and early Degas follow, while over in the galleries to the left, Daumier, Corot, Millet and the **Realist school** depart from the academic parameters of moralistic subject matter and idealization of the past.

Enter the ground-breaking works that were to inspire the early Impressionists: among these are Courbet's *Origin of the World* (1866; room 7), a painting of a foreshortened nude female lounging on a rumpled bed, her genitalia exposed; and Manet's *Olympia* (1863; room 14), as controversial in its day for its colour contrasts and sensual surfaces, as for the portrayal of Olympia as a defiant high-class whore. Both paintings mark a transition from the traditional subtle treatment of the artist's nude to the representation of explicit sexuality.

The *Café des Hauteurs* on the top floor of the museum, and a restaurant and tearoom in the elaborately gilded former station restaurant hall on the middle level, are good spots to recuperate after a tour of the paintings.

The collection continues chronologically on the top level. The private collection donated by the assiduous collector and art historian Moreau-Nélaton resides in room 29 and features some of the most famous Impressionist images – Monet's *Poppies* (1873) and Manet's *Déjeuner sur l'Herbe*, literally "lunch on the grass", which was refused by the Salon in 1863: the critics were scandalized by the alleged indecency of two fully dressed men sitting alongside a naked female bather. The next few rooms serve up **Impressionism**'s most identifiable masterpieces: Degas' ballet dancers, caught backstage and arranged in Japanese-influenced compositions; and numerous landscapes and out-door scenes by Renoir, Sisley, Pissarro and Monet. *The Cradle* (1872; room 30), by Berthe Morisot, the only woman in the group of early Impressionists, synthesizes the classic techniques of the movement with complex human emotion. Shimmering light and wide brush strokes domi-nate Renoir's depiction of *Dancing at the Moulin de la Galette* (1876; room 32) – a favourite Sunday-afternoon social event on the Butte Montmartre.

The museum owns five of the thirty paintings in Monet's Rouen cathedral series (1892–1894; room 34), a collection that tracks his obsession with light. Both *La Gare Saint-Lazare* (1877; room 32) and *Water Lilies* (room 34) are parts of separate series, done fifteen years before and after respec-tively, with a similar goal in mind. Room 35, full of the bold colours and disturbing rhythms of Van Gogh, illus-trates the **Post-Impressionists'** distinct departure from the already established Impressionists. Cézanne is wonderfully represented in room 36; his complex *Still Life with Apples and Oranges* (1895–1900), with its jaunty diagonal lines, prefigures Cubism.

The rest of the top level is given over to the various descendants of Impressionism. Among a number of **Pointilliste** works by Seurat, Signac and others, is Rousseau's dream-like *Snake Charmer* (1907; room 42), made all the more remarkable when you remember that the artist was essentially self-taught. There's Gauguin, post- and pre-Tahiti, as well as plenty of Toulouse-Lautrec's images of life in Paris's brassy theatres, cafés, bars, brothels and night clubs.

The middle level takes in Rodin and other **late-nineteenth-century sculptors**, several rooms of superb **Art Nouveau** and **Jugendstil** furniture and *objets*, and the original sumptuous reception room (room 51) of the station hotel. Overlooking the Seine, room 60 features Klimt's *Rose*

THE MUSÉE D'ORSAY

Bushes Under Trees (1905), with its glittery leaves, and some of Munch's lesser known works. Across the corridor, tucked away in rooms 71 and 72, are the Nabis painters, Vuillard and Bonnard, whose pieces are very much inspired by the art of Japan.

Montparnasse and the southern arrondissements

I n the eighteenth century, the pile of earth excavated from the Denfert-Rochereau quarries, on what is now the corner of boulevard du Montparnasse and boulevard Raspail, was named Mont Parnasse (Mount Parnassus) by drunken students, who liked to declaim poetry from the top of it. The area, today **Montparnasse**, stretching from the railway station to the Observatoire, was to keep its associations with art, bohemia and intellectualism, attracting the likes of Verlaine and Baudelaire in the nineteenth century, and Trotsky, Picasso, Man Ray, Chagall, Hemingway, Sartre and Simone de Beauvoir in the twentieth. They frequented the brasseries on the **boulevard du Montparnasse**, and many of them found their final resting-place in the **Montparnasse cemetery**, just south of the boulevard. Casting its shadow over the whole area is the skyscraping black **Tour Montparnasse**. Full of offices, and located between the train station and a large shopping centre, it forms a pivotal point for much of the activity in Montparnasse today.

The Montparnasse quartier divides the lands of the well-heeled opinion-formers and power-brokers of St-Germain and the 7e from the amorphous populations of the three **southern arrondissements**, the 13e, 14e and 15e. Unsightly, modern constructions have scarred some parts of this southern side of the city, but new spaces have also opened up, and some of the smaller-scale developments are delightful. Some pockets have been allowed to evolve in a happily patchy way – **Pernety** and **Plaisance** in the 14e, the **rue du Commerce** in the 15e, and the **Butte-aux-Cailles** quartier in the 13e. These are genuinely pleasant places to explore, well off the tourist track.

TOUR MONTPARNASSE

Map 6, G10. Summer 9.30am–11.30pm; winter 9.30am–10.30pm; 48F/€7.32 to 59th floor, 40F/€6.10 to 56th floor. Mº Montparnasse-Bienvenue.

Directly in front of the Gare Montparnasse looms the **Tour Montparnasse**. This has become one of the city's principal and least-liked landmarks – most tolerable at night, when the red corner lights give it a certain elegance. At 200m, it held the record as Europe's tallest office building until it was overtaken by the tower at London Docklands' Canary Wharf. You can pay to take the lift to the indoor viewing platform on the 56th floor or the outdoor one on the 59th floor for less than it costs to go to the top of the Eiffel Tower. Alternatively, you could sit down for an expensive drink or meal in the bar/restaurant, the *Ciel de Paris*, on the 56th floor (lift ride free). From here you get a tremendous view west over the city, especially at sunset.

THE BOULEVARD DU MONTPARNASSE AND AROUND

Most of the life of the Montparnasse quartier is concentrated around place du 18-Juin-1940, at the foot of the tour Montparnasse, and on the immediate eastern stretch of the **boulevard du Montparnasse**. Like other Left-Bank quartiers, Montparnasse still trades on its association with the wild characters of the interwar artistic and literary boom. Many were habitués of the cafés *Select*, *Coupole*, *Dôme*, *Rotonde* and *Closerie des Lilas*, all still going strong on the boulevard. The quartier stays up late, and negotiating the pavements, never mind the road, requires some care.

The animated part of the road ends at **boulevard Raspail**, where Rodin's *Balzac* broods over the traffic, though literary curiosity might take you down as far as the rather swanky brasserie **Closerie des Lilas**, on the corner of the tree-lined avenue connecting the Observatoire and Jardin du Luxembourg. Hemingway used to come here to write, and Marshal Ney, one of Napoleon's most glamorous generals, was killed by a royalist firing squad on the pavement outside in 1815.

The *Closerie des Lilas* and other cafés on boulevard du Montparnasse are reviewed on pp.221–222.

In the boulevard's surrounding streets, artistic activity, past and present, is represented by several small **museums**.

Musée du Montparnasse

Map 6, F10. 21 av du Maine. Wed–Sun 1–7pm; 25F/€3.81. M° Montparnasse-Bienvenue.

Picasso, Léger, Modigliani, Chagall, Braque and other members of the Montparnasse group of artists from the first half of the twentieth century used to dine at the *Cantine des Artistes*, a canteen run by Vassilieff from her studio on avenue du Maine. The rambling, ivy-clad alley has been saved from demolition and the studio converted into the **Musée du Montparnasse**, which hosts temporary exhibitions of work by Montparnasse artists, past and present.

Musée Bourdelle

Map 6, F10. Tues–Sun 10am–5.40pm; 22F/€3.35. M°
Montparnasse-Bienvenue.

On rue A. Bourdelle, opposite the Musée du Montparnasse, a garden of sculptures invites you into **Musée Bourdelle**, the former atelier of the early twentieth-century sculptor, Antoine Bourdelle. His work draws on Ancient Greece for inspiration and also shows the influence of his tutor Rodin, whose *profils rassemblés* ("assembled profiles") technique is particularly evident in the bust of Rodin in the garden. The house contains casts, drawings and tools, as well as studies for his great works, such as the homage to Mickiewicz, a column covered in friezes and crowned by a statue of the Polish poet, the completion of which took Bourdelle twenty years. The original can be seen on place de l'Alma, south-west of the Palais Galliera (see p.88).

A large selection of Rodin's work is
on view at the Musée Rodin; see p.91.

Musée Zadkine

Map 5, A3. 100 bis Assas. Tues–Sun 10am–5.40pm; 22F/€3.35. M°
Vavin & RER Port-Royal.

The rustic cottage at 100 bis Assas, the home and studio of Russian sculptor Ossip Zadkine from 1928 to 1967, is now a museum devoted to his work, the **Musée Zadkine**. The sculptor's angular Cubist bronzes are scattered throughout the house and garden, sheltering under trees or emerging from clumps of bamboo, and invite contemplative lingering.

Fondation Cartier pour l'Art Contemporain

Map 6, I13. 261 bd Raspail. Mº Raspail.

The **Fondation Cartier pour l'Art Contemporain** is a stunning glass-and-steel construction designed by Jean Nouvel in 1994. A glass wall following the line of the street is attached by steel tubes to the building behind, leaving a space for trees to grow. All kinds of contemporary art – installations, videos, multimedia – often by foreign artists little known in France, are shown in temporary exhibitions that use the light and very generous spaces to maximum advantage.

MONTPARNASSE CEMETERY

Map 6, G12–I13. April–Oct Mon–Fri 8am–6pm, Sat from 8.30am, Sun from 9am; Nov–March closes at 5.30pm. Mº Egar-Quinet & Mº Raspail.

Just off to the southern side of boulevard Edgar-Quinet is the main entrance to the **Montparnasse cemetery**, a suitably gloomy spot containing ranks of miniature temples, dreary and bizarre, and plenty of illustrious names. To the right of the entrance, by the wall, is the unembellished joint grave of Jean-Paul Sartre and Simone de Beauvoir. Sartre lived out the last few decades of his life just a few metres away on boulevard Raspail.

Down avenue de l'Ouest, which follows the western wall

of the cemetery, you'll find the **tombs** of Baudelaire, the painter Soutine, Dadaist Tristan Tzara, sculptor Zadkine, and the Fascist Pierre Laval, a member of Pétain's government who, after the war, was executed for treason, not long after a suicide attempt. As an antidote, you can pay homage to Proudhon, the anarchist who coined the phrase "Property is theft!"; he lies in Division 1, by the Carrefour du Rond-Point.

In the southwest corner of the cemetery is an old **windmill**, which housed a tavern in the seventeenth century and was frequented by the carousing, versifying students who gave the Montparnasse district its name.

Across rue Émile-Richard, in the eastern section of the cemetery, lie car-maker André Citroën, Guy de Maupassant, César Frank, and the celebrated victim of French anti-Semitism at the end of the nineteenth century, Captain Dreyfus. Right in the northern corner is a tomb with a sculpture by Brancusi, *The Kiss*. Its depiction of two people, locked in an embrace, sculpted from the same piece of stone, speaks of an undying love, and makes a far more poignant statement than the dramatic and passionate scenes of grief adorning so many of the other graves.

THE CATACOMBS

Map 6, I14. Tues–Fri 2–4pm, Sat & Sun 9–11am & 2–4pm; 33F/€5.03. Mº Denfert-Rochereau.

If you're determined to spend your time among the deceased, you can descend into **the catacombs** in nearby **place Denfert-Rochereau**, formerly place d'Enfer or "Hell Square". The entrance is on the east side of avenue Général-Leclerc; don't go down in fancy new shoes – it's wet and gungy underfoot. The catacombs are abandoned quarries stacked with millions of bones cleared from the old charnel houses in 1785. They are claustrophobic in the extreme, and cold to boot. Some years ago a group of punks and art students developed a macabre taste for this as the ultimate party location, but the authorities soon put an end to that.

THE OBSERVATOIRE DE PARIS

Map 5, B5. Rue Cassini. Mº Denfert-Rochereau & RER Port-Royal.

The Paris meridian line originated in the **Observatoire de Paris**, northeast of Denfert-Rochereau. From the 1660s, when the observatory was constructed, to 1884, all French maps had the zero meridian running through the middle of this building. After that date, they reluctantly agreed that 0° longitude should pass through a village in Normandy, which happens to be due south of Greenwich. Although you can no longer visit the Obersatory, you can see the original meridian line in the garden behind, on boulevard Arago, marked by a medallion set in the pavement. In 1986, the bicentenary of Arago's birth, 135 of these medallions were set along the Arago line in Paris. Many have since been uprooted, but a few are still in place.

THE 14ᵉ SOUTH OF MONTPARNASSE

The **14ᵉ** is one of the most characterful of the outer arrondissements. Old-fashioned networks of streets still exist in the **Pernety** and **Plaisance** quartiers, and between avenues Réné-Coty and Général-Leclerc. In the early years of the twentieth century, so many outlawed Russian revolutionaries lived in the 14ᵉ that the Tsarist police ran a special Paris section to keep tabs on them. The 14ᵉ was also a favourite address for artists, who could live in seclusion in its many *villas* (mews) built in the 1920s and 1930s. There's still a thriving artistic community here, though only the very successful can afford the *villas* these days. Cité Bauer,

the road that runs between rue Boyer-Barret and rue
Didot, is lined with adorable little houses and gardens;
neighbouring rue des Thermopyles has its secluded courtyards; and below rue d'Alésia, more quiet *villas* lead off
from rue Didot. Giacometti's old ramshackle studio and
home still stands on the corner of rue du Moulin Vert and
rue Hippolyte-Maindron. At the end of Impasse Floriment,
behind a petrol station on rue d'Alésia and holding out
against development threats, a bronze relief of Georges
Brassens, smoking his pipe – created by a contemporary
local artist – adorns the tiny house where Brassens lived and
wrote his songs from 1944 to 1966.

Rue d'Alésia (map 1, D6), the main east–west route
through the 14ᵉ, has a small **food market** every Thursday
and Sunday between the Plaisance métro and rue Didot,
but is best known for its good-value **clothes shops**, many
selling discounted couturier creations. These congregate
towards place Victor & Hélène Basch, where there's another delightful example of an old-style mews, the Villa
d'Alésia.

At the weekend, it's worth heading out to the southern
edge of the arrondissement, past the characterless flats on
boulevard Brune, for one of the city's best **flea markets**
(map 1, D7; see p.293). Starting at daybreak, it spreads
along the pavements of avenues Marc-Sangnier and
Georges-Lafenestre, petering out at its western end in place
de la Porte-de-Vanves.

For listings of Paris's other flea markets, see p.293.

More *villas* edge the western side of the **Parc
Montsouris** (map 1, E7), down in the southeast corner of
the 14ᵉ: Georges Braque lived at no. 6 in the one named
after him, and the studio at no. 53 square du Montsouris
was designed by Le Corbusier. The park was a favourite

walking place of Lenin's, and no doubt of all the local artists, too. Its peculiarities include a meteorological office, a marker of the old meridian line, near boulevard Jourdan, and, by the southwest entrance, a kiosk run by the French Astronomy Association.

On the other side of boulevard Jourdan, several thousand students from more than one hundred different countries live in the curious array of buildings of the **Cité Universitaire** (map 1, E7). The diverse styles of the international halls of residence reflect the variety of nations and peoples who study here; the Cambodia hall of residence is guarded by startling stone creatures next to the boulevard périphérique, and the Swiss hall was designed by Le Corbusier during his stilts phase.

THE 15^e

Between the Montparnasse railway tracks and the river lies Paris's largest, most populated and characterless arrondissement, the **15e**. The liveliest part of the quartier is the **rue du Commerce** (map 1, C5), a busy old-fashioned high street, where George Orwell worked as a dishwasher in a White Russian restaurant in the late 1920s, a period described in his *Down and Out in Paris and London*. Although there are still run-down and poor areas, an ever-widening stretch back from the **riverfront** has been sown with plush and featureless high-rise flats with underground parking, serviced lifts and electronic security. A welcome addition to the quartier is the open space of the **Parc André-Citroën** (map 1, C5–C6), laid out in 1993, on the site of the old Citroën works down in the southwest corner. The modern landscaping includes a sound garden with bubbling water on one side and a gushing cascade on the other; secluded gardens and stretches of grass for playing games; hothouses with mimosa, fish-tailed palms and other sweet-smelling shrubbery; and a capricious set of fountain jets, popular with children on a hot day. The down side is that there's rather too much concrete here, all the more evident when the sun doesn't shine.

For restaurants, cafés and bars in the 15ᵉ, see pp.223–224.

Over towards the railway lines stretches the more traditional-style **Parc Georges-Brassens** (map 1, C6–D6), built in the 1980s on the site of a former abattoir. It's a delight, especially for children: attractions include puppets and merry-go-rounds, a mountain stream with pine and birch trees, beehives and a tiny terraced vineyard, and a garden of scented herbs and shrubs designed principally for the blind. The success of the park has rubbed off on **rue des Morillons** and **rue Brancion** – new restaurants and tearooms have opened, and new life has been injected into existing cafés. On Saturday and Sunday mornings, take a look in the sheds of the old horse market between the park and rue Brancion where dozens of **book dealers** set out their genuinely interesting stock.

On the west side of the park, in a secluded garden in passage Dantzig, stands an unusual polygonal building known as **La Ruche** ("The Beehive"; map 1, C6). It was designed by Eiffel and started life as the wine pavilion for the 1900 World Trade Fair. After the Fair ended, the pavilion was bought by Alfred Boucher, sculptor of public monuments and friend of Rodin, and re-erected in passage Dantzig as a base for struggling artists. Very soon La Ruche became home to Fernand Léger, Modigliani (briefly), Chagall, Soutine, Ossip Zadkine and many others, mainly Jewish refugees from pogroms in Poland and Russia. The writer Blaise Cendrars was a regular visitor, as were Apollinaire and Max Jacob, who provided a link with the Picasso gang across the river in Montmartre. The French, however, were in a minority – you were much more likely to hear Yiddish, Polish, Russian or Italian spoken. The buildings were threatened with demolition in 1970, but were saved by a campaign led by Marc Chagall. The studios were restored and a number of artists, mostly Irish, American, Italian and Japanese, have since taken up residence here.

For transport through the 15ᵉ, 14ᵉ and 13ᵉ arrondissements, bus #62 plies a useful route along rues Convention, Alésia and Tolbiac.

If you're heading towards Montparnasse from Parc Georges-Brassens, you're better off taking bus #89 rather than slogging it on foot. Not a lot happens in this eastern stretch of the 15ᵉ. To the north, between rue du Docteur-Roux and rue Falguière, is the **Institut Pasteur** (map 6, C11–D12; daily 2–5pm; closed Aug; 15F/€2.29), renowned for its founder Louis, and for its research into AIDS. A pass obtained from the office opposite allows you to enter the building, where guided tours (English version available) take you through the **Musée Pasteur**, comprising the great nineteenth-century chemist–biologist's apartment, laboratory and Byzantine-style mausoleum. Of non-scientific, but equal, interest is the sombre interior decoration (plus innovative plumbing) of Pasteur's apartment, typical of a nineteenth-century Parisian middle-class home.

THE 13ᵉ

To the tight-knit community who lived in the crowded, rat-ridden and ramshackle slums around **rue Nationale** (map 5, J7–J8) in the postwar years, Paris was another place, rarely ventured into. Come the 1950s and 1960s, however, the city planners, here as elsewhere, came up with their usual solution to the housing problem – getting rid of the

THE 13ᵉ

107

slums to make way for tower blocks. However, the architectural gloom of the southeastern half of the arrondissement is alleviated by three distinct quartiers. West of avenue d'Italie and avenue des Gobelins – site of the famous tapestry workshop – there remains the almost untouched quartier of the **Butte-aux-Cailles** (map 5, F9), with its little streets and cul-de-sacs of prewar houses and studios. The five-storey houses on rue Butte-aux-Cailles are typical of pre-1960s Paris and, though many of the flats have shared loos and no bathrooms, the rents are not cheap. It's a pleasantly animated street, recently recobbled and furnished with lampposts. A jazz bar, *La Folie en Tête*, at no. 33, and a restaurant, *Le Temps des Cerises*, at nos. 18–20, are both run by co-operatives, plus there are plenty of other places to eat and drink, most of which stay open till the early hours. Culinary delights from Southeast Asia might tempt you to the area known as **Chinatown** (map 5, J9–K9) between rue de Tolbiac, avenue de Choisy and boulevard Masséna. As you step out into avenue d'Ivry, you'll find the huge **Tang–Frères supermarket** and a larger **covered market**, where birds circle above the mind- and stomach-boggling goods. Chinese, Lao, Cambodian, Thai and Vietnamese shops and restaurants fill avenue d'Ivry and avenue de Choisy all the way down to the city limits, many of them in shopping mazes on the ground floors of tower blocks.

If this is all too materialistic for you, head into the underground service road, rue du Disque, just by the escalators up to Les Olympiades at 66 avenue d'Ivry, where red and gold lanterns announce the entrance to a **Buddhist temple**.

For restaurants, cafés and bars in the 13e, see pp.225–226.

This is all a world away from the eastern edge of the 13e, along the riverfront, which is in the throes of mammoth development. Over the next ten to fifteen years, everything from the Gare d'Austerlitz out to the périphérique will be transformed and known as "Paris Rive Gauche". There's something very disconcerting about the attempt to create a new, and enormous, district from scratch, eradicating past traces of the area, so that every park, street and building belongs to just one period of approximately twenty years. It's not all new, though: the gigantic old **moulins** ("mills") and warehouses just south of Pont de Tolbiac are, thankfully, set to stay and are to host several university faculties, and at 91 quai de la Gare, the old SNCF building is due to be renovated, but the artists' studios, flats and exhibition spaces inside will remain. Interesting cultural venues are springing up in their own right: the barges moored along the quay are excellent places to hear live music and have a drink, while cutting-edge art galleries have sprung up on rue Louise Weiss, behind the most important addition to the area, the new **Bibliothèque Nationale de France** (François-Mitterrand/Tolbiac site).

Bibliothèque Nationale de France (François-Mitterrand/Tolbiac site)

Map 5, N6–N7. Tues–Sat 10am–8pm, Sun noon–7pm; day pass 20F/€3.05. Mº Bibliothèque-François-Mitterrand.

A general public library and some of the specialist collections from the Richelieu site of the **Bibliothèque Nationale de France** are housed in the four enormous L-shaped glass towers, designed by Dominique Perrault, and inaugurated in 1995. Seen from a distance the towers hold little interest, but from the raised wooden platform between the towers the perspective changes. Now you're looking down into a sunken pine wood with glass walls that filter light into the floors below your feet (all the public access areas are below), and the towers seem somehow closer than

THE 13ᵉ

109

the 250m length and 130m width that separates their corners. Conceptually original but functionally problematic, the library has been dogged by technical problems ever since it opened. It began with the failure to take into account the effect of light on printed matter, and so blinds had to be added; library staff strikes, computer failures, a fire and finally a mysterious syndrome of fainting readers followed, all adding up to general dissatisfaction with the new library. When the library is open, it does, however, provide unrivalled access to every book, periodical and audiovisual material ever published or produced in France.

Montmartre and Pigalle

One of Paris's most romantic quartiers, **Montmartre** embraces much of the largely petit-bourgeois and working-class 18e arrondissement, as well the somewhat less respectable **Pigalle** district on the northern edge of the 9e arrondissement. The heart of the quartier is the **Butte Montmartre**, at 130m the highest point in Paris. It's crowned by the white domes of **Sacré-Cœur**, a stone's throw away from the picturesque **place du Tertre**, whose crowds of pavement artists perpetuate a well-founded Montmartre cliché. The quartier's artistic associations go back to the nineteenth century, when artists such as Renoir, Picasso, Braque and Dufy colonized the steep, winding streets of the Butte. The streets and stairways retain something of the area's former village atmosphere – Montmartre was only included in the Parisian city limits in 1860 – and have formed a backdrop to many a sepia-romantic image.

The quiet, residential area south of Pigalle is also rich in artistic connections and harbours a couple of distinctive museums displaying work by former artist residents. The past also lives on at the **St-Ouen flea market**, on the northern edge of the 18e arrondissement.

PLACE DES ABBESSES TO THE BUTTE

The quickest way up the Butte is by funicular or via the steps up from square Willette, directly below Sacré-Cœur, but there's a choice of two quieter and more attractive routes, starting from postcard-pretty **place des Abbesses** (map 3, F3).

**The funicular up the Butte Montmartre
is part of the city's métro system; *Carte Orange*
(see p.12) or métro tickets can be used.**

The nearest métro stop to the *place* is Abbesses, its Guimard Art-Nouveau glass porch and railings one of the few that survive intact. On the downhill side of the square, the bizarre-looking brick-clad church of St-Jean de Montmartre has the distinction of being the first concrete church in France, built in 1904. From the square you can climb up **rue de la Vieuville** and the stairs in rue Drevet to the minuscule **place du Calvaire**, which has a lovely view back over the city. An alternative and slightly longer route takes you up **rue Tholozé**, then right on rue Lepic to rue des Norvins, via the **Moulin de la Galette** – the last survivor of Montmartre's forty-odd windmills, immortalized by Renoir in his *Le bal du Moulin de la Galette*.

Rue Poulbot, at the beginning of rue des Norvins, leads round to the underground **Espace Montmartre – Salvador Dalí** (map 3, G2; daily 10am–6.30pm; 40F/€6.09), which displays a selection of less well-known, yet unmistakeable, Dalí images. Unfortunately, however, more space is given over to the souvenir shop than the paintings.

The Montmartrobus is a bus specially designed
for the small winding one-way streets of Montmartre.
Its route begins at place Pigalle and takes in the rue
des Abbesses, rue Lepic and rue des Saules, finishing
up at the 18e arrondissement town hall. In the other
direction, its route follows rue Lamarck, passes in front of
Sacré-Coeur and heads back down the Butte via rue
Gabrielle, rue Chaptal, rue Le Tac and rue Houdon.

Artistic associations abound hereabouts. Zola, Berlioz,
Turgenev, Seurat, Degas and Van Gogh lived in the area.
Picasso, Braque and Juan Gris initiated the Cubist movement in an old piano factory in the tiny place Émile-
Goudeau, known as the **Bateau-Lavoir** (map 3, F2); it still
provides studio space for artists, though the original building burnt down some years ago. What you see today is a
reconstruction, but little has changed in the square itself.

On rue Cortot stands a pretty old house with a grassy
courtyard that was occupied at different times by Renoir,
Dufy, Suzanne Valadon and her son, Utrillo, and now houses the rather disappointing **Musée de Montmartre** (map
3, G1; Tues–Sun 11am–6pm; 25F/€3.81). It takes an uninspiring trip down memory lane via a selection of Toulouse-
Lautrec posters, a mock-up of a bar complete with original
zinc, and various painted impressions of how the Butte
once looked. On the slopes behind lie the terraces of the
tiny Montmartre **vineyard**, whose annual harvest of about
1500kg of grapes produces in the region of 1500 bottles of
wine. The small patch of overgrown ground next door is
the **museum's garden**, a haven for Paris's native flora and
fauna (April–Oct Mon 4–6pm, except during school and
public hols, Sat 2–6pm; free).

Just beyond the garden, on rue du Mont-Cenis, stands
the house where Berlioz lived with his English wife. From

PLACE DES ABBESSES TO THE BUTTE

PICASSO AT THE BATEAU-LAVOIR

Picasso came to the **Bateau-Lavoir** in 1904 and stayed for the best part of a decade. He painted *Les Demoiselles d'Avignon* here, and shared loves, quarrels, febrile discussions, opium trips and diverse escapades with Braque, Juan Gris, Modigliani, Max Jacob, Apollinaire and others, both famous and obscure. It was on place Émile-Goudeau that he had his first encounter with the beautiful Fernande Olivier, thrusting a kitten into her hand as she passed by. "I laughed," she said, "and he took me to see his studio." Fernande became his model and lover.

here there's a picturesque view north of some typical Montmartre steps, complete with their double handrail running down the centre, and lampposts between. The streets below, such as rue St-Vincent, rue Becquerel and rue de l'Abbé Patureau, are among the quietest and least touristy in Montmartre.

PLACE DU TERTRE

Map 3, G2. M° Abbesses & M° Anvers.

The heart of Montmartre, **place du Tertre**, photogenic but totally bogus, is jammed with tourists, souvenir-touts, overpriced restaurants and "artists" doing quick while-u-wait portraits.

At the east end of the *place* stands the **church of St-Pierre**, the oldest in Paris, along with St-Germain-des-Prés. The church is all that remains of a Benedictine convent built in the twelfth century, and although much altered, it still retains its Romanesque and early Gothic character. The four ancient columns inside, two by the door and two in the choir, are leftovers from the Roman shrine that stood on the hill, while the cemetery dates from Merovingian times.

SACRÉ-COEUR

Map 3, H2. Daily 6am–11pm. Mᵒ Abbesses & Mᵒ Anvers.

The white, pimply domes of the **Sacré-Cœur**, a romantic and graceful pastiche of Romanesque and Byzantine styles, are an essential part of the Paris skyline. Construction was started in the 1870s on the initiative of the Catholic Church to atone for the "crimes" of the Commune (see p.334). The leftists eventually got their revenge, however, by naming the space at the foot of the monumental staircase **square Willette**, after the local artist who turned out on inauguration day to shout, "Long live the devil!"

Climbing up to the **dome** (daily 9am–6pm; 15F/€2.28) of the Sacré-Cœur is worthwhile for the view from the top. It's almost as high as the Eiffel Tower, and you can see the layout of the whole city.

Below the Sacré-Cœur, in rue Ronsard, you can
see the sealed entrances to the quarries where
plaster of Paris was extracted, and which were used as
refuges by the revolutionaries of 1848.

MONTMARTRE CEMETERY

Map 3, D1–D2. March 16–Nov 5 Mon–Fri 8am–6pm, Sat from 8.30am, Sun from 9am; Nov 6–March 15 Mon–Fri 8am–5.30pm, Sat from 8.30am, Sun from 9am. Mᵒ Blanche & Mᵒ Place-de-Clichy.

West of the Butte lies the **Montmartre cemetery**. Tucked down below street level in the hollow of an old quarry, it's a tangle of trees and funerary pomposity, more intimate and

SACRÉ-COEUR • MONTMARTRE CEMETERY

less melancholy than Père-Lachaise or Montparnasse (see pp.132 and 101).

The illustrious dead at rest here include Zola, Stendhal, Berlioz, Degas, Feydeau, Offenbach, Dalida, Nijinsky and François Truffaut. There's also a large Jewish section by the east wall. The entrance is on avenue Rachel under rue Caulaincourt, next to an antique cast-iron poor-box (*Tronc pour les Pauvres*).

THE FLEA MARKET OF ST-OUEN

Map 1, E1. M° Porte-de-Clignancourt & M° Porte-de-St-Ouen.

The **flea market of St-Ouen** is located on the northern edge of the 18^e arrondissement in the suburb of St-Ouen. It spreads between the **Porte de St-Ouen** and the **Porte de Clignancourt**, with the bulk of the official markets closer to the latter.

Officially open on Saturday, Sunday and Monday from 9am to 6.30pm – although this can vary depending on the weather, and many stands are closed on a Monday – the **puces de St-Ouen** claims to be the largest flea market in the world, the name "flea" deriving from the state of the secondhand mattresses, clothes and other junk sold here when the market first operated in the free-fire zone outside the city walls. Nowadays, however, it's predominantly a proper – and very expensive – **antiques** market, selling mainly furniture but also such trendy "junk" as old café counters, telephones, traffic lights, posters, juke boxes and petrol pumps, with what is left of the rag-and-bone element confined to the further reaches of **rue Lecuyer** and its continuation **rue du Dr Babinski**. It can be fun to wander around, but it's foolish to expect any bargains.

For listings of other flea markets in Paris, see p.292.

THE FLEA MARKET OF ST-OUEN

First impressions as you arrive from the Porte-de-Clignancourt métro are that there's nothing for sale but jeans and leather jackets, whilst the Porte-de-St-Ouen métro approach brings you past the dregs of secondhand merchandise. There are, however, twelve official markets within the complex: Marché **Biron**, Marché **Cambo**, Marché **Antica** and Marché **Malassis**, all selling serious and expensive antique furniture; Marché **Vernaison** – the oldest – which has the most diverse collection of old and new furniture and knick-knacks; Marché **Dauphine**, one of the newest markets and expensive on the whole; Marché **Paul-Bert**, offering all kinds of furniture, china, and the like; Marché **Serpette**, indoors and high-class; Marché **des Rosiers** concentrating on twentieth-century decorative pieces; Marché **Malik**, with mostly clothes, some swanky couturier stuff, and a lot of uninteresting new items; and Marché **Jules-Vallès** and Marché **Lécuyer-Vallès**, which are the cheapest, most junk-like . . . and most likely to throw up an unexpected treasure.

PIGALLE

Between place Clichy in the west and Barbès-Rochechouart in the east, run the sleazy **boulevards of Clichy** and **de Rochechouart**. At the **Barbès** end, where the métro clatters by on iron trestles, the crowds teem round the Tati department store, the cheapest in the city, while the pavements are thick with Arab and African street vendors hawking watches, trinkets and textiles.

At the **place Clichy** end, tour buses from all over Europe discharge their contents into massive hotels. In the middle, between place Blanche and place Pigalle, sex shows, sex shops and prostitutes, both male and female, vie for the custom of *solitaires* and couples alike. Among all the sleaze lies a little oasis of respectability, **avenue Frochot**, one of the city's most elegant private *villas*, just off place Pigalle. In the adjacent streets – rues de Douai, Victor-Massé and Houdon – grey façades are interspersed with tiny ill-lit bars where "hostesses" lurk in complicated tackle.

At the corner of boulevard de Clichy and place Blanche, Toulouse-Lautrec's inspiration for his cabaret paintings, the **Moulin Rouge** (map 3, E3), still survives, albeit a mere shadow of its former self.

Perfectly placed among the sex shops and shows, the **Musée de l'Érotisme** (map 3, E3; 10am–2am; 40F/€6.10), 72 bd Clichy, endeavours to explore different cultures'

CABARETS AND SEX AROUND PIGALLE

For many foreigners, Paris is still synonymous with the stage shows of the mythical **cabaret theatres**, the Moulin Rouge, Folies Bergères and Lido. These theatres flash their presence from the Champs-Élysées to boulevard Montmartre, but are a distant shadow of what they once were: bawdy, populist places of entertainment, of the kind widely depicted in Impressionist paintings of the day. Nowadays, an evening at the cabaret consists of an expensive dinner-and-show formula that attracts coachloads of package-tourists. The show itself pulls out all the stops to impress – glitz, special effects and bare-breasted women sporting large coloured feathers.

Although the whole event is touted as artistic and respectable, when push comes to shove, it's a not-too-distant relative of the other "Live Shows" touted on the boulevard de Clichy. These "Live Sex" and "Ultra-Hard Live Sex" shows go one step further, leaving the world of elegant gloss and exportable Frenchness for a world of sealed-cover porn that knows no cultural borders.

approaches to sex through a small collection of sacred and ethnographic art from Asia, Africa and pre-Columbian Latin America and changing temporary exhibitions.

SOUTH OF PIGALLE

The rest of the 9e arrondissement, which stretches south of Pigalle, boasts an illustrious artistic past: Georges Sand, Chopin, Delacroix, Dumas and Gustave Moreau all resided here. You can find out more about Moreau at the fine **Musée Gustave Moreau** (map 3, E5; Mon & Wed 11am–5.15pm, Thurs–Sun 10am–12.45pm & 2–5.15pm; 22F/€3.35), located in his former house and studio at 14 rue de La Rochefoucauld. The house was designed by

Moreau himself and is largely given over to studio space; the living quarters are relatively tiny. Most of the Symbolist's major paintings, along with thousands of drawings and watercolours, are on display in the studio.

Also converted into a museum are the house and studio of the Romantic portrait painter, Ary Scheffer. The **Musée de la Vie Romantique** (map 3, E4; Tues–Sun 10am–5.40pm; 22F/€3.35), at 16 rue Chaptal, is a delight, set in a shuttered provincial house in a cobbled courtyard. Some of Scheffer's paintings are on display in the studio, although more interesting is the rest of the collection in the house, consisting mainly of bits and pieces linked to Georges Sand, who was a frequent visitor.

The rest of the quartier is rather quiet and a tad dull, with the exception of some pleasant residential streets around **place St-Georges** (map 3, G5). In the nineteenth century, this area was nicknamed the "mistresses' quartier", on account of the number of mistresses who lived here. At the time, many bourgeois males considered it de rigeur to have mistresses, or *lorettes*, as they were known, after the nearby church of Notre-Dame-de-Lorette. In the centre of the place St-Georges stands a statue of the cartoonist Gavarni, who delighted in lampooning the *lorettes* of his contemporaries. Another notable figure associated with the area is Thiers, president of the Third Republic. His house, which stood in the *place*, was burnt during the Commune, but was rebuilt and is now a library.

Eastern Paris

P aris east of the **Canal St-Martin** is traditionally a working-class area. The main quartiers, **Belleville**, **Ménilmontant** and **Charonne**, were once villages on the fringes of the city, colonized by the rural poor in the nineteenth century. The area developed a reputation as a revolutionary hot-bed, with many inhabitants taking the side of the Commune in 1871. Unfortunately, much of the area these days is characterized by high-rise housing developments, though some charming old villagey streets do remain. The main attractions in these eastern districts are the **Père-Lachaise cemetery**, the final resting place of many well-known artists and writers, and the **Parc de La Villette**, containing a state-of-the-art science museum and many other high-tech attractions.

THE CANAL ST-MARTIN

Map 4, D1–D14. M° Bastille & M° République.

The **Canal St-Martin** flows through Eastern Paris, starting at the Seine at Pont Morland, and disappearing underground between the Bastille and rue du Faubourg-du-Temple, near place de la République, before continuing on to La Villette. Designed, built and completed in 1825 under the watchful eye of Napoleon III, the canal was

CANAL CRUISES

Boats operated by **Canauxrama** (reservations ☏01.42.39.15.00, ⓦ *www.canauxrama.com*) chug up and down the Canal St-Martin between the Port de l'Arsenal (opposite 50 bd de la Bastille, 12ᵉ; Mᵒ Bastille) and the Bassin de la Villette (13 quai de la Loire, 19ᵉ; Mᵒ Jaurès) on the Canal St-Martin. Daily departures are at 9.45am and 2.45pm from La Villette and at 9.45am and 2.30pm from the Bastille. At the Bastille end there's a long tunnel from which you don't surface till the 10ᵉ arrondissement. The ride lasts three hours and costs 75F/€11.43 (students 60F/€9.15, under-12s 45F/€6.86, under-6s free; no reductions weekends or holiday afternoons).

intended as a shortcut for river traffic wishing to avoid the great western loop of the Seine around Paris, and also provided a reliable water source for the growing city.

The canal quais are popular with cyclists and rollerbladers on Sundays, when the quais are closed to traffic between 10am and 4pm.

The most attractive stretch of the canal is the area just **south of the Bastille**, with its leafy trees, cobbled quais, high-arched footbridges and nineteenth-century, solid, bourgeois residences. The area has attracted a lot of new developement recently: flats have been refurbished and cafés have opened up. The more run-down **northern stretch**, from place de la République to La Villette, cuts through working-class neighbourhoods and former industrial areas, flanked by wide quais and abandoned warehouses, factories and workshops. The City of Paris is investing a lot of money to clean up the waterway and regenerate the area.

THE CANAL ST-MARTIN

PARC DE LA VILLETTE

Map 1, G1. ℡ 01.40.03.75.75, ⓦ *www.la-villette.com* M° Porte-de-Pantin & M° Porte-de-la-Villette.

Built in 1986 on the site of what was once Paris's largest abattoir and meat market, the **Parc de la Villette** is an enormous high-tech arts and science park in the northeast of Paris. The landscaped grounds include a huge science museum, a music museum, various satellite attractions and a series of themed gardens. It's made up of so many disparate, disconnected elements and such a clash of architectural styles that it's hard to know where to start. To help you get your bearings, there are **information** centres at the entrances by M° Porte-de-la-Villette, to the north, and M° Porte-de-Pantin, in the south.

Cité des Sciences et de l'Industrie

Tues–Sat 10am–6pm, Sun 10am–7pm; 50F/€7.62 day pass, 35F/€5.34 on Sat. M° Porte-de-la-Villette.

The park's main attraction has to be the enormous **Cité des Sciences et de l'Industrie**. This is the science museum to end all science museums and worth visiting for the building alone: its giant glass walls hang beneath a dark-blue lattice of steel, while inside are crow's nests and cantilevered platforms, bridges and suspended walkways, the different levels linked by lifts and escalators. The centre of the building is left open to the full extent of the roof, 40m high. Not only is the building overwhelming, but the amount of information, too. You're likely to come out after several hours reeling with images and ideas.

The permanent exhibition, called **Explora**, covers subjects such as sound, robotics, energy, light, ecology, maths, medicine, space and language. The emphasis is on exploring, and there are numerous interactive computers, videos,

PARC DE LA VILLETTE

●

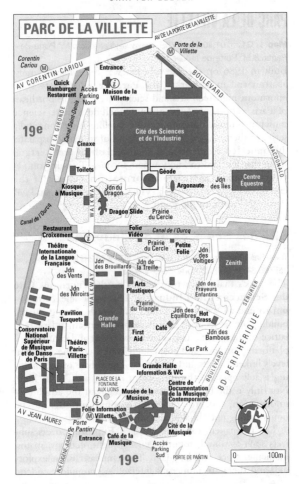

PARC DE LA VILLETTE

holograms, animated models and games. In the section *Expressions et comportements* you can intervene in stories acted out on videos, changing the behaviour of the characters to engineer a different outcome. Hydroponic plants grow for real in a green bridge across the central space. You can steer robots through mazes; experiment with motion in an "inertia carousel"; watch computer-guided puppet shows; and see holograms of different periods' visions of the universe.

An **audioguide in English** is available at the counter in the main hall (25F/€3.81), and includes details about the architecture, explanations for Explora and the soundtrack for some of the planetarium shows (2pm, 3pm, 4pm & 5pm). It's recommended if you want to make the most of the museum, unless your French is very good.

Cité des Enfants

90min sessions: Tues, Thurs & Fri 11.30am, 1.30pm & 3.30pm; Wed, Sat, Sun & public hols 10.30am, 12.30pm, 2.30pm & 4.30pm; special sessions school hols. Advance reservations at the Cité des Sciences ticket office advised to avoid disappointment (℡ 08.03.30.63.06).

The Cité's special section for children, the **Cité des Enfants**, with areas for 3-to-5-year-olds and 6-to-12-year-olds, is totally engaging. Children can touch, smell, play about with water, construct buildings on a miniature construction site (complete with cranes, hard hats and barrows), experiment with sound and light, manipulate robots, race their own shadows, and superimpose their image on a landscape. They can listen to different languages by inserting telephones into the appropriate country on a globe, and put together their own television news. The whole area is beautifully organized and managed. If you haven't got a child, it's worth borrowing one to get in here.

PARC DE LA VILLETTE

Techno Cité

90min sessions: Tues, Thurs & Fri 11.30am, 1.30pm & 3.30pm; Wed, Sat, Sun & public hols 10.30am, 12.30pm, 2.30pm & 4.30pm; special sessions school hols. Advance reservations advised to avoid disappointment (℡ 08.03.30.63.06).

On the ground floor, **Techno Cité** is for over-11s only, and, though technically geared towards teenagers, appeals to adults as well. The exhibits are designed to illustrate the application of technology to industry. You can write a programme for a robotic videotape selector, design a prototype racing bike, manufacture a plastic puzzle and package it using a laser-guided cutter, and set up a control system for an assembly line.

The planetarium, cinemas, médiathèque and cafés

When all the interrogation and stimulation of the science museum becomes too much, you can relax in cafés within Explora, before joining the queue for the **planetarium**. Back on the ground floor, the **Louis-Lumière Cinema** shows 3-D films, while the **Salle Jean-Bertin** shows documentaries in French only (closed Mon). Below ground is the multimedia library, the **médiathèque** (daily noon–8pm), **restaurants** and an **aquarium**. Entry to all these attractions is included in the day pass for the science museum.

Musée de la Musique

Tues–Thurs noon–6pm, Fri & Sat noon–7.30pm, Sun 10am–6pm; 35F/€5.34. M° Porte-de-Pantin.

The **Musée de la Musique**, within the **Cité de la Musique** complex, near the Porte-de-Pantin entrance, presents the history of music from the end of the Renaissance to the present day, both visually, through a collection of 4500 instruments, and aurally, with headsets and interactive displays. Designed by Christian de Portzamparc, the buildings make abstract artistic statements, with their wedged, wavy, funnel shapes, musical patterns, and varied colours and textures. There's also a concert hall, the very chic *Café de la Musique* and a music and dance information centre. A separate building houses the national music academy.

The park grounds

Daily 6am–1am; entry to park free; admission fee for some themed gardens. M° Porte-de-Pantin & M° Porte-de-la-Villette.

The extensive **park grounds** contain a number of bizarrely landscaped **themed gardens**, aimed mainly at children, and featuring mirrors, trampolines, water jets and spooky music. Polished steel monoliths hidden amongst the trees and scrub cast strange reflections in the **Jardin des Miroirs**, while Le **Jardin des Brouillards** has jets and curtains of water at different heights and angles. Predictably, dune-like shapes, sails and windmills make up the **Jardin des Vents et des Dunes** (for under-12s only and their accompanying adults). Strange music creates the fairytale and horror-story ambience in the imaginary forests of the **Jardin des Frayeurs Enfantines**. The **Jardin des Voltiges** has an obstacle course with trampolines and rigging. Small bronze figures lead you through the vines and other climbing plants of the **Jardin de la Treille**; and the **Jardin des Bambous** is filled with the sound of running water. On the north side of the canal de l'Ourcq is the wildly popular eighty-metre-long **Dragon Slide**.

The park is dotted with brigh-red "follies". One, called *Trabendo* (see p.244), hosts live music. Others have activities for kids: video editing in the **Folie Vidéo** and a game-filled crèche for 2-to-5-year-olds in the **Petite Folie**, both on the south bank of the canal de l'Ourcq; and arts activities for 7-to-10-year-olds in the **Folie des Arts Plastiques**.

PARC DE LA VILLETTE

In front of the Cité des Sciences floats the **Géode** (hourly shows 10am–9pm; closed Mon; 57F/€8.69), a bubble of reflecting steel which looks as though it's been dropped from an intergalactic boules game into a pool of water. Inside the bubble, half the sphere is a screen for Omnimax 180° films, not noted for their plots but a great visual experience. Alternatively, there's the **Cinaxe**, between the Cité and the Canal St-Denis (screenings every 15 min 11am–6pm; closed Mon; 34F/€5.18 or 29F/€4.42 with day pass), combining 70mm film shot at thirty frames a second with seats that move.

Next to the Géode, you can clamber around a decommissioned 1957 French **submarine**, the **Argonaute** (Tues–Fri 10.30am–5.30pm, Sat & Sun 10.30am–6pm; 25F/€3.81 or free entry with day pass), and view the park through its periscope.

Over to the east is the **Zénith** inflatable rock music venue (see p.241), while to the south, the largest of the old **market halls** – an iron-frame structure designed by Baltard, the engineer of the vanished Les Halles pavilions – is now a vast and brilliant exhibition space, the **Grande Salle**.

The various films and exhibitions at La Villette are detailed in *Pariscope* listings magazine.

BELLEVILLE, MÉNILMONTANT AND CHARONNE

Strung out along the western slopes of a ridge that rises from the Seine, the suburbs of **Belleville, Ménilmontant** and **Charonne** retain pockets of charm, despite the tower-block mania of the 1960s and 1970s. Before the housing developers moved in, the cobbled lanes, individual gardens, numerous stairways, and local shops and cafés gave the Belleville and Ménilmontant areas a village-like character – quite the equal of Montmartre, but without the touristy commercialism. Amid the graffitied concrete buildings, some of these old streets still survive, especially the little cul-de-sacs of terraced houses and gardens **east of rue des Pyrénées**. There are alleys so narrow that nothing but the knife-grinder's tricycle would have been able to fit down them. Ascending the hills to either the **Parc de Belleville** or the bucolic **Parc des Buttes-Chaumont** reveals one of the area's greatest assets – unobstructed and near-panoramic views of the city beyond.

The quickest and easiest way to get out to the eastern suburbs is to hop on the #26 bus from the Gare du Nord, and get off at one of the stops on avenue de Simon-Bolivar or rue des Pyrénées.

Parc des Buttes-Chaumont

Map 4, H1. Mᵒ Buttes-Chaumont & Mᵒ Botzaris.

At the northern end of the hills dominating Belleville, a short walk from La Villette, is the **parc des Buttes-Chaumont**, constructed by Haussmann in the 1860s to camouflage what until then had been a desolate warren of disused quarries and miserable shacks. At the park's centre is a huge rock crowned by a delicate Corinthian temple and surrounded by a lake, spanned by two bridges. Meticulously planned, the park is landscaped, terraced and groomed to emulate nature at is prettiest, and the sloping lawns, enormous trees, splashing waterfall and fantastic views of the city make it worth the trip. The park remains open all night, making it the perfect spot for evening strolls.

BELLEVILLE, MÉNILMONTANT AND CHARONNE

LA DESCENTE DE LA COURTILLE

The heights of Belleville were known as **La Haute Courtille** in the nineteenth century, while the lower part around rue du Faubourg-du-Temple and rue de la Fontaine-au-Roi was called **La Basse Courtille**. The name *Courtille* comes from *courti*, "garden" in the Picard dialect. Both areas were full of boozers and dance halls, where people flocked from the city on high days and holidays.

The wildest revels of the year took place on the night of Mardi Gras, when thousands of masked people turned out to celebrate the end of the *carnaval*. Next morning – Ash Wednesday – they descended in drunken procession from Belleville to the city, in up to a thousand horse-drawn vehicles, a procession that became known as *la descente de la Courtille*.

Rue de Belleville and around

Map 4, G3–I3. Mº Belleville.

Belleville's colourful main street, **rue de Belleville**, abounds with Vietnamese, Thai and Chinese shops and restaurants, which spill south along boulevard de Belleville and rue du Faubourg-du-Temple. The quartier's rich ethnic mix is also evident on rue Ramponeau, which is just off boulevard de Belleville, and is full of kosher shops, belonging to Sephardic Jews from Tunisia. African and oriental fruits, spices, music and fabrics attract shoppers to the **boulevard de Belleville market** on Tuesday and Friday mornings.

More Asian shops, restaurants, and markets can be found in the 13e; see p.108 for more information.

Édith Piaf Museum

Map 4, H6. Mon–Thurs 1–6pm; closed Sept; by appointment on
Ⓣ 01.43.55.52.72; donation. M° Ménilmontant & M° St-Maur.
Édith Piaf was abandoned at just a few hours old on the
steps of 72 rue de Belleville, and there's a small **museum**
dedicated to her at 5 rue Créspin-du-Gast. A virtual
shrine to the performer, the museum displays Piaf's
belongings including paintings, photographs, recordings
and, the highlight for any devotee, her little black dress.

Parc de Belleville and around

Map 4, I4. M° Couronnes & M° Pyrénées.
You get fantastic views down onto the city centre from the
higher reaches of Belleville and Ménilmontant: the best
place to watch the sunset is the **Parc de Belleville** which
descends in a series of terraces and waterfalls from rue Piat.
And from **rue de Ménilmontant** (map 4, I6), by rues de
l'Ermitage and Boyer, you can look straight down to the
Pompidou Centre and the Beaubourg quartier.

Charonne

Map 1, H4. M° Charonne.
There is little to distinguish **Charonne** from its neighbours,
save **St-Germain-de-Charonne**, the perfect little
Romanesque church which dominates **place St Blaise**. It
seems to have changed little, and its belfry not at all, since
the thirteenth century. Opposite the church, the old cobbled village high street, **rue St-Blaise**, pedestrianized as far
as place des Grés, was one of the most picturesque in Paris,
until it was prettified further, the face-lift removing much
of its charm.

BELLEVILLE, MÉNILMONTANT AND CHARONNE

PÈRE-LACHAISE CEMETERY

Map 1, H4. Daily 7.30am–6pm. M° Gambetta, M° Père-Lachaise & M° Alexandre-Dumas.

Père–Lachaise cemetery is like a miniature city devastated by a neutron bomb: a great number of dead, seemingly empty houses and temples of every size and style, and exhausted survivors, some congregating aimlessly, some searching persistently. The cemetery was opened in 1804 after an urgent stop

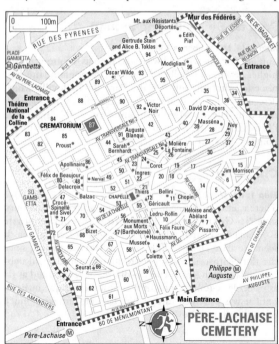

had been put on further burials in the overflowing city cemeteries and churchyards, and to be interred in Père-Lachaise
quickly became the ultimate symbol of riches and success. A
free **map** of the cemetery is available at the entrance on rue
des Rondeaux by Av du Père Lachaise, or you can buy a
more detailed souvenir one for 10F/€1.52 at newsagents near
here and the Boulevard de Ménilmontant entrance.

Swarms flock to the now-sanitized tomb of ex-Doors
lead singer Jim Morrison (division 6), cleansed of all its
graffiti and watched vigilantly by security guards. Colette's
tomb (division 4), close to the main Ménilmontant
entrance, is very plain though always covered in flowers.
The same is true of Sarah Bernhardt's (division 44) and the
great chanteuse Édith Piaf's (division 97). Marcel Proust lies
in his family's conventional tomb (division 85), which hon-
ours the medical fame of his father. In division 92, nineteenth-century journalist Victor Noir – shot for daring to
criticize a relative of Napoleon III – lies flat on his back,
fully clothed, his top hat fallen by his feet.

Corot (division 24) and Balzac (division 48) both have
superb busts, Balzac looking particularly satisfied with his
life. Géricault reclines on cushions of stone (division 12),
paint palette in hand; Chopin (division 11) has a willowy
muse weeping for his loss. The most impressive of the individual tombs is that of Oscar Wilde (division 89), adorned
with a strange Pharaonic winged messenger (sadly robbed
almost immediately of its prominent penis by a scandalised
cemetery employee, who, so the story goes, used it as a
paperweight) sculpted by Jacob Epstein and a grim verse
from *The Ballad of Reading Gaol* behind. Nearby, in division
96, is the grave of Modigliani and his lover Jeanne
Herbuterne, who killed herself in crazed grief a few days
after he died in agony from meningitis.

It is the monuments to the collective, violent deaths, however, that have the power to change a sunny outing to Père-

PÈRE-LACHAISE CEMETERY

Lachaise into a much more sombre experience. In division 97, you'll find the memorials to those who died in the Nazi concentration camps, to executed Resistance fighters and to those who were never accounted for in the genocide of the last world war. The sculptures are relentless in their images of inhumanity, of people forced to collaborate in their own degradation and death. Finally, there is the *Mur des Fédérés* (division 76), the wall where the last troops of the Paris Commune were lined up and shot in the final days of the battle in 1871. The man who ordered their execution, Adolphe Thiers, lies in the centre of the cemetery in division 55.

OUT TO VINCENNES

Beyond the 12e arrondissement, across the *boulevard périphérique*, lies the **Bois de Vincennes**, which includes a lake, botanical garden, Château, and, just on its periphery, a **museum** dedicated to African and Oceanic art.

Musée des Arts Africains et Océaniens

Map 1, H6. 293 av Daumesnil. Mon, Wed–Fri & hols 10am–5.30pm, Sat & Sun till 6pm; 30F/€4.57. Mº Porte-Dorée.

On the edge of the Bois de Vincennes stands one of the city's least visited museums, the **Musée des Arts Africains et Océaniens**. Constructed for the 1931 Colonial Exposition, showcasing the various colonialized people's "overseas contribution to the capital", this museum was seen as a monument to the conquests of the French Empire. Don't be put off, however, by its past. The comprehensive collection of fascinating objects – masks, jewellery, headdresses, statues, ceramics, and utensils – are of interest both historically and ethnographically. Unfortunately, Imperialism is much in evidence: hardly any of the black African artefacts are dated, as the collection predates European acknowledgement that Africa had its own history. In the basement, what is referred to as an "aquarium" is actually five live crocodiles in a tiny pit surrounded by tanks of tropical fish.

Note that in 2004, the museum's holdings will be transferred to the **quai Branly** to join the city's other ethnographic collections, to be exhibited in a brand-new museum of art and civilization (see p.88).

The Bois de Vincennes

Map 1, I6. M° Château-de-Vincennes.

In the **Bois de Vincennes**, the city's only extensive green space besides the Bois de Boulogne, you can spend an afternoon boating on Lac Daumesnil (by the zoo) or rent a bike from the same place and feed the ducks on Lac des Minimes on the other side of the wood (you can also get here by bus #112 from Vincennes métro). The fenced enclave on the southern side of Lac Daumesnil is a **Buddhist centre** with a Tibetan temple, Vietnamese chapel and international pagoda, all occasionally open to the public. To the north is the **Parc Floral** (summer 9.30am–8pm; winter 9.30am–dusk; 10F/€1.52; bus #112 or short walk from M° Château-de-Vincennes), one of the best gardens in Paris. Flowers are always in bloom in the "Jardin des Quatres Saisons"; you can picnic beneath pines, then wander through groves of camellias, cacti, ferns, irises and bonsaï trees. On the northern edge of the *bois*, the **Château de Vincennes** (daily 10am–5/6pm; choice of guided visits 32F/€4.88; M° Château-de-Vincennes), royal medieval residence, then state prison, porcelain factory, weapons dump and military training school, is still undergoing restoration work started by Napoleon III. Visits include the Flamboyant-Gothic **Chapelle Royale**, completed in the mid-sixteenth century and decorated with superb Renaissance stained-glass windows.

OUT TO VINCENNES

Western Paris

Paris's well-manicured **western** arrondissements, the 16e and 17e, are commonly referred to as the **Beaux Quartiers**. The 16e is aristocratic and rich, and the 17e – or at least the southern part of it – middleclass and rich, both embodying the conservative nineteenth-century values of the affluent. The northern half of the 16e, towards place Victor-Hugo and place de l'Étoile, is leafy and distinctly metropolitan in character. The southern part, around the old villages of **Auteuil** and **Passy**, has an almost provincial air, with its tight knot of streets and pockets of activity amid residential calm. It's a pleasant area to stroll around and has some interesting architecture, including buildings by Hector Guimard, designer of the swirly green Art Nouveau métro stations, and Le Corbusier and Mallet-Stevens, architects of the first "Cubist" buildings. One of the highlights of the area is the **Musée Marmottan** with its marvellous collection of late Monets. Just behind the museum lies the **Bois de Boulogne**, which runs all the way down the west side of the 16e. Further west, beyond the city limits, gleams the modern purpose-built commercial district of **La Défense**, dominated by the enormous **Grande Arche**.

AUTEUIL

Map 1, B5. Mº Eglise d'Auteuil.

The **Église d'Auteuil** métro station makes a good starting point for exploring Auteuil. Around this area are several of Hector Guimard's **Art Nouveau** buildings: at 8 avenue de la Villa-de-la-Réunion, 41 rue Chardon-Lagache, 142 avenue de Versailles, 39 boulevard Exelmans and 34 rue Boileau. This last was one of Guimard's first commissions, in 1891. A high fence, creepers and a huge satellite dish obscure much of the view, but you can see some of the decorative tile-work under the eaves and around the doors and windows. At the end of rue Boileau, beyond boulevard Exelmans, you'll find a series of charming *villas* backing onto the Auteuil cemetery.

For more of the life of the quartier, follow the old village high street, **rue d'Auteuil**, west from the métro exit to **place Lorrain**, which hosts a Saturday market. In rue Poussin, just off the *place*, carriage gates open onto **Villa Montmorency**, a typical 16e *villa*, with leafy lanes and English-style gardens. Former residents include the writer André Gide and the Goncourt brothers of Prix Goncourt fame.

AUTEUIL BUS ROUTES

Handy **bus routes** for exploring Auteuil are the #52 and the #72. The #52 runs between Mº Opéra in the centre and Mº Boulogne-Pont-de-St-Cloud near the Parc de Princes, stopping at rue Poisson en route, while the #72's route extends between métro Hôtel de Ville in the Marais and Mº Boulogne-Pont-de-St-Cloud, stopping en route by the Exelmans crossroads near some of Guimard's buildings on avenue de Versailles.

Villa Roche

Mon–Fri 10am–12.30pm & 1.30–6.30pm; closed Aug; 15F/€2.29. Mº Jasmin.

In a cul-de-sac off rue du Dr-Blanche, in the northern part of the quartier, stand the first private houses built by **Le Corbusier** (1923). One of the houses, the **Villa Roche**, is in the care of the Fondation Le Corbusier and is open to the public. It's built in strictly Cubist style, very plain, with windows in bands, the only extravagances the raising of one wing on piers and a curved frontage. They look common-place enough now from the outside, but were a radical departure from anything that had gone before, and once you're inside, the spatial play still seems groundbreaking. The interior, appropriately enough, is decorated with Cubist paintings.

Off the northern end of rue du Dr-Blanche, the tiny street named after the Cubist architect **Mallet-Stevens** consists exclusively of buildings designed by him.

PASSY

Map 1, C4. Mº La Muette & Mº Passy.

The heart of the Passy quartier is pleasant little **place de Passy**, with its crowded but leisurely *Le Paris Passy* café. Leading off from here is the old high street, rue de Passy, with its eye-catching parade of boutiques, and the cobbled, pedestrianized **rue de l'Annonciation**, an agreeable blend of genteel affluence and the down-to-earth. Highlights of the area are the **Musée Marmottan** and **Balzac's house**.

Trocadéro (see p.86), with its stunning view of the Eiffel
Tower, is a leisurely walk from place de Passy.

The Maison de Balzac

Map 7, A9. 47 rue Raynouard. Tues–Sun 10am–5.40pm; 22F/€3.35.
Mº Av-du-Pres-Kennedy–Maison-de-Radio-France & Mº Passy.

The **Maison de Balzac** repays a visit even if you've never
read the writer's works. It's a delightful, summery little
house with pale-green shutters and a decorative iron
entrance porch, tucked away down some steps among a
tree-filled garden. Balzac moved here in 1840 to outrun
his debtors and stayed for seven years. The house is decep-
tively small, for it is built on a hillside and most of the
house is hidden behind. You can visit the study where
Balzac would stay up all night writing, fuelled by coffee.
One room is devoted to the development of ideas for the
creation of a monument to Balzac, resulting in the
famously blobby Rodin sculpture of the writer: caricatures of the sculpture by cartoonists of the time are on display. Another room is devoted to the many adaptations,
both filmic and theatrical, of Balzac's novel *Le Colonel
Chabert*, the most recent being the 1994 film starring
Gérard Depardieu. Outside, the shady garden is a delightful place to dally on wrought-iron seats, surrounded by
busts of the writer.

Musée Marmottan

Map 1, B4. Daily except Mon 10am–5.30pm; 40F/€6.10. Mº Muette.
The collection of the **Musée Marmottan** consists largely
of paintings by **Monet**, bequeathed, along with the family's
former residence, a nineteenth century *hôtel particulier*, to

PASSY

the Académie des Beaux-Arts by the wealthy industrialist Jules Marmottan and his son, art historian and collector, Paul Marmottan. Among the paintings is Monet's *Impression, Soleil Levant* ("Impression, Sunrise"; 1872), a rendering of a misty sunrise over Le Havre; its title was borrowed by critics to give the Impressionist movement its name. In October 1985, the painting, along with eight others, was stolen from the gallery. After a police operation lasting five years and extending as far afield as Japan, the paintings were discovered in a villa in southern Corsica – they're now back on show with greatly tightened security. There's a dazzling collection of canvases from Monet's last years at Giverny, including several *Nymphéas* ("Water lilies"), *Le Pont Japonais* ("The Japanese Bridge"), *L'Allée des Rosiers* ("The Rose Bushes") and *La Saule Pleureur* ("The Weeping Willow"), where rich colours are laid on in thick, excited whorls and lines. To all intents and purposes, these are abstractions, much more "advanced" than the work of, say, **Renoir**, Monet's exact contemporary, some of whose paintings are on display, as are those of other Impressionists, including **Berthe Morisot**.

BOIS DE BOULOGNE

Map 1, A3–B4. Mº Porte-Maillot & Mº Porte-Dauphine.

The **Bois de Boulogne** runs down the west side of the 16ᵉ. When the park was opened to the public in the eighteenth century, people said of it, "Les mariages du bois de Boulogne ne se font pas devant Monsieur le Curé" ("Unions cemented in the Bois de Boulogne do not take place in the presence of a priest"). The same is true today and the sex trade practised within the park is accompanied by a fair amount of crime; despite an obvious police presence, you should consider it unsafe at night. By day, however, the park is pleasant enough, with its trees, lakes, cycling trails and picnic spots.

The best, and wildest, part for walking is towards the southwest corner. If you're after something more energetic, you could check out the riding school and **race courses** at Longchamp and Auteuil. **Bikes** are available for rent at the entrance to the Jardin d'Acclimatation (see p.297) and you can go **boating** on the Lac Inférieur.

More information about the Jardin d'Acclimatation and activities for children in the Bois de Boulogne is given on p.297.

Especially attractive in spring is the **Parc de Bagatelle** (M° Port-de-Neuilly, then bus #43 or M° Porte-Maillot, then bus #244), which features beautiful displays of tulips, hyacinths and daffodils in the first half of April, irises in May, water lilies and roses at the end of June.

Musée National des Arts et Traditions Populaires

Daily except Tues 9.45am–5.15pm; 25F/€3.81, 32F/€4.88 with exhibitions. M° Les Sablons & M° Porte-Maillot.

Beside the main entrance to the Jardin d'Acclimatation lies the **Musée National des Arts et Traditions Populaires**, devoted to traditional crafts such as boat-building, farming, weaving, blacksmithing and pottery, all beautifully illustrated and displayed.

LA DÉFENSE

Map 1, A2. M°/RER Grande-Arche-de-la-Défense.

A perfect monument to late-twentieth-century capitalism, **La Défense** is a complex of skyscrapers, housing large corporations and modern apartment blocks. Its most popular visitor attraction is the huge **Grande Arche**, built in 1989 for the bicentenary of the Revolution. It's a beautiful and astounding 112-metre-high arch, clad in white marble, standing 6km out

LA DÉFENSE

LA DÉFENSE

River Seine

River Seine

QUAI DU PRÉSIDENT PAUL DOUMER

PONT DE NEUILLY

QUAI DE DION BOUTON

BOULEVARD PIERRE GAUDIN

Roussel Hoechst

BOULEVARD DE NEUILLY

Assur

RUE LOUIS BLANC

R.N. 13

GAN

Athéna

N

R.N. 13

Manhattan

Esplanade de la Défense

Galilée

Total

Descartes (IBM France)

ESPLANADE DU GÉNÉRAL DE GAULLE

Lorraine

BOULEVARD CIRCULAIRE

AVENUE GAMBETTA

Esso

Galerie de l'Esplanade

ELF

Info Défense

FIAT

RER Entrance

PLACE DE LA DÉFENSE

PARVIS

R.N. 13

Bull

CNIT

Grande Arche de la Défense

Centre Commercial Les 4 Temps

Voltaire

AVENUE DU PT. WILSON

R.N. 13

Les Collines de l'Arche

La Grande Arche

Dôme Imax

Pascal (IBM Europe)

Colline de la Défense

BOULEVARD CIRCULAIRE

Automobile Museum

0   200 m

and at a slight angle from the Arc de Triomphe at the far end of the Voie Triomphale. Lifts (daily 10am–7pm; 43F/€6.55) take you up past a "cloud canopy" to the roof of the arch. On a clear day you can see as far as the Louvre and beyond.

Between the Grande Arche and the river is the **business complex** of La Défense. Apartment blocks, offices of Elf, Esso, IBM, banks and other big businesses compete to dazzle and make you dizzy. The jungle of concrete and glass is relieved by bizarre **artworks** by artists such as Joan Miró and Torricini, dotted around the place de la Défense and the Esplanade du Géneral de Gaulle between the Arche and the river.

Get off a stop early, at Mº Esplanade-de-la-Défense, for the most dramatic approach to the Grande Arche and to see the sculptures.

ÎLE DE LA JATTE

Map 1, B1–2. Mº Pont-de-Levallois.

Northeast of La Défense, the **Île de la Jatte** floats in the Seine, just off rich and leafy Neuilly, an ideal venue for a romantic riverside walk, though it is much more developed than it was when Georges Seurat painted his riverside scene here, *A Sunday on La Grand Jatte*, in 1884. Formerly an industrial site, it's now part public garden (Mon–Fri 8.30am–6pm, Sat & Sun 10am–8pm) and part stylish new housing complex. On the right of the development, a former *manège* (riding-school) has been converted into the smart *Café de la Jatte*, while beside the bridge, there's the ever-popular, though pricey restaurant, *Guinguette de Neuilly*.

ÎLE DE LA JATTE

Day-trips from Paris

Y ou're unlikely to exhaust the delights of Paris during your stay, but should you feel like a break from the bustle of the city, you'll find a number of attractive destinations within easy reach of the capital. The region that surrounds Paris – known as the **Île de France** – and the borders of the neighbouring provinces are studded with large-scale **châteaux**, many set in beautiful grounds. In this chapter we've highlighted just a few of the best-known ones. Many have played an integral part in French history – none more so than **Versailles**, an overwhelming monument to the reign of Louis XIV. On a slightly more intimate scale, **Fontainebleau**, with its Italianate decoration, is easy to appreciate; and **Chantilly** has a wonderful collection of Italian paintings and a gorgeous medieval Book of Hours. You can also enjoy the country air by taking a stroll in the gardens, parks and forests that surround the châteaux.

Two of France's most important church buildings can be easily reached from Paris in a day: the awe-inspiring **cathedral of Chartres** and the basilica of **St-Denis**, predating Chartres and representing the first breakthrough in Gothic art; it is also the burial place of almost all the French kings.

The River Seine winds northwest out of Paris through some idyllic countryside. In the nineteenth century, it attracted and inspired many artists. The **Île de Chatou**, an island in the river Seine, was especially popular with artists and has a small museum of Impressionist memorabilia within a riverside restaurant that was once frequented by Monet, Renoir and others. Further west is **Monet's beautiful garden** at Giverny, the inspiration for all his water-lily canvases.

VERSAILLES

Map 9, B5. RER Versailles-Rive Gauche.

Twenty kilometres southwest of Paris, the royal town of Versailles is renowned for the **Palace of Versailles**, built for Louis XIV, and, today, one of the most visited monuments in France. Envious of the château built by his finance minister, Fouquet, at Vaux-le-Vicomte, the young Louis XIV determined to outdo him. He recruited the design team of Vaux-le-Vicomte – architect Le Vau, painter Le Brun and gardener Le Nôtre – and ordered something a hundred times the size. The result was Versailles, the apotheosis of French regal indulgence, and even if the grotesque decor and blatant self-propaganda of the Sun King are not to your liking, its historical significance and anecdotes should enthral.

Much the simplest way to **get to** Versailles from Paris is the RER line C5 to Versailles-Rive Gauche (40min). Turn right out of the station for the château and left for the **tourist office**, 2bis av de Paris (daily: May–Sept 9am–7pm; Nov–April 9am–6pm; ☏01.39.24.88.88, ⓦ*www.mairie-versailles.fr*).

There's a wonderfully posh place to take **tea** in the town: the *Hôtel Palais Trianon*, where the final negotiations for the

Treaty of Versailles took place in 1919. Located near the park entrance at the end of boulevard de la Reine, it offers trayfuls of mouth-watering pâtisseries for about 100F/€15.24. The style of the hotel is very much that of the town in general. The dominant population is aristocratic, with those holding pre-revolutionary titles disdainful of those dating merely from the time of Napoleon. On Bastille Day, both parties go about wearing black ribbons and ties in mourning for the guillotined monarchy.

The château

May–Sept Tues–Sun 9am–6.30pm; Oct–April Tues–Fri 9am–5.30pm; closed Mon & hols. Last admission 30min before closing. Grands Appartements and Chambre du Roi 70F/€10.67 (entrance C); Grands Appartements only 45F/€6.86 (entrance A); Ⓦ www.chateauversailles.fr

Visitors to the château have a choice of itineraries, and whether to be guided or not. Apart from the state apartments of the king and queen and the Hall of Mirrors, where the Treaty of Versailles was signed to end World War I, most of the palace can only be viewed by guided tour. Note that you won't be able to see the whole palace in one day, because tours of some of the apartments run concurrently.

There are four entrances: **entrance A** is for those who want to visit the Grands Appartements only; **entrance B** is for pre-booked groups; **entrance C** gives access to Louis XIV's apartments, the Dauphin and Dauphine's apartments and the Hall of Mirrors; and **entrance D** organizes various guided tours for individual visitors at varying prices. Places can be booked for **guided tours** on the same day, but it's wise to arrive early. Information on which tours will be running is available by ringing the day before (☎ 01.30.83.77.88 or 01.30.83.77.89).

The construction of the château began in 1664 and lasted virtually until Louis XIV's death in 1715. It was never meant to be a home. Regarded as second only to God, and the head of an immensely powerful state, Louis XIV was an institution rather than a private individual. His risings and sittings, comings and goings, were minutely regulated and rigidly encased in ceremony. Attendance at these rituals was an honour much sought after by courtiers. Versailles was the headquarters of every arm of the state. More than 20,000 people – nobles, administrative staff, merchants, soldiers and servants – lived in the palace in a state of unhygienic squalor, according to contemporary accounts.

Following Louis XIV's death, the château was abandoned for a few years before being reoccupied by Louis XV in 1722. It remained the residence of the royal family until the Revolution of 1789, when the furniture was sold and the pictures dispatched to the Louvre. Thereafter, it fell into ruin and was nearly demolished, until 1837 when Louis-Philippe donated funds to turn it into a museum to the glory of France. In 1871, during the Paris Commune, it became the seat of the nationalist government, and the French parliament continued to meet in Louis XV's opera building until 1879. Restoration only began in earnest between the two world wars.

The park

Daily 7am–dusk; free except on days when fountains play (30F/€4.57). Fountains play May–Sept Sun 11am–noon & 3.30–5pm, the Neptune fountains only 5.20–5.30pm.

The **park** surrounding the château covers four square kilometres. The grounds near the palace are made up of symetrical formal gardens, with ornate fountains and sculptures. The fountains only gush on selected days (Sun mid-

VERSAILLES

THE DECEMBER 1999 STORMS

The park at Versailles was one of the biggest casualties of the storms which ravaged northern France on December 26, 1999. Ten thousand trees were destroyed and the area around the Hameau de Marie-Antoinette was devastated. Parts of the park may be off-limits until trees are replanted, and it will be years before the gaps in the tree-lined avenues are filled in. The necessity of having to start again from scratch, however, has given landscapers a chance to reassess the design of the park and consider a lay-out that may be closer to the original.

April to mid-Oct & Sat July–Sept), bringing the gardens to life. The rest of the time, the statues on the empty pools look rather bereft of purpose.

The park scenery becomes less formal the further you go from the palace and makes a pleasant setting for two lesser outcrops of royal mania: the Italianate **Grand Trianon** (daily: April–Oct noon–6.30pm; Nov–March noon–5.30pm; 25F/€3.81), designed by Hardouin-Mansart in 1687 as a "country retreat" for Louis XIV, and the more modest Greek **Petit Trianon** (same hours; 15F/€2.29, combined ticket for both Petit and Grand Trianon 30F/€4.57), built by Gabriel in the 1760s for Mme de Pompadour, Louis XV's mistress.

More charming and rustic than either of these, however, is **Le Hameau de Marie-Antoinette**, a play-village and farm built in 1783 for Louis XVI's queen to indulge the fashionable Rousseau-inspired fantasy of returning to nature.

Distances in the park are considerable. If you can't manage them on foot, a *petit train* shuttles between the terrace in front of the château and the Trianons (33F/€5.03); horse-drawn calashes also cover the same journey (21F/€3.20 each way). There are **bikes** for rent at the

Grille de la Reine, Porte St-Antoine and by the Grande Canal, and **boats** for rent on the Grande Canal, within the park.

FONTAINEBLEAU

Daily except Tues: May–Oct 9.30am–5pm; Nov–April 9.30am–12.30pm & 2–5pm; 35F/€5.34; ☎ 01.60.71.50.70.

Some 60km south of Paris, the **château of Fontainebleau**, located in the middle of a magnificent forest, was built as a base for royal hunting expeditions. Its transformation into a luxurious palace only took place in the sixteenth century on the initiative of François 1er. The king imported a colony of Italian artists to carry out the decoration: among them Rosso il Fiorentino and Niccolò dell'Abate. The château continued to enjoy royal favour well into the nineteenth century; Napoleon spent huge amounts of money on it, as did Louis-Philippe. After World War II, when it was liberated from the Germans by General Patton, it served for a while as Allied military HQ in Europe.

The château **buildings**, unpretentious and attractive despite their extent, have none of the architectural unity of a purpose-built residence like Chantilly. Their distinction is the sumptuous interiors worked by the Italians, notably the celebrated **Galerie François-1er** – which had a seminal influence on the subsequent development of French aristocratic art and design – the Salle de Bal, the Salon Louis-XIII, and the Salle du Conseil with its eighteenth-century decoration.

The **gardens** are equally luscious. If you want to escape into the wilds, head for the surrounding **Forest of Fontainebleau**, which is full of walking and cycling trails, all marked on Michelin map 196 (*Environs de Paris*). Its rocks are a favourite training ground for Paris-based climbers.

FONTAINEBLEAU

Getting to Fontainebleau from Paris is straightforward. By road it is 16km from the A6 autoroute (exit Fontainebleau). By train, it is fifty minutes from the Gare de Lyon to Fontainebleau-Avon station; from here bus #AB takes you to the château gates in a few minutes. For further information, contact the **tourist office** at 4 rue Royale (Mon–Sat 10am–6.30pm, Sun 10am–4pm; ☏01.60.74.99.99).

CHANTILLY

The small town of **Chantilly**, 40km north of Paris, is closely associated with horses and racing. Some 3000 thoroughbreds prance the forest rides of a morning, and two of the season's classiest flat races are held here. Horses can also be seen at a museum in the stables of Chantilly's other main attraction, its elegant nineteenth-century **château**.

Trains take about thirty minutes from Paris's Gare du Nord to Chantilly. Occasional free buses run from the station to the château, though it's an easy walk. **Footpaths** GR11 and 12 pass through the château park and its surrounding forest, offering a peaceful and leisurely way of exploring this bit of country.

Moored in the park of the château is an *aérophile*, a hot-air **balloon**, which takes visitors up for short rides over the château every ten minutes (March–Oct daily weather permitting 10am–7pm; 66F/€10.06, 72F/€10.98 for the balloon and the château/museum). You can also take a 25-minute commentated boat trip all the way round the château and be dropped off at the entrance to the museum (March–Oct daily 10am–7pm; 52F/€7.93, 107F/€16.31 for the **boat**, the balloon and the château/museum).

By the entrance-gate to the grounds of the château is a caravan selling the local delight, **Chantilly cream**. It's basically whipped, sugared cream and tastes delicious.

The château

March–Oct daily except Tues 10am–6pm; Nov–Feb Mon & Wed–Fri 10.30am–12.45pm & 2–5pm; 42F/€6.40.

The Chantilly estate used to belong to two of the most powerful clans in France: first to the Montmorencys, then, through marriage, to the Condés. The present **château** was put up in the late nineteenth century, replacing an earlier palace destroyed in the Revolution. The original had been built for the Grand Condé, the general who crushed Spanish military power for Louis XIV in 1643. The current building is a graceful and romantic structure, surrounded by water and looking out over a formal arrangement of pools and pathways.

The château's chief attraction is the *galeries de peinture*, an outstanding collection of paintings and drawings. If there seems to be little logic to the order in which the paintings are displayed it's because their donor, Henri d'Orléans, stipulated that they remain as he had organized them. Consequently, good, bad and indifferent works are displayed alongside each other, as if of equal value. Highlights of the collection include Piero di Cosimo's *Simonetta Vespucci* and Raphaël's *Madone de Lorette*, both in the Rotunda of the picture gallery. Raphaël is also well represented, with his *Three Graces* displayed alongside Filippo Lippi's *Esther and Assuerius*, and forty miniatures from a fifteenth-century Book of Hours attributed to the French artist Jean Fouquet. Pass through the Galerie de Psyche with its series of sepia-stained glass illustrating Apuleius' *Golden Ass*, to the room known as the Tribune, where Italian art, including Botticelli's *Autumn*, takes up two walls; works by Ingres and Delacroix fill the other walls.

The rest of the château can be visited on a guided tour only, included in the entry fee. The most interesting port of

CHANTILLY

151

call is the well-stocked **library**, where the museum's single greatest treasure is kept: *Les Très Riches Heures du Duc de Berry*, the most celebrated of all the Books of Hours. Unfortunately, the original is too fragile to go on display, but there are excellent facsimiles. The illuminated pages illustrating the months of the year with scenes from early fifteenth-century rural life, such as harvesting and ploughing, sheep-shearing and pruning, are richly coloured and drawn with a delicate naturalism.

Musée Vivant du Cheval

April–Oct Mon & Wed–Fri 10.30am–5.30pm; Sat & Sun till 6pm; May & June also Tues 10.30am– 5.30pm; July & Aug also Tues 2–5.30pm; Nov–March Mon–Fri 2–5pm, Sat & Sun 10.30am–5pm; 50F/€7.62.

Five minutes' walk down the drive from the château of Chantilly, stands a colossal stable block, now transformed into a horse museum, the **Musée Vivant du Cheval**. The building was erected at the beginning of the eighteenth century by the incumbent Condé prince, who believed he would be reincarnated as a horse and wished to provide fitting accommodation for his future relatives.

In the main hall, horses of different breeds from around the world are stalled, with a ring for **demonstrations** (April–Oct 11.30am, 3.30pm & 5.15pm; Nov–March weekends & public hols 11.30am, 3.30pm & 5.15pm, weekdays 3.30pm only). Beyond the hall, a series of life-size models illustrates the various activities horses are used for. In the rooms off the hall are collections of paintings, horseshoes, veterinary equipment, bridles and saddles, a mock-up of a blacksmith's, children's horse toys (including a chain-driven number, with handles in its ears, which belonged to Napoleon III), and a fanciful Sicilian cart painted with scenes of Crusader battles.

CHARTRES

The small city of **Chartres** lies 80km southwest of Paris and the hour-long train journey from Paris brings an immediate reward the moment you approach, when you first see the city's great **cathedral** rearing up above the River Eure.

Trains run roughly every two hours to Chartres from Paris-Montparnasse (140F/€21.34 return), with a journey time of just under an hour. From the station, avenue J-de-Beauce leads up to place Châtelet. Diagonally opposite, past all the parked coaches, is rue Ste-Même, which meets place Jean-Moulin. Turn left and you'll find the cathedral, and nearby, on place de la Cathédrale, the tourist office (April–Sept Mon–Sat 9am–7pm, Sun 9.30am–5.30pm; Oct–March Mon–Sat 10am–6pm, Sun 10am–1pm & 2.30–4.30pm; ☎02.37.21.50.00).

The cathedral

Mon–Sat 7.30am–7.15pm, Sun 8.30am–7.15pm.

Chartres **cathedral** is best experienced on a cloud-free winter's day, when the low sun transmits the stained-glass colours to the interior stone. However, the best preserved medieval cathedral in Europe is endowed with more than enough wonders to enthral visitors' eyes on any day. The geometry of the building is unique in being almost unaltered since its consecration in the thirteenth century. The stonework is amazingly detailed, especially the hosts of sculpted figures above each transept door and the western façade, which includes the Portail Royal saved from the cathedral's predecessor, destroyed by fire in 1195.

Inside, in the middle of the floor of the nave, is an original thirteenth-century **labyrinth**, a great rarity, since the authorities at other cathedrals had them pulled up as distracting frivolities. It traces a path of black and white stone over 200m long, enclosed within a diameter of 13m, the same size as the rose window above the main doors. The centre used to have a bronze relief of Theseus and the Minotaur and the pattern of the maze was copied from classical texts – the medieval Catholic idea of the path of life to eternity echoing Greek myth. Finding your own way round the labyrinth is permitted during certain periods only; a noticeboard in front of the labyrinth indicates times. The other highlight inside is the beautiful Renaissance choir screen.

Although the interior is magnificent, were a medieval pilgrim to see Chartres today, they would probably think it was an abandoned shrine. In **the Middle Ages** all the sculptures above the doors were painted and gilded, while inside, the walls were whitewashed. The colours in the clean stained-glass windows would have been so bright they would have glittered from the outside along with the gold of the crowns and halos of the statuary. Inside, the reflected patterns from the windows on the white walls would have jewelled the entire building. It is difficult now to appreciate just how important **colour** used to be, when the minerals or plant and animal extracts to make the different shades cost time, effort and considerable amounts of money to procure. Perhaps, in a later age, the statues will again be painted. Demands for whitewash are occasionally made and ignored. Cleaning the windows does go on, but each one takes years and costs run into millions.

There are separate admission fees for various of the less public parts of the cathedral. Probably the best value of these, preferable to the crypt and the treasures, is the climb up the **north tower** (crowds permitting; times vary, check in the cathedral; 25F/€3.81) for its bird's-eye view of the sculptures and structure of the cathedral. There are gardens at the back from where you can contemplate the complexity of stress factors balanced by the flying buttresses.

CATHEDRAL TOURS

One of the best ways to appreciate the detail of Chartres Cathedral is to join a **guided tour** given by the erudite Englishman Malcolm Miller (April–Nov Mon–Sat noon & 2.45pm; rest of the year, days and times vary – call ☎ 02.37.21.75.02; 40F/€6.10; tour starts just inside the West door). This is no ordinary patter, but a labour of love from someone who has studied, written and lectured about Chartres for decades. Mr Miller's performance as the eccentric academic is impeccably done and he knows so much about the cathedral that you can follow several consecutive tours without fear of repetition. He likes to compare the cathedral to a library in which the windows and the statuary are the books. He reveals the storylines with fascinating digressions into the significance, past and present, of symbols, shapes and numbers.

The Town

Though the cathedral is the main attraction, a wander round the **town** of Chartres also has its rewards. Occasionally, stunning exhibitions of stained glass are displayed in a medieval wine and grain store, now the **Centre International du Vitrail** (Mon–Fri 9.30am–12.30pm & 1.30–6pm, Sat & Sun 10am–12.30pm & 2.30–6pm; 20F/€3.05), at 5 rue du Cardinal-Pie on the north side of the cathedral. Another atmospheric building, the former episcopal palace, just north of the cathedral, is the setting for the **Beaux Arts Museum** (May–Oct Mon & Wed–Sat 10am–noon & 2–6pm, Sun 2–6pm; Nov–April same days 10am–noon & 2–5pm; 15F/€2.29). It has some beautiful tapestries, a collection of works by Vlaminck and Zurbaran's *Sainte Lucie*, as well as good temporary exhibitions. Behind it, rue Chantault leads past old town houses to the River Eure and Pont des Massacres. You can follow

CHARTRES

this reedy river lined with ancient wash-houses upstream via **rue du Massacre** on the right bank. On the left bank you'll see the Romanesque **church of St-André**, now mainly used for art exhibitions and concerts.

A left turn at the end of rue de la Tannerie, then third right onto rue du Repos, will bring you to one of Chartres' more eccentric tourist attractions: the **Maison Picassiette** (April–Oct Mon & Wed–Sat 10am–noon & 2–6pm, Sun 2–6pm; 15F/€2.29), decorated by Raymond Isidore with mosaics made of bits of pottery and glass, a fine example of naïve painting. Back at the end of rue de la Tannerie, the bridge over the river brings you back to the **medieval town**. At the top of rue du Bourg there's a turreted stair-case attached to a house, and at the eastern end of place de la Poissonnerie, a carved salmon decorates a sixteenth-century house. The **food market** on Saturday morning takes place on place Billard and rue des Changes, and there's a **flower market** on place du Cygne (Tues, Thurs & Sat).

At the edge of the old town, on the junction of boulevard de la Résistance and rue Collin-d'Arleville (to the right as you're coming up from the station), stands a memorial to **Jean Moulin**, Prefect of Chartres until he was sacked by the Vichy government in 1942. When the Germans occupied the town in 1940, Moulin refused under torture to sign a document to the effect that black soldiers in the French army were responsible for Nazi atrocities. He later became de Gaulle's number one man on the ground, coordinating the Resistance. He died at the hands of Klaus Barbie in 1943.

When it comes to finding somewhere to **eat**, there's no finer place than the classy *La Truie qui File*, place de la Poissonnerie (℡02.37.21.53.90; closed Sun eve, Mon & Aug; *menu* 215F/€32.78); a good alternative is *Le Buisson Ardent*, 10 rue du Lait (℡02.37.34.04.66; closed Sun eve & Wed). There are also innumerable *faste foude* joints. The liveliest place to **drink** on market days is *Le Brazza*, on place Billard.

ST-DENIS

Map 9, E2. Mº Basilique-de-St-Denis & RER D St-Denis.

St-Denis, just 10km north of the centre of Paris and easily accessible by métro, remains a very distinct community, centred on its magnificent **basilica**. It was the first heavily industrialized town in France and is a stronghold of the Communist Party, with nearly all the principal streets bearing some notable left-wing name. Today, recession has taken a heavy toll, though the decision to stage the 1998 Football World Cup finals in St-Denis brought temporary fame and fortune. A vast hi-tech **stadium** was built in honour of the occasion, just south of town, as well as two new RER stops for the thousands of fans passing through.

The basilica

April–Sept Mon–Sat 10am–7pm, Sun noon–7pm; Oct–March Mon–Sat 10am–5pm, Sun noon–5pm; closed Jan 1, May 1, Nov 1, Nov 11 & Dec 25.

Begun by Abbot Suger in the first half of the twelfth century, **St-Denis basilica** is generally regarded as the birthplace of the Gothic style. Its west front was the first ever to have a rose window, though it is in the choir that you see the clear emergence of the new style: the slimness and lightness that comes with the use of the pointed arch, the ribbed vaulting and the long shafts of half-column rising from pillar to roof. It is a remarkably well-lit church: the clerestory is almost wholly glass – another first for St-Denis – and the transept windows are so big that they occupy their entire end walls.

Once the place where the kings of France were crowned, since 1000 AD the basilica has been the burial place of all but three. Their very fine **tombs and effigies** can be found in the transepts and ambulatory (32F/€4.88). Among the most interesting are the enormous Renaissance memorial to François 1er on the right just inside the entrance, in the form of a triumphal arch with the royal family perched on top and battle scenes depicted below, and the tombs of Louis XII, Henri II and Catherine de Médicis on the left side of the church. Also on the left, close to the altar steps, Philippe the Bold's is one of the earliest look-alike portrait statues, while to the right of the ambulatory steps you can see the stocky little general, Bertrand du Guesclin, who gave the English a run-around after the death of the Black Prince. On the level above him, invariably graced by bouquets of flowers from the royalist contingent, are the undistinguished statues of Louis XVI and Marie-Antoinette. Around the corner on the far side of the ambulatory, is the resting-place of Clovis, king of the Franks way back in 500 AD, a canny little German who wiped out Roman Gaul and turned it into France, with Paris for a capital.

A prestigious music festival is held at St-Denis every June; for more information see p.269.

The Musée d'Art et d'Histoire

Mon & Wed–Sat 10am–5.30pm, Sun 2–6.30pm; 20F/€3.05.

A stone's throw away on rue Gabriel-Péri is the **Musée d'Art et d'Histoire de la Ville de St-Denis**, housed in a former Carmelite convent, rescued from the clutches of the developers and carefully restored. The exhibits on display are not of outstanding interest, though the presentation is excellent. The **local archeology** collection is good, and there are some interesting paintings of nineteenth- and

ST-DENIS

twentieth-century industrial landscapes, including the St-Denis canal. The one unique collection is of documents relating to the **Commune**, comprising posters, cartoons, broadsheets, paintings, plus an audiovisual presentation. There is also an exhibition of manuscripts and rare editions of the Communist poet, **Paul Éluard**, native son of St-Denis.

Stade de France

Daily 10am–6pm; 35F/€5.34 to visit the public areas, 90F/€13.72 for the visit that goes backstage. M° Porte-de-Paris & RER La-Plaine-Stade-de-France or RER Stade-de-France-St-Denis.

Since it was opened for the 1998 Football World Cup, the **Stade de France** has attracted twice the number of visitors to the St-Denis basilica. It now plays host to all kinds of major sporting events, and international pop and rock stars such as Céline Dion and the Rolling Stones regularly pack it out. It's situated south of St-Denis' town centre, between St-Denis canal and the motorways A1 and A86. The grounds and facilities are open to the public.

ÎLE DE CHATOU

Map 9, C4. RER Rueil-Malmaison.

A long narrow island in the Seine, the **Île de Chatou**, between Rueil-Malmaison and St-Germain-en-Laye, was once a rustic spot where Parisians came on the newly opened rail line to row on the river, and to dine and flirt at the *guinguettes*. A favourite haunt of artists was the **Maison Fournaise**, just below the Pont de Chatou road bridge, which is now once again an attractive restaurant (daily except Sun eve in winter: lunch & eve until 10pm; *menu* 159F/€24.24, *carte* 200–250F/€30.49–38.11; ☎01.30.71.41.91). It also houses a small **museum** of mem-

ÎLE DE CHATOU

orabilia relating to Impressionist painters (Thurs & Fri 11am–5pm, Sat & Sun 11am–6pm; 25F/€3.81). One of Renoir's best-known canvases, *Le Déjeuner des Canotiers*, shows his friends lunching on the balcony of the Maison Fournaise, shaded by a magnificent riverside plane tree. A copy of the painting pasted on a board next to the restaurant marks the spot where Renoir would have placed his easel. Habitués of the restaurant included not only Impressionist painters, but also de Vlaminck and his fellow Fauves, Derain and Matisse. The **Maison Levanneur**, opposite, was rented between 1900 and 1905 by Derain and de Vlaminck as a studio. It has since been renovated and now houses the Centre National de l'Estampe et de l'Art Imprimé (Wed–Sun noon–8pm; free), which puts on temporary exhibtions linked to the art of printing.

Heading south, under the Pont de Chatou, will bring you to the Parc des Impressionistes, a fairly nondescript park with a few picnic tables. Beyond the park, however, a narrow wooded path, with the Seine running both sides, takes you as far as the **Grenouillère** (10-min walk), a popular spot in the early 1900s for riverside drinking, dancing, bathing and boating; it was much frequented and painted by the Impressionists. A small **museum** of memorabilia relating to the Grenouillère (Tues, Thurs and Sun 2–6pm; closed mid-Dec to mid-Jan; 20F/€3.05) is housed in the Maison Joséphine (so-called because Joséphine de Beauharnais lived there for two years before her marriage to Napoleon) on the other side of the river in Croissy, but you need to head back up the Pont de Chatou to cross over, and follow the river downstream on the Chatou/Croissy side to get there.

Access to the island is from the Rueil-Malmaison RER stop. Take the Sortie av Albert-1er, go left out of the station and right along the dual carriageway onto the bridge – a ten-minute walk. **River cruises** round the island of

Chatou or as far as Auvers-sur-Oise, the town where Van Gogh spent the last two months of his life, depart from the Capitainerie (May–Oct Sun and public hols; 50–320F/€7.62–48.78 depending on the cruise; ☎01.47.16.72.66 for tickets and information) on the Rueil-Malmaison bank of the Seine, opposite the Maison Fournaise.

MONET'S GARDEN, GIVERNY

April–Oct Tues–Sun 10am–6pm; house and garden 35F/€5.34, garden only 25F/€3.81.

Monet's garden in Giverny is a class of its own. The artist lived in Giverny from 1883 till his death in 1926, and his garden, stretching from his house down to the river, were considered by many of his friends to be his greatest masterpiece. He planted his garden so that each month a different colour would dominate. Similarly, each of the rooms, with his collection of Japanese prints hung exactly as Monet left them, were decorated in different colours. The best times to visit are May and June, when the rhododendrons flower round the lily pond and the wisteria winds over the Japanese bridge. But in any month from spring to autumn you'll be overwhelmed by the beauty of the garden's arrangement of shades and shapes.

Giverny is some way out of Paris – 65km – in the direction of Rouen. Without a car, the easiest approach is by **train** to Vernon from Paris-St-Lazare (45min; 3 daily, last one to get you there in time is at 2.20pm Tues–Sat, 10.44am Sun; 132F/€20.12). **Buses** meet each train (21F/€3.20 return journey, last bus back to the station is Tues, Thurs & Fri 6.55pm, Wed & Sat 5.15pm, Sun 5.25pm) for the six-kilometre ride to the garden. Alternatively, you could rent a **bike** (1000F/€152.45 deposit) or walk. You'll need to cross the river and turn right on the D5. Take care as you enter Giverny to follow the left fork, otherwise you'll make a long detour to reach the garden entrance.

Monet's house and garden have spawned a couple of expensive cafés and restaurants in the village, as well as the **Musée d'Art Américain** (April–Oct Tues–Sun 10am–6pm; 35F/€5.34). The display is changed annually and is taken from the Terra Foundation for the Arts collection which represents a wide range of periods from American art. The main interest for a visitor to Giverny is likely to be the American Impressionist collection, which includes a few Sargents.

LISTINGS

Accommodation

Not surprisingly, Paris hotels are the most expensive in France, though compared with other European capitals, **accommodation** prices are not exorbitant, and there is a wide range of comfort, price and location. It's possible to find a decent, centrally located double

BUREAUX D'ACCUEIL

Office du Tourisme, 127 av des Champs-Élysées, 8e; ℡01.49.52.53.54, Ⓕ01.49.52.53.00 (Mº Charles-de-Gaulle–Étoile). May–Sept daily 9am–8pm, closed May 1; Oct–April Mon–Sat 9am–8pm, Sun & hols 11am–6pm.

Gare de Lyon, exit from main-line platforms, 20 bd Diderot, 12e; ℡01.43.43.33.24. Mon–Sat 8am–8pm; closed hols.

Gare du Nord, arrival point for international trains, 18 rue de Dunkerque, 10e; ℡01.45.26.94.82. Mon–Sat 8am–8pm; closed hols.

Tour Eiffel, Champ de Mars, 7e; ℡01.45.51.22.15 (RER Champs-de-Mars & Mº Tour Eiffel). April–Sept daily 11am–6pm.

Information in English (24hr) ℡01.49.52.53.56.

with a shower for 220F/€33.54 in low season, if you hunt around and book in advance. Bargains exist in the 11e near the Bastille and on the edge of the Marais, as well as in the 17e or 20e, where you can find a small room with just a washbasin and perhaps a bidet for as little as 170F/€25.92. For average comfort and location you'd be looking at 300F/€45.73 minimum. If you're stuck, the main **tourist office** at Champs Élysées and the branches at Gare de Lyon and the Eiffel Tower (see box opposite for addresses) will endeavour to find you a room: all book accommodation for that day only and charge 20F–55F/€3.05–8.38 commission for a hotel room, depending on category, and 8F/€1.22 for a hostel room. The **Accueil des Jeunes en France** (AJF), at the Banlieue section of the Gare du Nord (June–Sept 10am–6.30pm; ☎01.42.85.86.19) and within the travel agency OTU Voyages Beaubourg, 119 rue St-Martin, opposite the Pompidou Centre, 4e (Mon–Fri 10am–6.45pm, Sat 10am–5.30pm; ☎01.40.29.12.12, ⓦ www.otu.fr; Mº Châtelet-Les-Halles), guarantees to find young people (under 26) a room, though not necessarily a cheap one, for a fee of 10F/€1.52.

HOTELS

Our **hotel** recommendations below are divided by area and listed in ascending price order.

THE ISLANDS

Henri IV
Map 2, F7. 25 place Dauphine, 4e ☎ 01.43.54.44.53. Mº Pont-Neuf & Mº Cité.

An ancient and well-known bargain in a beautiful central location on the Île de la Cité. Nothing more luxurious than a *cabinet de toilette* and now very run-down. Essential to book in advance. ❷.

ACCOMMODATION PRICE CATEGORIES

Each hotel in this chapter has a symbol which corresponds to one of nine price categories. The prices quoted are for the cheapest available double room in high season, though remember that many of the cheap places will have more expensive rooms with en-suite facilities.

❶ Under 160F/€24.39
❷ 160–220F/€24.39–33.54
❸ 220–300F/€33.54–45.73
❹ 300–400F/€45.73–60.98
❺ 400–500F/€60.98–76.22

❻ 500–600F/€76.22–91.47
❼ 600–700F/€91.47–107
❽ 700F–800F/€107–122
❾ Over 800F/€122

de Lutèce

Map 4, A13. 65 rue St-Louis-en-l'Île, 4e ☏ 01.43.26.23.52, Ⓕ 01.43.29.60.25. Mº Pont-Marie.

The small but exquisite rooms are tastefully decorated in soothing colours. The hotel has air conditioning, a vaulted breakfast room and a private garden; plus it is located on the most desirable island in France. ❾.

THE TUILERIES, CHAMPS-ÉLYSÉES AND AROUND

----

d'Artois

Map 7, I3. 94 rue la Boétie, 8e ☏ 01.43.59.84.12, Ⓕ 01.43.59.50.70. Mº St-Philippe-du-Roule.

One of the cheapest hotels in this smart part of town. Rooms are spacious, though basic. ❹.

Lion d'Or

Map 2, C3. 5 rue de la Sourdière,1er ☏ 01.42.60.79.04, Ⓕ 01.42.60.09.14. Mº Tuileries. Poky and busily decorated hotel, but clean, friendly and very central. ❹.

des Champs-Élysées

Map 7, I2. 2 rue Artois, 8e ☏ 01.43.59.11.42, Ⓕ 01.45.61.00.61. Mº St-Philippe-du-Roule.

HOTELS

●

It's not the most stylish place to stay, but you'll certainly feel welcome. All rooms have bathrooms, satellite television and minibar. Excellent value for the area. ❺.

Keppler

Map 7, E4. 12 rue Keppler, 16ᵉ
Ⓣ 01.47.20.65.05,
Ⓕ 01.47.23.02.29. Mº George-V & Mº Kléber.
Rooms are a little small, but spotless, quite comfortable, and just a few steps away from the Champs-Élysées. ❺.

Hôtel Brighton

Map 2, B3. 218 rue de Rivoli,1ᵉʳ Ⓣ 01.47.03.61.61,
Ⓕ 01.42.60.41.78. Mº Tuileries.
A slow renovation is in progress in order to bring the *Hôtel Brighton* into line with specified norms, but this shouldn't mar your stay. You can still enjoy the charm of faded splendour and magnificent views over the Tuileries from the rooms with balconies. ❼.

de L'Élysée

Map 7, L3. 12 rue des Saussaies, 8ᵉ

Ⓣ 01.42.65.29.25,
Ⓕ 01.42.65.64.28,
Ⓔ *hotel.de.l.elysee@wanadoo.fr*
Mº Miromesnil.
Chandeliers and four-poster beds – classic luxury. ❼.

Le Bristol

Map 7, K3. 112 rue du Faubourg St-Honoré, 8ᵉ
Ⓣ 01.53.43.43.00,
Ⓕ 01.53.43.43.01,
Ⓦ *www.hotel-bristol.com*
Mº Miromesnil.
Paris's most luxurious and spacious hotel manages to remain discreet and warm. There are Gobelins tapestries, private roof gardens with some of the rooms and a large colonnaded interior garden, as well as the expected swimming pool, health club and gourmet restaurant. Doubles start at 3500F/€533.57, but you could always plump for the 300m² presidential suite at 40,000F/€6097.96 per night. ❾.

Costes

Map 2, B2. 239 rue St-Honoré,1ᵉʳ Ⓣ 01.42.44.50.00,
Ⓕ 01.42.44.50.01. Mº Tuileries.

The recent redesign, marrying Second-Empire style with the modern amenities required for a luxurious stay, is rather garish but proved an instant success. Mingle with media and fashion celebrities. Doubles start at 2000F/€304.90. ❾.

THE GRANDS BOULEVARDS AND AROUND
- - - - - - - - - - - - - - - - - - -

Tiquetonne
Map 2, H3. 6 rue Tiquetonne, 2e ℡01.42.36.94.58. M° Étienne-Marcel.
Old-fashioned, well-maintained cheapie on a pedestrian street, but close to the red-light stretch of St-Denis. ❷.

Vauvilliers
Map 2, F5. 6 rue Vauvilliers,1er ℡01.42.36.89.08. M° Châtelet-Les Halles & M° Louvre.
All you need for somewhere to sleep and wash – nothing more. Book far in advance for this well-established cheapie. ❷.

du Palais
Map 2, G6. 2 Quai de la Mégisserie,1er ℡01.42.36.98.25, ℱ01.42.21.41.67. M° Châtelet.
The rooms at the top are basic and cheap, though for 100F/€15.24 more, you'll have a view over the Seine and a shower in your room. Location and views at this price are hard to beat. ❸.

Vivienne
Map 3, G8. 40 rue Vivienne, 2e ℡01.42.33.13.26, ℱ01.40.41.98.19. M° Grands-Boulevards.
Traditional comfort and wooden floors. Ideal location for the Opéra Garnier, *grands boulevards* and nightlife. ❹.

de Beauharnais
Map 3, F7. 51 rue de la Victoire, 9e ℡01.48.74.71.13. M° Le Peletier & M° Havre-Caumartin.
Every room is decorated in a different period style: Louis Quinze, First Empire… It's at the cheaper end of this price bracket with reasonable discounts outside high season. ❺.

HOTELS

Chopin

Map 3, H8. 46 passage Jouffroy, 9e Ⓣ 01.47.70.58.10, Ⓕ 01.42.47.00.70. M° Grands-Boulevards.

Splendid period building in an old *passage*. Entrance on boulevard Montmartre, near rue du Faubourg-Montmartre. ❺.

Agora

Map 2, G5. 7 rue Cossonerie,1er Ⓣ 01.42.33.46.02, Ⓕ 01.42.33.80.99. M° Châtelet–Les-Halles.

Old-fashioned, individually styled rooms, each with bathroom. It's expensive for a two-star, but peaceful and in a good location. ❻.

Ducs d'Anjou

Map 2, G5. 1 rue Ste-Opportune,1er Ⓣ 01.42.36.92.24, Ⓕ 01.42.36.16.63, Ⓦ *www.hotelducsdanjou.fr* M° Châtelet.

A carefully renovated old building overlooking the busy place Ste-Opportune in the middle of Les Halles. ❼.

Les Noailles

Map 3, F8. 9 rue Michodière, 2e Ⓣ 01.47.42.92.90, Ⓕ 01.49.24.92.71. M° Opéra & M° 4-Septembre.

Although part of an international chain, the *Noailles* still retains its own character. Contemporary styling, with the traditional pleasures of a garden and *terrasse*. ❽.

QUARTIER BEAUBOURG, THE MARAIS AND BASTILLE

Picard

Map 4, C7. 26 rue de Picardie, 3e Ⓣ 01.48.87.53.82, Ⓕ 01.48.87.02.56. M° Temple & M° République.

Somewhat frayed around the edges, but a clean and comfortable hotel on the outer limits of the Marais overlooking the Carreau du Temple and next door to Paris's best internet café (see p.203). Popular with young American backpackers. Run by a charming and very accommodating Pole. ❸.

du Midi

Map 4, G14. 31 rue Traversière, 12e ℡01.43.07.88.68, ℻01.43.07.37.77. M° Ledru-Rollin.

Clean, pleasant accommodation close to the Gare de Lyon and the Viaduc des Arts; most rooms have shower, toilet and TV. ③—④.

Moderne

Map 4, C11. 3 rue Caron, 4e ℡01.48.87.97.05. M° St-Paul & M° Bastille.

Just modern enough and certainly offering the basic amenities, which is more than the price would suggest. A real bargain on cute little Place du Marché St Catherine. ④.

Pax

Map 4, F13. 12 rue de Charonne, 11e ℡01.47.00.40.98, ℻01.42.28.57.81. M° Ledru-Rollin & M° Bastille.

A clean, if simple, bargain in the centre of the Bastille's nightlife and surrounded by cafés for early-morning, after-dancing coffee. There's no lift, just a seemingly endless spiral staircase. ④.

Grand Hôtel Amelot

Map 4, E9. 54 rue Amelot, 11e ℡01.48.06.15.19, ℻01.48.06.69.77. M° St-Sébastien-Froissart.

A recently renovated, well-run establishment in a good location amid several amiable bars on the edge of the Marais and close to the Cirque d'Hiver. Rooms are spacious and pleasantly decorated with attractive modern bathrooms plus cable TV. Also has a few bargain 150F/€22.87 basic single rooms. Excellent value. ⑤.

Grand Hôtel Jeanne d'Arc

Map 4, C11. 3 rue de Jarente, 4e ℡01.48.87.62.11, ℻01.48.87.37.31. M° St-Paul.

Clean, quiet and attractive; rooms have all mod-cons, including cable TV, and all the charm and personality of the quintessential Parisian hotel. Located in a wonderfully intimate neighbourhood, within easy striking distance of the Marais

HOTELS

171

and the Islands. Booking
essential. **⑤**.

du Septième Art

Map 4, C12. 20 rue St-Paul,
4ᵉ ⓣ 01.42.77.04.03,
ⓕ 01.42.77.69.10. Mº St-Paul &
Mº Sully Morland.
Pleasant, comfortable place
decorated with posters and
photos from old movies, and
a similarly themed *salon de thé*
downstairs. The stairs and
bathrooms live up to the
black-and-white-movie style.
Every room equipped with a
safe. **⑤**.

Hôtel-Résidence Trousseau

Map 4, G13. 13 rue
Trousseau, 11ᵉ
ⓣ 01.48.05.55.55,
ⓕ 01.01.48.05.83.97. Mº
Bastille & Mº Ledru-Rollin.
Modern, serviced studio
apartments sleeping two to
six people, and fitted with
satellite TV and fully
equipped kitchens. Perfectly
positioned for food shopping
in the nearby place d'Aligre
market. Car parking is
available for 80F/€12.20 per
day. **⑤**.

Grand Hôtel Mahler

Map 4, C11. 5 rue Mahler, 4ᵉ
ⓣ 01.42.72.60.92,
ⓕ 01.42.72.25.37. Mº St-Paul.
Immaculate rooms and
attentive service are hallmarks
of this small, comfortable and
relaxed hotel located in the
heart of the Marais and near
the St-Paul métro stop.
Breakfast is served in a
renovated seventeenth-century
vaulted wine cellar. **⑤**.

de Saintonge

Map 4, C8. 16 rue de
Saintonge, 3ᵉ
ⓣ 01.42.77.91.13,
ⓕ 01.48.87.76.41.
Mº Filles-du-Calvaire.
In a sixteenth-century house
on the edge of the Marais,
near the Picasso Museum,
though only the stone-
vaulted cellar, where breakfast
is taken, retains much
character. It's a very relaxing
hotel, however, with all mod-
cons, including cable TV and
safes in the rooms. **⑤**.

St-Louis Marais

Map 4, C12. 1 rue Charles-V,
4ᵉ ⓣ 01.48.87.87.04,
ⓕ 01.48.87.33.26,

Ⓦ www.hotelsaintlouismarais
.com M° Sully-Morland.
A very comfortable restored
seventeenth-century mansion
featuring wood beams,
exposed stonework, antique
furniture and en-suite
bathrooms. A fine place to
stay all year, but particularly
cosy during the cooler
months. ❼.

Pavilion de la Reine
Map 4, D11. 28 pl des Vosges,
3ᵉ Ⓣ 01.40.29.19.19,
Ⓕ 01.40.29.19.20. M° Bastille.
In one of the *place*'s much
admired seventeenth-century
mansions, this makes a good
honeymoon or romantic
weekend hotel choice for
those prepared to splurge.
The decor is antique, right
down to the four-poster beds
and oil paintings, but all modern comforts come with the
deal, from air conditioning to
24-hour room service. ❾.

QUARTIER LATIN

Médicis
Map 2, F12. 214 rue St-
Jacques, 5ᵉ Ⓣ 01.43.54.14.66.
RER Luxembourg.
Very primitive – some
would say run-down, others
well worn – but the low
prices and stellar Latin
Quarter location make it
very popular with hard-up
backpackers, students, and
young people. The owners
are charming and the atmosphere is laid-back and congenial. ❷.

Marignan
Map 2, G10. 13 rue du
Sommerard, 5ᵉ
Ⓣ 01.43.54.63.81. M° Maubert-
Mutualité.
One of the best bargains in
town, with a free breakfast
thrown in. Totally sympathetic to the needs of rucksack-
toting foreigners, with free
laundry and ironing facilities,
plus a room to eat your own
food in – plates, fridge and
microwave provided. Even
the maid speaks English.
Rooms for 2, 3 and 4–5 people; no reservations for single
rooms, though you need to
turn up early. ❸.

HOTELS

des Grandes Écoles

Map 2, H12. 75 rue du Cardinal-Lemoine, 5ᵉ Ⓣ01.43.26.79.23, Ⓕ01.43.25.28.15 Ⓦ*www.hotel-grandes-ecoles .com* Mᵒ Cardinal-Lemoine.

A stately hotel in the heart of the Latin Quarter, with refurbished, nicely decorated rooms featuring lots of floral wallpaper and lace accents. The large and beautifully manicured courtyard garden with trees and flowerbeds – not to mention chairs and tables – gives it a country-manor air. ❽.

Agora St-Germain

Map 2, H10. 42 rue des Bernardins, 5ᵉ Ⓣ01.46.34.13.00, Ⓕ01.46.34.75.05. Mᵒ Maubert-Mutualité.

Nothing out of the ordinary, but pleasant and with all the comfort you'd expect for the price. The old-fashioned, high-ceilinged rooms have been outfitted with modern amenities such as hair dryer, TV and individual safes. ❽.

Libertal Quartier Latin

Map 2, H11. 9 rue des Écoles, 5ᵉ Ⓣ01.44.27.06.45, Ⓕ01.43.25.36.70. Mᵒ Cardinal-Lemoine & Mᵒ Maubert-Mutualité.

Part of the Libertal group focusing on small, charming hotels in Paris. The individual rooms are straight out of a style mag, with air conditioning, double glazing and even a kettle, plus luxuriously spacious white bathrooms. ❽.

ST-GERMAIN

de Nesle

Map 2, E7. 7 rue de Nesle, 6ᵉ Ⓣ01.43.54.62.41. Mᵒ St-Michel.

Characterful erstwhile hippy haven complete with dim lighting, overstuffed chairs and Art Deco posters on the wall. Rooms are themed and decorated with murals. Small, friendly and full of backpackers and free spirits. No reservations – arrive before 10am. ❹.

Récamier

Map 2, D9. 3bis place St-

HOTELS

Sulpice, 6e Ⓣ 01.43.26.04.89,
Ⓕ 01.46.33.27.73. Mº St-
Sulpice & Mº St-Germain-des-
Prés.

Comfortable, old-fashioned
and solidly bourgeois hotel
offering few concessions to
modernity or fashion.
Personable staff are very
helpful and give the establishment its folksy friendli-
ness. Superbly situated on
the peaceful *place*, just a few
blocks' walk from boulevard
St-Germain. ❺.

Grand Hôtel des Balcons

Map 2, E9. 3 rue Casimir-
Delavigne, 6e Ⓣ 01.46.34.78.50,
Ⓕ 01.46.34.06.27. Mº Odéon.
An attractive and comfortable
family-run hotel, complete
with Art Deco entrance, in a
lovely location near the
Odéon and Jardin du
Luxembourg. The rooms are
small and simple, but some
have tiny balconies, and all
are spotlessly clean. ❻.

Bersoly's St-Germain

Map 2, C6. 28 rue de Lille, 7e
Ⓣ 01.42.60.73.79,
Ⓕ 01.49.27.05.55. Mº Rue-du-
Bac.

Small but exquisite rooms,
each named after an artist.
Impeccable service. ❼.

des Marronniers

Map 2, D7–D8. 21 rue Jacob,
6e Ⓣ 01.43.25.30.60,
Ⓕ 01.40.46.83.56. Mº St-
Germain-des-Prés.
Lavishly decorated rooms,
with rich-coloured drapes,
beautifully tiled bathrooms
and rooftop views from the
upper rooms. At the back is a
dining room overlooking a
secluded garden shaded by
chestnut trees. This is a
delightful place, perfect for a
special occasion. ❼.

de l'Angleterre

Map 2, D7. 44 rue Jacob, 6e
Ⓣ 01.42.60.34.72,
Ⓕ 01.42.60.16.93. Mº St-
Germain-des-Prés.
A classy and elegant hotel in
the former British Embassy.
Sumptuous rooms with
seventeenth-century canopy
beds. Perhaps one of its most
pleasant features is the flower
garden at the back where
breakfast is served in the
warmer months. Hemingway
lived in room 14, although in

HOTELS

●

those days he only paid three francs a night, not 980F/€149.40. **9**.

TROCADÉRO, THE EIFFEL TOWER AND LES INVALIDES

----

de la Paix
Map 6, B4. 19 rue du Gros-Caillou, 7e Ⓣ01.45.51.86.17, Ⓕ01.45.55.93.28. M° École-Militaire.
A fairly standard cheap hotel whose main bonus is the price – the best bargain within proximity of the Eiffel Tower. **4**.

la Serre
Map 6, B3. 24bis rue Cler, 7e Ⓣ01.47.05.52.33, Ⓕ01.40.62.95.66. M° École-Militaire.
An old-fashioned, no-frills establishment on a lively street in a posh and attractive neighbourhood. Reserve a fortnight in advance. **4**.

du Palais Bourbon
Map 6, E4. 49 rue de Bourgogne, 7e Ⓣ01.45.51.63.32,

Ⓕ01.44.11.30.70, Ⓦ www.hotel-palais-bourbon.com M° Varenne.
A handsome old building in a sunny street by the Musée Rodin. Rooms are spacious and light. **4–6**.

Grand Hôtel Lévêque
Map 6, B3. 29 rue Cler, 7e Ⓣ01.47.05.49.15, Ⓕ01.45.50.49.36, Ⓦ www.hotel-leveque.com M° École-Militaire & M° Latour-Maubourg.
In a good location smack in the middle of the rue Cler market, this is a clean, decent hotel, run by nice people who speak some English. You'll need to book a month ahead. **5**.

Le Pavillon
Map 6, C2. 54 rue St-Dominique, 7e Ⓣ01.45.51.42.87, Ⓕ01.45.51.32.79. M° Invalides & M° Latour-Maubourg.
A tiny former convent set back from the tempting shops of the rue St-Dominique in a leafy courtyard. A lovely setting, though the rooms are a little poky for the price. **5**.

Hameau de Passy

Map 1, B4. 48 rue de Passy, 16e ⓣ 01.42.88.47.55, ⓕ 01.42.30.83.72, ⓦ *www.hameaudepassy.com* Mº Muette.

A ten-minute stroll from the Eiffel Tower, the *Hameau de Passy* is a modern, sunlight-filled hotel tucked away in a mews. The rooms are bright and cheerful, with en-suite facilities, hairdryer, TV and phone. Utterly peaceful, with faultless service from the friendly polyglot staff. ❻.

d'Orsay

Map 6, G2. 93 rue de Lille, 7e ⓣ 01.47.05.85.54, ⓕ 01.45.55.51.16. Mº Solférino & RER Musée-d'Orsay. Ex-*Hôtel Selférino*, minus the old lift, enlarged and refurbished in a simple and classic style. An attractive and relaxing place to stay, and rooms are spacious by Parisian standards. ❼.

de la Tulipe

Map 6, B2. 33 rue Malar, 7e ⓣ 01.45.51.67.21, ⓕ 01.47.53.96.37. Mº Latour-Maubourg.

Cottage-like place with a patio for summer breakfast and drinks. But, as with all hotels in this area, you pay for the location rather than luxury. ❼.

MONTPARNASSE AND THE SOUTHERN ARRONDISSEMENTS

- - - - - - - - - - - - - - - -

Ouest

Map 6, E14. 27 rue de Gergovie, 14e ⓣ 01.45.42.64.99, ⓕ 01.45.42.46.65. Mº Pernety. Located in a very pleasant part of town, with basic but perfectly acceptable rooms. ❷.

Printemps

Map 6, off A8. 31 rue du Commerce, 15e ⓣ 01.45.79.83.36, ⓕ 01.45.79,84.88, ⓔ *hotel.printemps.15e@yahoo .fr* Mº La Motte-Picquet. A welcoming place, popular with backpackers and offering sparsely furnished, clean rooms. There's no TV and no lift but there is internet access (1F/€0.15 per minute). ❷.

HOTELS

Tolbiac

Map 5, H9. 122 rue de Tolbiac, 13e ⓣ01.44.24.25.54, ⓕ01.45.85.43.47, ⓔ*htolbiac@club-internet.fr* Mº Tolbiac.

On a noisy junction, but all rooms are very pleasant, with toilets and showers; breakfast is only 21F/€3.20. In July & Aug you can rent small studios by the week. ❷.

de la Loire

Map 6, off F14. 39bis rue du Moulin-Vert, 14e ⓣ01.45.40.66.88, ⓕ01.45.40.89.07. Mº Alésia & Mº Plaisance.

Attractive hotel on a very quiet street, with breakfast served in a little garden. ❹.

Pasteur

Map 6, D11. 33 rue du Docteur-Roux, 15e ⓣ01.47.83.53.17, ⓕ01.45.66.62.39. Mº Pasteur.

The rooms are comfortable and well equipped for the price, and there's a small garden. ❹.

Résidence Les Gobelins

Map 5, F6. 9 rue des Gobelins, 13e ⓣ01.47.07.26.90, ⓕ01.43.31.44.05. Mº Les Gobelins.

Delightful establishment that's cosy and well tended. The warm welcome ensures a regular clientele, so book far in advance. ❹.

Le Vert-Galant

Map 5, F7. 41 rue Croulebarbe, 13e ⓣ01.44.08.83.50, ⓕ01.44.08.83.69. Mº Les Gobelins.

In a quiet, verdant backwater, above a renowned Basque restaurant. Cosy rooms, some with kitchenette, and a vine climbing up the wall from the garden. ❺.

Istria

Map 6, I12. 29 rue Campagne-Première, 14e ⓣ01.43.20.91.82, ⓕ01.43.22.48.45. Mº Raspail.

A beautifully decorated hotel, with legendary artistic associations: Duchamp, Man Ray, Aragon, Mayakovsky and Rilke all stayed here. ❻.

MONTMARTRE

----

du Commerce

Map 3, G3. 34 rue des Trois-Frères, 18ᵉ Ⓣ 01.42.64.81.69. Mᵒ Abbesses & Mᵒ Anvers. Very basic and dirt-cheap; for the hardened dosser only. ❶.

Burq-Bonséjour

Map 3, F2. 11 rue Burq, 18ᵉ Ⓣ 01.42.54.22.53, Ⓕ 01.42.54.25.92. Mᵒ Abbesses. Marvellous location on a quiet untouristy street on the slopes of Montmartre. The hotel is run by friendly and conscientious owners, and the rooms, which are basic, but clean and spacious, are Montmartre's best deal. Rooms 23, 33, 43 and 53 have balconies. ❷.

Versigny

Map 1, E1. 31 rue Letort, 18ᵉ Ⓣ 01.42.59.20.90, Ⓕ 01.42.59.32.66. Mᵒ Jules-Joffrin. Unmodernized and basic – fine if you're tough and want a cheap sleep. ❷.

Ermitage

Map 3, I2. 24 rue Lamarck, 18ᵉ Ⓣ 01.42.64.79.22. Mᵒ Lamarck-Caulaincourt & Mᵒ Château-Rouge. A discreet hotel only a stone's throw away from the Sacré Cœur, yet completely undisturbed by the throngs of tourists. Approach via Mᵒ Anvers and the *funiculaire* to avoid the steep climb. ❺.

Terrass

Map 3, E2. 12 rue Joseph de Maistre, 18ᵉ Ⓣ 01.46.06.72.85, Ⓕ 01.42.52.29.11. Mᵒ Blanche. On the southwest side of the Butte, with magnificent views from the terrace-garden. Spacious rooms done out in antiques and warm colours. Doubles starting at 1390F/€211.90, going up to 1860F/€283.56. ❾.

PIGALLE

Perfect Hotel

Map 3, H5. 39 Rue Rodier, 9ᵉ Ⓣ 01.42.81.18.86, Ⓕ 01.42.85.01.38. Mᵒ Anvers. Popular hotel on a lively street populated with restaurants. Rather brusque welcome but the rooms are clean and simple. ❷.

André Gill

Map 3, G3. 4 rue André-Gill, 18ᵉ ℡ 01.42.62.48.48, ⒡ 01.42.62.77.92. Mº Pigalle & Mº Abbesses.
Very adequate, quiet rooms in a great location on the slopes of Montmartre, in a dead-end alley off rue des Martyrs. ❸.

des Croisés

Map 3, E6. 63 rue St-Lazare, 9ᵉ ℡ 01.48.74.78.24, ⒡ 01.49.95.04.43. Mº Trinité.
Low on mod-cons but great on style: a hotch-potch of different periods. Good value. ❺.

EASTERN PARIS

- - - - - - - - - - - - - - - - - - -

Palace

Map 2, I1. 9 rue Bouchardon, 10ᵉ ℡ 01.40.40.09.45 or 01.42.06.59.32, ⒡ 01.42.06.16.90. Mº Strasbourg-St-Denis.
Gloomy corridors, but acceptable rooms in a busy, colourful and central district near the Porte St-Martin. Popular with backpackers and run by nice, helpful owners. ❶.

Ermitage

Map 4, off I4. 42bis rue de l'Ermitage, 20ᵉ ℡ 01.46.36.23.44, ⒡ 01.46.36.23.44. Mº Jourdain.
A clean, decent cheapie, close to the leafy rue des Pyrénées. ❷.

du Jura

Map 4, A3. 6 rue de Jarry, 10ᵉ ℡ 01.47.70.06.66. Mº Gare-de-l'Est & Mº Château-d'Eau.
A bit basic, but friendly and decent. ❷.

Mary's

Map 4, D6. 15 rue de Malte, 11ᵉ ℡ 01.47.00.81.70, ⒡ 01.47.00.58.06, ⓦ www.maryshotel.com Mº République & Mº Oberkampf.
Comfortable and clean hotel on the edge of the Marais, run by courteous people and devoid of all pretensions; cheaper rooms are good value for money but en-suite rooms suffer from money-saving

gadgets such as hand-held showers. ❷.

de Reims

Map 4, off F14. 26 rue Hector-Malot, 12ᵉ Ⓣ 01.43.07.46.18. Mᵒ Gare-de-Lyon & Mᵒ Ledru-Rollin.
An old-fashioned hotel with a worn, lived-in feel, on a quiet street with access to the Promenade Plantée, and close to the place d'Aligre market. Closed Aug. ❷.

de Vienne

Map 4, D6. 43 rue de Malte, 11ᵉ Ⓣ 01.48.05.44.42. Mᵒ République & Mᵒ Oberkampf.
Very pleasant, clean, good-value cheapie, with nicely decorated rooms (none with toilet, though some have showers) and flowered drapes. Run by a charming older couple. No lift. Closed Aug. No credit cards. ❷.

Ibis Paris La Villette

Map 4, off D1. 31 Quai de L'Oise, 19ᵉ Ⓣ 01.40.38.04.04, Ⓕ 01.40.38.48.90. Mᵒ Corentin Cariou & Mᵒ Ourcq.
Situated right on the canal facing the Parc de la Villette,

this good-value modern chain hotel is a great spot to stay if you want to spend a few days exploring the park or attending concerts at the Cité de la Musique. It is also a wise choice for people with their own cars, easily reached from the *boulevard périphérique* exiting at the Porte de la Villette, with free parking included. ❸.

Rhin et Danube

Map 4, off I1. 3 place Rhin-et-Danube, 19ᵉ Ⓣ 01.42.45.10.13, Ⓕ 01.42.06.88.82. Mᵒ Danube.
Studio apartments away from the centre on the airy heights of Belleville close to the Buttes Chaumont. Geared to self-catering. Amenities include en-suite bathroom, kitchenette, phone, TV, and hair dryer. Good value. ❹.

Beaumarchais

Map 4, E8. 3 rue Oberkampf, 11ᵉ Ⓣ 01.43.38.16.16, Ⓕ 01.43.38.32.86, Ⓦ www.hotelbeaumarchais.com Mᵒ Filles-du-Calvaire & Mᵒ Oberkampf.
Fashionable and funky gay-

HOTELS

friendly hotel with personal service and colourful Fifties-inspired decor; all rooms are en suite with air conditioning, double-glazed windows, individual safes and cable TV. Breakfast in bed is 50F/€7.62 per person. ❻.

Terminus Nord
Map 3, L5. 12 bd de Denain, 10ᵉ ⓣ 01.42.80.20.00, ⓕ01.42.80.63.89.

Mº Gare-du-Nord.
Traditional-style luxury hotel right in front of the Gare du Nord. It bears a few signs of chain-hotelry, but its aspirations and services are those of a four-star hotel and it's a very comfortable and convenient place to stay. Facilities include a well-stocked whisky bar. Rooms start at 1161F/€176.99. ❾.

HOSTELS, STUDENT ACCOMMODATION AND CAMPSITES

Numerous places in Paris offer **hostel** accommodation. The cheapest hostels are those run by the **French Youth Hostel Association** (Fédération Unie des Auberges de Jeunesse, or **FUAJ**; online at ⓦ*www.fuaj.fr*), for which you need Hostelling International (HI) membership (no age limit), and those connected with the **MIJE** (Maison Internationale de la Jeunesse et des Étudiants) and **UCRIF** (Union des Centres de Rencontres Internationaux de France). There is also a handful of privately run hostels.

Current costs for dorm-bed and breakfast are: HI hostels from 120F/€18.29, MIJE hostels from 140F/€21.34 and UCRIF hostels 120–130F/€18.29–19.82. Single and double rooms are more expensive. There is no age limit and reservations are not always possible. MIJE hostels, mostly centrally situated in historic buildings, have a seven-day stay limit; for the other hostels it varies but is normally less. Bear in mind, too, that some places have a curfew – usually around 11pm – though you may be able to borrow a key. We've detailed only the most central of the UCRIF hostels: for a full list contact their main office at 27 rue de Turbigo, 2ᵉ (Mon–Fri 10am–6pm; ☏ 01.40.26.57.64, 🅕 01.40.26.58.20, 🅦 *www.ucrif.asso.fr*; Mᵒ Étienne-Marcel). Independent hostels are even cheaper: around 90F/€13.72 for a dorm room off-season, rising to about 120F/€18.29 in summer.

   Student accommodation is let out during vacation time (July–Sept). The organization to contact is CROUS, Académie de Paris, 39 av Georges-Bernanos, 5ᵉ ☏ 01.40.51.36.00, 🅦 *www.crous-paris.fr* (Mᵒ Port-Royal). Rooms are spartan, part of large, modern university complexes, often complete with self-service kitchen facilities and shared bathrooms. Space tends to fill up quickly with international students, school groups and young travellers, so make plans well in advance. Expect to pay 100–200F/€15.24–30.49 per night for a single and 80–150F/€12.20–22.87 per person, per night for a double.

HI HOSTELS

- - - - - - - - - - - - - - - - - - -

D'Artagnan

Map 4, off I8. 80 rue Vitruve, 20ᵉ ☏ 01.40.32.34.56, 🅕 01.42.32.34.55. Mᵒ Porte-de-Bagnolet. A colourful, funky, modern hostel, on the eastern edge of the city near the village-like Charonne, with some good bars, and handy for the Père-Lachaise cemetery. It has a

fun atmosphere and lots of facilities, including a video cinema, bar/restaurant and a local swimming pool nearby. It's very popular, so try to get here early – reservations by fax or from other HI hostels only.

Jules Ferry

Map 4, E6. 8 bd Jules-Ferry, 11ᵉ ☏ 01.43.57.55.60, 🅕 01.40.21.79.92. Mᵒ République.

Smaller and more central than D'Artagnan, in a lively area at the foot of the Belleville hill. Very difficult to get a place, but when full, they will help you find a bed elsewhere.

MIJE HOSTELS

Le Fauconnier

Map 4, B12. 11 rue du Fauconnier, 4ᵉ ⓣ01.42.74.23.45, ⓕ01.40.27.81.64. Mᵒ St-Paul & Mᵒ Pont-Marie.
A superbly renovated seventeenth-century building, with a courtyard. Dorms sleep 4–8. Breakfast included.

Le Fourcy

Map 4, B11. 6 rue de Fourcy, 4ᵉ ⓣ01.42.74.23.45. Mᵒ St-Paul.
Another beautiful mansion, this one has a small garden and a restaurant with menus from 52F/€7.93. Dorms only, sleeping 4–8.

Maubuisson

Map 4, A11. 12 rue des Barres, 4ᵉ ⓣ01.42.74.23.45.

Mᵒ Pont-Marie & Mᵒ Hôtel-de-Ville.
A magnificent medieval building in a quiet street. The restaurant has menus from 32F/€4.88. Dorms only, sleeping 4. Breakfast included.

UCRIF HOSTELS

Centre International de Paris/Louvre

Map 2, E4. 20 rue Jean-Jacques-Rousseau, 1ᵉʳ ⓣ01.53.00.90.90, ⓕ01.53.00.90.91. Mᵒ Louvre & Mᵒ Châtelet-Les Halles.

Foyer International d'Acceuil de Paris Jean Monnet

Map 5, C8. 30 rue Cabanis, 14ᵉ ⓣ01.45.89.89.15, ⓕ01.45.81.63.91. Mᵒ Glacière.
A huge, efficiently run hostel in a fairly sedate area. Facilities include meeting rooms and a disco; ideal for groups. 139F/€21.19 for a bed in a dormitory.

HOSTELS, STUDENT ACCOMMODATION AND CAMPSITES

INDEPENDENT HOSTELS

Auberge International des Jeunes Ste-Marguerite

Map 4, G13. 10 rue Trousseau, 11ᵉ ⓣ 01.47.00.62.00, ⓕ 01.47.00.33.16, ⓦ *www.aij.com* Mᵒ Bastille & Mᵒ Ledru-Rollin.

Despite the official-sounding name, a laid-back independent, but very noisy, hostel in a great location 5min walk from the Bastille. Clean and professionally run with 24hr reception, generous breakfast and free luggage storage. Under 100F/€15.24.

Maison Internationale des Jeunes

Map 4, I13. 4 rue Titon, 11ᵉ ⓣ 01.43.71.99.21, ⓕ 01.43.71.78.58. Mᵒ Faidherbe-Chaligny.

For 18- to 30-year-olds. Operates like a youth hostel, but does not require YHA membership. Dorms and doubles both 110F/€16.77

per person. Breakfast included.

Three Ducks Hostel

Map 1, C5. 6 place Étienne-Pernet, 15ᵉ ⓣ 01.48.42.04.05, ⓕ 01.48.42.99.99, ⓦ *www.3ducks.fr* Mᵒ Commerce & Mᵒ Félix Faure.

A private youth hostel with no age limit; kitchen facilities as well as a bar with the cheapest beer in town. Essential to book ahead between May & Oct: send the price of the first night or leave a credit-card number. Lock-out 11am–5pm, curfew at 2am. July–Oct 127F/€19.36; Nov–June 107F/€16.31; some rooms for couples at 137F/€20.89 per person.

Woodstock Hostel

Map 5, H5. 48 rue Rodier, 9ᵉ ⓣ 01.48.78.87.76, ⓦ *www.woodstock.fr* Mᵒ Anvers & Mᵒ St-Georges.

Another hostel in the *Three Ducks* stable, with its own bar. A great location in a pretty, untouristy street near Montmartre: dorm 117F/€17.84; double

HOSTELS, STUDENT ACCOMMODATION AND CAMPSITES

137F/€20.88 per person, cheaper in winter. Price includes breakfast.

Young and Happy Hostel

Map 5, F3. 80 rue Mouffetard, 5e Ⓣ01.45.35.09.53, Ⓕ01.47.07.22.24. Mº Monge & Mº Censier-Daubenton. Noisy, basic and studenty in a lively, if a tad touristy, position. Dorms, with shower, sleep 4–8 and there are a few doubles (137F/€20.88 each). You can book in adavance but you have to turn up early, between 8am and 11am, to keep the room. Dorms 117F/€17.84, cheaper in winter.

CAMPSITES

With the exception of the one in the Bois de Boulogne, most of Paris's **campsites** are some way out of town. Those listed below are open all year round.

Camping du Bois de Boulogne

Map 1, A4. Allée du Bord-de-l'Eau, 16e Ⓣ01.45.24.30.00, Ⓕ01.42.24.42.95. Mº Porte-Maillot then bus #244 to Route des Moulins 6am–8.30pm. Much the most central campsite, next to the River Seine in the Bois de Boulogne, and usually booked out in summer. The ground is pebbly, but the site is well equipped and has a useful information office.

90F/€13.72 for a tent with two people; and there are also bungalows from 399F/€60.83 per night. A camping shuttle bus runs April–Oct 8.30am–1am.

Camping du Parc de la Colline

Map 9, I4. Route de Lagny, 77200 Torcy; Ⓣ01.60.05.42.32. RER line A4 to Torcy, then phone from the station and they will come and collect you, or take bus #421 to stop Le Clos.

122F/€18.60 for two people and a tent. To the east of the city, near Disneyland.

Camping du Parc-Étang

Map 9, B6. Base de Loisirs, 78180 Montigny-le-Bretonneux; ℡ 01.30.58.56.20. RER line C to St-Quentin-en-Yvelines; métro connections for RER line C at Invalides/St-Michel/Gare-d'Austerlitz.
Southwest of Paris.
81F/€12.35 for two people and a tent.

Eating and drinking

Eating and drinking are among Paris's chief delights, as they are in the country as a whole. The capital offers a tremendous variety of cuisines: as well as regional French cooking, notably from the southwest, you can sample Senegalese, Caribbean, Thai, eastern European and North African cuisine, among others. There's also a huge diversity of eating and drinking establishments: luxurious **restaurants** in the traditional style or elbow-to-elbow bench-and-trestle-table jobs; spacious **brasseries** and **cafés** where you can watch the world go by while nibbling on a baguette sandwich; or dark, cavernous **beer cellars** and tiny **wine bars** with sawdust on the floor offering wines by the glass from every region of France. You can take coffee and cakes in a chintzy **salon de thé**, in a bookshop or gallery, or even in the confines of a mosque. **Bars** can be medieval vaults, minimalist or postmodern design units, London-style pubs or period pieces in styles ranging from the Swinging Sixties to the Naughty Nineties.

It's true that the old-time cheap neighbourhood cafés and bistros are a dying breed, while fast-food chains have burgeoned at an alarming speed. Quality is also in decline at the lower end of the restaurant market, particularly in tourist hotspots. Yet, however much Parisians bemoan the changing times, you'll find you're still spoiled for choice, even on a modest budget. There are numerous **fixed-price menus** (*prix fixe*) for under 80F/€12.20, particularly at lunchtime, providing staple dishes; for 150F/€22.87 you'll have the choice of more interesting dishes; and for 200F/€30.49, you should be getting some gourmet satisfaction.

The big boulevard cafés and brasseries are always more expensive than those a little further removed, and addresses in the smarter or more touristy *arrondissements* set prices soaring. A snack or drink on the Champs-Élysées, place St-Germain-des-Prés or rue de Rivoli, for instance, will be double or triple the price of Belleville, Batignolles or the southern 14e. Many bars have **happy hours**, but prices can double after 10pm, and any clearly trendy, glitzy or stylish place is bound to be expensive.

The different eating and drinking establishments are listed here by area. They are divided into **restaurants**, including some brasseries, and **bars and cafés**, incorporating snack bars, ice-cream parlours and *salons de thé*.

THE ISLANDS

BARS AND CAFÉS

Berthillon
Map 2, I9. 31 rue St-Louis-en-l'Île, 4e. Mo Pont-Marie. Wed–Sun 10am–8pm.
Long queues for these excellent ice creams and sorbets (22F/€3.35 a triple), with a big choice of unusual fruity flavours, such as rhubarb. There are also outlets at *Lady Jane* and *Le Flore-en-l'Île*, both on quai d'Orléans, as well as at four other island sites.

FOODS AND DISHES

Basics

Pain	Bread	*Vinaigre*	Vinegar
Beurre	Butter	*Bouteille*	Bottle
Œufs	Eggs	*Verre*	Glass
Lait	Milk	*Fourchette*	Fork
Huile	Oil	*Couteau*	Knife
Poivre	Pepper	*Cuillère*	Spoon
Sel	Salt	*L'addition*	The bill
Sucre	Sugar		

Snacks

Crêpe	Pancake (sweet)
Galette	Buckwheat (savoury) pancake
Un sandwich/	A sandwich . . .
une baguette . . .	
jambon	with ham
fromage	with cheese
saucisson	with sausage
pâté	with pâté
Croque-monsieur	Grilled cheese & ham sandwich
Croque-madame	Croque-monsieur with an egg on top
Œufs	Eggs
au plat	fried
à la coque	boiled
durs	hard-boiled
brouillés	scrambled
Omelette	Omelette
nature	plain
au fromage	with cheese
Salade de tomates	Tomato salad
Carottes rapées	Grated carrots

FOODS AND DISHES

Related terms

Cru	Raw
A emporter	Takeaway

Soups (soupes)

Bouillon	Broth or stock
Potage	Thick vegetable soup
Velouté	Thick soup, usually made with fish or poultry

Fish (poisson), seafood (fruits de mer) and shellfish (crustaces or coquillages)

Anchois	Anchovies	*Langouste*	Spiny lobster
Cabillaud	Cod	*Lotte*	Burbot
Coquilles St-Jacques	Scallops	*Moules (marinière)*	Mussels (with shallots in white wine sauce)
Crabe	Crab		
Crevettes grises	Shrimps		
Crevettes roses	Prawns	*Rouget*	Red mullet
Escargots	Snails	*Saumon*	Salmon
Gambas	King prawns	*Thon*	Tuna
Huîtres	Oysters	*Truite*	Trout

Meat (viande) and poultry (volaille)

Agneau	Lamb	*Dinde*	Turkey
Andouille, andouillette	Tripe sausage	*Entrecôte*	Ribsteak
		Faux filet	Sirloin steak
Bœuf	Beef	*Foie gras*	Fattened (duck/ goose) liver
Bifteck	Steak		
Boudin noir	Black pudding		
		Gigot (d'agneau)	Leg (of lamb)
Canard	Duck		

Hâchis	Chopped meat or mince hamburger	Lard, lardons	Bacon, diced bacon
Lapin, lapereau	Rabbit, young rabbit	Os	Bone
		Porc	Pork
		Poulet	Chicken
		Veau	Veal

For steaks

Bleu	Almost raw	Très bien cuit	Very well cooked
Saignant	Rare		
A point	Medium	Brochette	Kebab
Bien cuit	Well done		

Vegetables (légumes), herbs (herbes) and spices (épices)

Ail	Garlic	Moutarde	Mustard
Champignons, cèpes, chanterelles	Mushrooms of various kinds	Pâte	Pastry
		Pâtes	Pasta
		Persil	Parsley
Chou (rouge)	(Red) cabbage	Poireau	Leek
Chou-fleur	Cauliflower	Poivron (vert, rouge)	Sweet pepper (green, red)
Concombre	Cucumber		
Cornichon	Gherkin	Pommes (de terre)	Potatoes
Endive	Chicory		
Épinards	Spinach	Riz	Rice
Haricots	Beans	Truffes	Truffles

Fruits (fruits) and nuts (noix)

| Ananas | Pineapple | Cerises | Cherries |
| Cacahouète | Peanut | Citron | Lemon |

Fraises (des bois)	Strawberries (wild)	*Pamplemousse*	Grapefruit
		Pêche (blanche)	(White) peach
Framboises	Raspberries	*Pomme*	Apple
Noisette	Hazelnut	*Prune*	Plum
Noix	Nuts	*Raisins*	Grapes

Desserts (desserts or entremets) and pastries (pâtisserie)

Bavarois	Refers to the mould, could be mousse or custard
Brioche	Sweet, high yeast breakfast roll
Charlotte	Custard & fruit in lining of almond fingers
Crème Chantilly	Vanilla-flavoured & sweetened whipped cream
Crème pâtissière	Thick eggy pastry-filling
Génoise	Rich sponge cake
Glace	Ice cream
Mousse au chocolat	Chocolate mousse
Parfait	Frozen mousse, sometimes ice cream
Petits fours	Bite-sized cakes/pastries
Sablé	Shortbread biscuit

Cheese (fromage)

There are over four hundred types of French cheese, most of them named after their place of origin. *Chèvre* is goat's cheese and *brebis* is cheese made from sheep's milk. *Le plateau de fromages* is the cheeseboard, and bread – but not butter – is served with it.

Addressing the waiter or waitress

Always call the waiter or waitress *Monsieur* or *Madame* (*Mademoiselle* if a young woman), never *garçon*, no matter what you've been taught in school.

FOODS AND DISHES

Taverne Henri IV

Map 2, F7. 13 place du Pont-Neuf, 1ᵉʳ. Mᵒ Pont-Neuf. Mon–Fri noon–10pm, Sat noon–4pm; closed Aug.
Yves Montand used to come here when Simone Signoret lived in the adjacent place Dauphine. Good food but a bit pricey for a full meal. Plates of meats and cheeses around 70F/€10.67, sandwiches 30F/€4.57, wine from 20F/€3.05 a glass.

RESTAURANTS

Au Rendez-vous des Camionneurs

Map 2, F7. 72 quai des Orfèvres, 1ᵉʳ ☎ 01.43.54.88.74. Mᵒ St-Michel.
Daily noon–2pm & 7–11.30pm. Crowded, traditional establishment serving snails, steaks and scallops. Midday menus under 100F/€15.24, evening menu 130F/€19.82,

à *la carte* around 175F/€26.68.

Le Castafiore

Map 2, I9. 51 rue St-Louis-en-l'Île, 4ᵉ ☎ 01.43.54.78.62. Mᵒ Pont-Marie.
Daily till 10.30pm.
Run by a very pleasant *patron*. Italian specialities: pasta from 56F/€8.54, meat dishes from 78F/€11.89. Menu 90F/€13.72 before 8pm, 158F/€24.09 after.

Le Gourmet de l'Île

Map 2, I9. 42 rue St-Louis-en-l'Île, 4ᵉ ☎ 01.43.26.79.27. Mᵒ Pont-Marie.
Wed–Sun noon–2pm & 7–10pm; closed Aug.
Tourists make the pilgrimage to this down-to-earth restaurant for the bargain four-course menu for 140F/€21.34, including wonderful monkfish with crab sauce and the savoury andouliette.

THE ISLANDS

THE TUILERIES, CHAMPS-ÉLYSÉES AND AROUND

CAFÉS AND BARS

Angélina
Map 2, B3. 226 rue de Rivoli, 1er. Mº Tuileries.
Mon–Fri 9am–7pm, Sat & Sun 9am–7.30pm; closed Tues in July & Aug.
A long-established gilded cage, where the well-coiffed sip the best hot chocolate in town and scoff exquisite pastries.

Barry's
Map 7, L3. 9 rue Duras, 8e. Mº Champs-Élysées-Clemenceau.
Mon–Sat 11am–3pm.
Salads, snacks and sandwiches for under 30F/€4.57 in a tiny street behind the Élysée Palace.

Café Marly
Map 2, D5. Cour Napoléon du Louvre, 93 rue de Rivoli, 1er. Mº Palais-Royal–Musée-du-Louvre.
Daily till 2am.
Inside the Louvre, with tables beneath the colonnade overlooking the Pyramid in summer; chic, very classy and very expensive.

Le Fouquet's
Map 7, G3. 99 av des Champs-Élysées, 8e. Mº George-V.
Daily till 1.30am.
Le Fouquet's is such a well-established watering hole for stars of the stage and screen, politicians, newspaper editors and advertising barons, that it's now been classified as a "Monument Historique". You pay dearly to sit in the deep leather armchairs, and as for the restaurant don't expect to pay less than 300F/€45.73.

Musée Jacquemart-André
Map 7, J1. 158 bd Haussmann, 8e ☎01.45.62.11.59.
Mº St-Philippe-du-Roule & Mº Miromesnil.
Daily 11am–6pm.
A sumptuously appointed *salon de thé* in a nineteenth-century palazzo, with salads at 58–85F/€8.84–12.96, a

lunch *formule* at 86F/€13.11 and a popular weekend brunch for 130F/€19.82; museum ticket not needed.

Le Rubis

Map 2, C3. 10 rue du Marché-St-Honoré, 1er. M° Pyramides. Mon–Fri 7am–10pm, Sat 8am–4pm; closed mid-Aug.
One of the oldest wine bars, with a reputation for excellent wines, snacks and *plats du jour*. Very small and very crowded. Glasses of wine from 5.50F/€0.84.

RESTAURANTS

aux Amis du Beaujolais

Map 7, H2. 28 rue d'Artois, 8e ℡ 01.45.63.92.21. M° George-V & M° St-Philippe-du-Roule. Mon–Sat noon–3pm & 6.30–9pm; closed middle two weeks of July.
If you can fathom the hand-written menu, you'll find good traditional French stews and sautéed steaks, washed down with Beaujolais. Evening menu at 120F/€18.29.

Le Dauphin

Map 2, D4. 167 rue St-Honoré, 1er ℡ 01.42.60.40.11. M° Palais-Royal–Musée-du-Louvre. Daily: Nov–May noon–2.30pm & 7–10.30pm; June–Oct till 12.30am.
A genuine bistro, with a menu at 140F/€21.34 and seafood platter during oyster season for 167F/€25.46. Country cooking includes pig's cheeks, *lapereau* (young rabbit) *à la grand-mère* and *magret de canard*.

Dragons Élysées

Map 7, G3. 11 rue de Berri, 8e ℡ 01.42.89.85.10. M° George-V. Daily 11am–3pm & 7–11pm.
The restaurant's Chinese–Thai cuisine encompasses dim sum, curried seafood and baked mussels, but the overriding attraction is the extraordinary decor. The floor is made of glass tiles, beneath which pools of water gurgle and exotic fish dart back and forth. 80F/€12.20 lunch menu, 220F/€33.34 for *menu royal*, *à la carte* 250F/€38.11.

Foujita

Map 2, C3. 41 rue St-Roch, 1er
℡ 01.42.61.42.93. M° Tuileries
& M° Pyramides.
Mon–Sat noon–2.15pm &
7.30–10pm; closed mid-Aug.
One of the cheaper but better
Japanese restaurants, as proven
by the numbers of Japanese
eating here. Quick and
crowded; soup, sushis, rice
and tea for 72F/€10.98 at
lunchtime; plate of sushis or
sushamis for under
110F/€16.77.

Restorama

Map 2, D5. Le Carrousel du
Louvre, 1er. M° Palais-Royal-
Musée-du-Louvre.
Daily 9am–9pm.
One vast, underground, fast-
food eating hall served by
over a dozen different outlets:
rôtisseries, hamburgers,
pizzas, Tex-Mex, Chinese,
Lebanese, Japanese, crêperies,
salad bars – easy to eat for
under 50F/€7.62. Access
from place du Carrousel or
the Louvre Pyramid.

Yvan

Map 7, J3. 1bis rue J-Mermoz,
8e ℡ 01.43.59.18.40. M°
Franklin-D-Roosevelt.
Mon–Fri noon–2.30pm &
7pm–midnight; Sat
7pm–midnight.
Fish specialities and pigeon
with polenta attract a stylish
clientele. Extremely good
food and menus from
168F/€25.61.

THE GRANDS BOULEVARDS AND AROUND

CAFÉS AND BARS

L'Arbre à Cannelle

Map 3, H8. 7 passage des
Panoramas, 2e. M° Grands-
Boulevards.
Mon–Sat till 6.30pm.
Exquisite wooden panelling,
frescoes and painted ceilings
make this an enchanting spot
for puddings, flans and
assiettes gourmandes. Prices are
60–75F/€9.15–11.43.

Aux Bons Crus

Map 2, E3. 7 rue des Petits-Champs, 1er. Mº Pyramides. Mon 9am–4pm, Tues–Sat 9am–11pm.

A relaxed, workaday place that has been serving good wines and cheese, sausage and ham for over eighty years. Wine from 15F/€2.29 a glass; plate of cold meats from 55F/€8.38.

Le Café

Map 2, G3. 62 rue Tiquetonne, 2e. Mº Les Halles & Mº Étienne-Marcel. Daily 10am–2am.

On the junction with rue Étienne-Marcel, a quiet and secluded café, with old maps on the walls and people playing chess. *Plats du jour* 45–55F/€6.86–8.38.

Le Grand Café Capucines

Map 3, E8. 4 bd des Capucines, 9e. Mº Opéra. A favourite all-nighter with over-the-top belle-époque decor and excellent seafood. Boulevard prices mean 20F/€3.05 for an espresso.

Juveniles

Map 2, D3. 47 rue de Richelieu, 1er. Mº Palais-Royal-Musée-du-Louvre. Mon–Sat noon–midnight.

A very popular, tiny wine bar run by a Brit. Wine from 85F/€12.96 a bottle; *plats du jour* around 68F/€10.37.

Kitty O'Shea's

Map 2, C1. 10 rue des Capucines, 2e. Mº Opéra. Daily noon–1.30am.

An Irish pub with excellent Guinness and Smithwicks. A favourite haunt of Irish expats. The *John Jameson* restaurant upstairs serves high-quality, pricey, Gaelic food, including seafood flown in from Galway.

Le Sous-Bock

Map 2, G5. 49 rue St-Honoré, 1er. Mº Châtelet & Mº Les Halles. Mon–Sat 11am–5am, Sun 3pm–5am.

Hundreds of beers - bottled and on tap - at around 40F/€6.10 a pint, as well as whiskies to sample, plus simple, inexpensive food. Mussels are a speciality

(60–75F/€9.15–11.43).
Frequented by night owls.
Prices go up after 7pm.

RESTAURANTS

Chartier

Map 3, H8. 7 rue du Faubourg-
Montmartre, 9e
Ⓣ 01.47.70.86.29. Mº Grands-
Boulevards.
Daily 11.30am–3pm & 6–10pm.
Dark-stained woodwork,
brass hat-racks, mirrors,
waiters in long aprons – the
original decor of a late-
nineteenth-century soup
kitchen. Though crowded
and rushed, it's worth a visit,
and the food's not bad at all.
Under 100F/€15.24.

Dilan

Map 2, G3. 13 rue Mandar, 2e
Ⓣ 01.42.21.14.88. Mº Les
Halles & Mº Sentier.
Mon–Sat noon–2pm &
7.30–11.30pm.
An excellent-value Kurdish
restaurant, offering beautiful
starters, stuffed aubergines
(*babaqunuc*), fish with yoghurt
and courgettes (*kanarya*).
Midday menu 64F/€9.76.

Le Gros Minet

Map 2, F5. 1 rue des
Prouvaires, 1er
Ⓣ 01.42.33.02.62. Mº Châtelet
& Mº Les Halles.
Mon & Sat 7.30–11.30pm,
Tues–Fri noon–2pm &
7.30–11.30pm.
Relaxed, small and charming
restaurant, specializing in
duck dishes.

Higuma

Map 2, D3. 32bis rue Ste-Anne,
1er Ⓣ 01.47.03.38.59.
Mº Pyramides.
Daily 11.30am–10pm.
Authentic Japanese canteen
with cheap filling ramen
dishes and a variety of set
menus starting at 63F/€9.60.

L'Incroyable

Map 2, D3. 26 rue de Richelieu,
1er Ⓣ 01.42.96.24.64. Mº
Palais-Royal-Musée-du-Louvre.
Tues–Fri lunchtime & 6.30–9pm,
Mon & Sat lunchtime only.
Hidden away down a tiny
passage, this a very pleasant
restaurant serving decent
traditional French meals
dishes for 85F/€12.96 lunch;
115F/€17.53 eves.

THE GRANDS BOULEVARDS AND AROUND

199

PARIS FOR VEGETARIANS

The chances of finding vegetarian main dishes on the menus of regular French restaurants are not good. You could choose a selection of non-meat starters or order an omelette or a salad, but you'll be much better off going to an ethnic restaurant – Middle Eastern or Indian make a good choice – or a proper **vegetarian restaurant**. There are not many of the latter, and the ones that do exist tend to be based on a healthy diet principle rather than *haute cuisine*, but at least you get a choice. All the establishments listed below are reviewed in the pages that follow.

Aquarius 1, 54 rue Ste-Croix-de-la-Bretonnerie, 4e. See p.204.
Aquarius 2, 40 rue Gergovie, 14e. See p.221.
Au Grain de Folie, 24 rue de la Vieuville, 18e. See p.228.
Grand Appétit, 9 rue de la Cerisaie, 4e. See p.207.
Le Grenier de Notre-Dame, 18 rue de la Bûcherie, 5e. See p.213.
La Petite Légume, 36 rue Boulangers, 5e. See p.214.
Les Quatre et Une Saveurs, 72 rue du Cardinal-Lemoine, 5e. See p.214.
La Ville de Jagannath, 10 rue St Maur, 11e. See p.232.
La Victoire Suprème du Coeur, 41 rue des Bourdonnais, 1er. See p.201.

Au Pied de Cochon
Map 2, F4. 6 rue Coquillière, 1er
℡01.42.36.11.75. Mº Châtelet & Mº Les Halles.
Daily 24hr.
For extravagant middle-of-the-night pork chops and oysters. Seafood platter 155F/€23.63. *Carte* up to 300F/€45.73.

La Robe et le Palais
Map 2, G6. 13 rue des Lavandières Ste-Opportune, 1er

☎01.45.08.07.41. Mᵒ Châtelet.
Mon–Sat noon–2.30pm &
7.15–10.30pm.
Refined, unpretentious cuisine and an excellent wine list served up in a small, busy space. Good lunch menu for 79F/€12.04.

La Tour de Montlhéry (Chez Denise)
Map 2, F5. 5 rue des Prouvaires, 1ᵉʳ
☎01.42.36.21.82. Mᵒ Louvre-Rivoli & Mᵒ Châtelet.
Mon–Fri till midnight, Sat lunchtime only.
An old-style Les Halles bistro serving substantial food; always crowded and smoky; *carte* from 200F/€30.49.

Vaudeville
Map 2, E1. 29 rue Vivienne, 2ᵉ

☎01.40.20.04.62. Mᵒ Bourse.
Daily 7am–2am.
A lively, late-night brasserie, often with a queue to get a table. Good food, attractive marble-and-mosaic interior. *À la carte* from 150F/€22.87, menu at 138F/€21.04.

La Victoire Suprême du Coeur
Map 2, G5. 41 rue des Bourdonnais, 1ᵉʳ
☎01.40.41.93.95. Mᵒ Louvre-Rivoli & Mᵒ Châtelet.
Mon–Sat noon–10pm.
Vegetarian restaurant of the Sri Chimnoy variety – the Indian guru's photos and drawings cover the walls. The menu offers a wide range of tasty salads, quiches and *plats du jour* (49F/€7.47); all very wholesome.

QUARTIER BEAUBOURG AND THE MARAIS

BARS AND CAFÉS
- -

L'Apparement Café
Map 4, C9. 18 rue des

Coutures-St-Gervais, 3ᵉ. Mᵒ St-Sébastien-Froissart.
Mon–Fri noon–2am, Sat 4pm–2am, Sun 12.30pm–midnight.

Chic, but cosy, café resembling a series of comfortable sitting rooms, with quiet corners and deep sofas. Popular Sunday brunch until 4pm costs 90F/€13.72.

Café Beaubourg

Map 2, H5. 43 rue St-Merri, 4ᵉ. Mᵒ Rambuteau & Mᵒ Hôtel-de-Ville.
Mon–Thurs & Sun 8am–1am, Sat 8am–2am.

A seat under the expansive awnings (café designed by Christian de Portzamparc) is one of the best places for people-watching on the Pompidou Centre's piazza; expensive, rather sour service, but very stylish loos.

Dame Tartine

Map 4, A9. 2 rue Brisemiche, 4ᵉ. Mᵒ Rambuteau & Mᵒ Hôtel-de-Ville.
Daily noon–11.30pm.

Overlooking the Stravinsky pool, this place serves particularly delicious open toasted sandwiches from 30F/€4.57. Inside, the relaxed atmosphere matches the mellow, yellow walls.

L'Ébouillanté

Map 4, A11. 6 rue des Barres, 4ᵉ. Mᵒ Hôtel-de-Ville.
Tues–Sun noon–9pm, till 10pm in summer.

A tiny *salon de thé* in a picturesque, cobbled, pedestrian-only street behind the church of St-Gervais, serving chocolate cakes and pâtisseries, as well as savoury dishes. *Plats du jour* for 67F/€10.21, Tunisian crêpes for 45F/€6.86, and generous salads.

Épices et Délices

Map 4, B10. 53 rue Vieille-du-Temple, 4ᵉ. Mᵒ St-Paul.
Daily till midnight.

Restaurant and *salon de thé* with very pleasant service and food. Salads from 60F/€9.15; evening menu 70F/€13.72.

Bar de Jarente

Map 4, C11. 5 rue de Jarente, 4ᵉ. Mᵒ St-Paul.
Open Tues–Sat.

Just off the pretty place du Marché Ste-Catherine, this is a lovely old-fashioned café-bar, which remains nonchalantly indifferent to the shifting trends around it.

Le Petit Fer à Cheval

Map 4, B10. 30 rue Vieille-du-Temple, 4ᵉ. Mº St-Paul.
Mon–Fri 9am–2am, Sat & Sun 11am–2am; food noon–midnight.
A popular and very attractive small bistro/bar with trad decor, including a huge *zinc* bar, and tables outside. Agreeable wine and good-value *plats*; sandwiches from 35F/€5.34.

Le Petit Marcel

Map 2, H5. 63 rue Rambuteau, 3ᵉ. Mº Rambuteau.
Mon–Sat till 2am.
Speckled tabletops, mirrors and Art Nouveau tiles, cracked and faded ceiling and about eight square metres of drinking space. Friendly bar staff and "local" atmosphere.

Le Rouge Gorge

Map 4, C12. 8 rue St-Paul, 4ᵉ. Mº St-Paul.
Mon–Sat 11am–2am, Sun 11am–8pm.
The young, enthusiastic clientele sip familiar wines and snack on *chèvre chaud* and smoked-salmon salad, or tuck into more substantial fare

(*plats du jour* around 60F/€9.15) while listening to jazz or classical music.

Sacha Finkelsztajn

Map 4, B10. 27 rue des Rosiers, 4ᵉ. Mº St-Paul.
Wed–Sun 10am–2pm & 3–7pm; closed Aug.
Marvellous for takeaway goodies: gorgeous east European breads, cakes, *gefilte* fish, aubergine purée, tarama, *blinis* and *borscht*. There's another branch at 24 rue des Écouffes (daily except Wed 10am–1pm & 3–7pm).

La Tartine

Map 4, B11. 24 rue de Rivoli, 4ᵉ. Mº St-Paul.
Daily except Tues until 10pm; closed Aug.
The genuine 1900s article, attracting a very mixed clientele. A good selection of affordable wines, plus excellent cheese and *saucisson* with *pain de campagne*.

Web Bar

Map 4, C7. 32 rue de Picardie, 3ᵉ ⓦ www.webbar.fr
Mº Filles-du-Calvaire.
Mon–Fri 8.30am–2am, Sat &

Sun 11am–2am.

Paris's best cybercafé, on three levels in a converted industrial space, with 15 terminals on a gallery level. A real culture zone: pick up a printed programme of the art exhibitions, short film screenings and other arty events or consult their website. Comfy couches to loll on and a resident DJ make it a good place to chill, and simple healthy food comes in generous portions (37F/€5.34 for a delicious quiche with heaps of salad; lunch menu 51F/€7.77 or 61F/€9.30).

RESTAURANTS

Aquarius 1

Map 4, A10. 54 rue Ste-Croix-de-la-Bretonnerie, 4e ℡ 01.48.87.48.71. Mº St-Paul & Mº Rambuteau.
Mon–Sat noon–10pm; closed last fortnight in Aug.
Vegetarian restaurant established in 1974: not the austere and penitential place it once was, though. Alcohol is now served, but smoking is

still not allowed. It also functions as a health-food store, New Age bookshop and *salon de thé* between lunch and dinner, so you can order an omelette, soup or salad throughout the afternoon. Lunch menu at 62F/€9.45, evening 62F/€9.45 and 92F/€14.02. Hot dishes 22–64F/€3.35–9.76.

Auberge de Jarente

Map 4, C11. 7 rue Jarente, 4e ℡ 01.42.77.49.35. Mº St-Paul. Tues–Sat noon–2.30pm & 7.30–10.30pm; closed Aug.
A hospitable and friendly Basque restaurant, serving first-class food: *cassoulet*, hare stew, *magret de canard*, and *piperade* – Basque omelette. Menus at 117F/€17.84 and 132F/€20.12, and 185F/€28.20 with wine.

Chez Nénesse

Map 4, C8. 17 rue Saintonge, 3e ℡ 01.42.78.46.49. Mº Filles-du-Calvaire.
Mon–Fri noon–2pm & 7.45–10pm; closed Aug.
Steak in bilberry sauce, figs stuffed with cream of

almonds, and home-made chips on Thursday lunchtimes are some of the unique delights at this restaurant. *À la carte* around 160F/€24.40.

Chez Omar
Map 4, C7. 47 Rue de Bretagne, 3ᵉ. Mᵒ Arts-et-Métiers.
Closed Sun lunch.
Very popular North African resto in a nice old brasserie set with mirrors, attracting a young crowd. Couscous 60–98F/€9.15–14.94. Does not accept credit cards.

Les Fous d'en Face
Map 4, A10. 3 rue du Bourg-Tibourg, 4ᵉ ℡ 01.48.87.03.75. Mᵒ Hôtel-de-Ville.
Daily 11.30am–3pm & 7pm–midnight.
Delightful little restaurant and wine bar serving wonderful marinated salmon and scallops. Midday menu under 90F/€13.72, otherwise *à la carte* 140F/€21.34 upwards.

Goldenberg's
Map 4, C11. 7 rue des Rosiers, 4ᵉ ℡ 01.48.87.20.16.

Mᵒ St-Paul.
Daily until 2am.
The best known Jewish restaurant in the capital, though success has made service pretty surly. Its *borscht*, *blinis*, potato strudels, *zakouski* and other central-European dishes are a treat. Daily changing *plat du jour* 80F/€12.20, *à la carte* around 200F/€30.49.

Le Grizli
Map 2, H6. 7 rue St-Martin, 4ᵉ ℡ 01.48.87.77.56. Mᵒ Châtelet.
Mon–Sat till 11pm.
Fin-de-siècle bistro serving superb food with specialities from the Pyrenees. 115F/€17.53 midday menu; 155F/€23.63 evening.

Ma Bourgogne
Map 4, D11. 9 place des Vosges, 3ᵉ. Mᵒ St-Paul.
Daily till 12.30am, 1am in summer.
A quiet and pleasant arty café with tables under the arcades on the northwest corner of the square. It's best in the morning when the sun hits this side of the square. Meals are somewhat pricey – lunch

QUARTIER BEAUBOURG AND THE MARAIS

and dinner menu
195F/€29.73.

Le Marais-Cage
Map 4, C8. 8 rue de Beauce, 3ᵉ
℡ 01.48.87.44.51. Mº Arts-et-
Métiers & Mº Filles-du-Calvaire.
Mon–Fri noon–2.15pm &
7–10.30pm, Sat evenings only;
closed Aug.
Friendly, popular West Indian
restaurant, serving good food,
especially seafood.
130F/€19.82 menu midday,
160F/€24.40 and
199F/€30.34 evening, wine
included with all.

Pitchi-Poï
Map 4, C11. 7 rue Caron, cnr
place du Marché-Ste-Catherine,
4ᵉ ℡ 01.42.77.46.15. Mº St-
Paul.
Daily noon–3pm & 7.30–11pm.
Excellent Polish–Jewish

cuisine in a lovely location,
with sympathetic ambience
and 150F/€22.87 lunch and
dinner menu, kids' menu
73F/€11.13, and a choice of
delicious hors d'œuvres from
43F/€6.55.

Le Quincampe
Map 2, H4. 78 rue
Quincampoix, 3ᵉ
℡ 01.40.27.01.45. Mº Étienne-
Marcel, Mº Rambuteau & RER
Châtelet.
Noon–11pm; closed Mon, Sat
lunch & Sun.
Moroccan restaurant and
salon de thé, with a pleasant
atmosphere, serving high-
quality food and delicious
mint tea. You can eat around
a real fire in the room at the
back. Tagines, *pastilla* and *plat
du jour* 80F/€12.20.

BASTILLE

BARS AND CAFÉS

Bar des Ferrailleurs
Map 4, F12. 18 rue de Lappe,
11ᵉ. Mº Bastille.
Daily 5pm–2am.
Dark and stylishly sinister bar,
with rusting metal decor, an
eccentric owner and fun wig-

wearing staff. Relaxed, friendly crowd.

Café de l'Industrie

Map 4, F11. 16 rue St-Sabin, 11ᵉ. Mᵒ Bastille.
Noon–2am; closed Sat.
Rugs on the floor around solid old wooden tables, miscellaneous objects on the walls, and a young, unpretentious crowd enjoying the comfortable lack of minimalism. One of the best Bastille addresses. *Plats du jour* from 48F/€7.32.

Café des Phares

Map 4, E12. 7 place de la Bastille, west side, 4ᵉ.
Mᵒ Bastille.
Daily 7am–4am.
Every Sunday at 11am, a public philosophy debate is held in the back room here, run by the somewhat controversial Nietzsche specialist Marc Sautet. During the rest of the week, the sunny and relaxed terrace is the perfect spot for coffee.

Fouquet's

Map 4, E13–E14. 130 rue de Lyon, 12ᵉ. Mᵒ Bastille.

Mon–Fri till midnight; closed Sat & Sun midday.
Sister establishment to the Champs-Élysées *Fouquet's*. A smart, expensive café–restaurant underneath the new Opéra. With perfect French courtesy they will leave you undisturbed for hours with a 15F/€2.29 coffee. Menu, including wine, at 170F/€25.91.

Grand Appetit

Map 4, D13. 9 rue de la Cerisaie, 4ᵉ. Mᵒ Bastille.
Mon–Thurs noon–7pm, Fri & Sun noon–2pm.
Vegetarian meals served by dedicated eco-veggies at the back of an unassuming shop.

Havanita Café

Map 4, F12. 11 rue de Lappe, 11ᵉ. Mᵒ Bastille.
Daily 5pm–2am; happy hour 5–8pm.
Large, comfortable, Cuban-style bar with battered old leather sofa. Cocktails from 48F/€7.32.

Iguana

Map 4, E13. 15 rue de la Roquette, cnr rue Daval, 11ᵉ.

BASTILLE

LATE-NIGHT PARIS

It's not at all unusual for bars and brasseries in Paris to stay open after midnight; the list below is of cafés and bars that remain open after 2am, and restaurants that are open beyond midnight. Note that the three **Drugstores**, at 133 av des Champs-Élysées and 1 av Matignon in the 8ᵉ, and 149 bd St-Germain in the 6ᵉ, stay open till 2am, with bars, restaurants, shops and *tabacs*.

BARS AND CAFÉS

Café des Phares, 7 place de la Bastille, west side, 4ᵉ. Daily 7am–4am. See p.207.

Le Dépanneur, 27 rue Fontaine, 9ᵉ. All-nighter. See p.229.

au Général Lafayette, 52 rue Lafayette, 9ᵉ. Daily till 4am. See p.229.

Le Grand Café Capucines, 4 bd des Capucines, 9ᵉ. All-nighter. See p.198.

Le Mazet, 60 rue St-André-des-Arts, 6ᵉ. Mon–Thurs till 2am, Fri & Sat till 3.30am. See p.216.

La Paillote, 45 rue Monsieur-le-Prince, 6ᵉ. Mon–Sat till dawn. See p.216.

Pub Saint-Germain, 17 rue de l'Ancienne-Comédie, 6ᵉ. All-nighter. See p.216.

Le Sous-Bock, 49 rue St-Honoré, 1ᵉʳ. Daily till 5am. See p.198.

La Taverne de Nesle, 32 rue Dauphine, 6ᵉ. Mon–Thurs & Sun till 4am, Fri & Sat till 5am. See p.217.

RESTAURANTS

Bofinger, 3–7 rue de la Bastille, 4ᵉ. Daily till 1am. See p.210.

Brasserie Balzar, 49 rue des Écoles, 5ᵉ. Daily till 1am. See p.213.

Chez Gladines, 30 rue des Cinq-Diamants, 13e. Daily till 2am. See p.226.

La Coupole, 102 bd du Montparnasse, 14e. Daily till 1am. See p.222.

Le Dauphin, 167 rue St-Honoré, 1er. June–Oct daily till 12.30am. See p.196.

Flo, 7 cours des Petites-Écuries, 10e. Daily till 1.30am. See p.234.

Fouta Toro, 3 rue du Nord, 18e. Daily except Tues till 1am. See p.227.

Goldenberg's, 7 rue des Rosiers, 4e. Daily till 2am. See p.205

Julien, 16 rue du Faubourg-St-Denis, 10e. Daily till 1.30am. See p.234.

Lipp, 151 bd St-Germain, 6e. Daily till 12.30am. See p.217.

Le Muniche, 7 rue St-Benôit, 6e. Daily till 2am. See p.217.

N'Zadette, M'Foua, 152 rue due Château, 14e. Daily till 2am. See p.223.

Le Pacifique, 35 rue de Belleville, 20e. Daily till 1am. See p.235.

Le Petit Zinc, 11 rue St-Benoît, 6e. Daily till 2am. See p.218.

Au Pied de Cochon, 6 rue Coquillière, 1er. All-nighter. See p.200.

Polidor, 41 rue Monsieur-le-Prince, 6e. Mon–Sat till 12.30am. See p.218.

Le Procope, 13 rue de l'Ancienne-Comédie, 6e. Daily till 1am. See p.219.

Taï Yen, 5 rue de Belleville, 20e. Daily till 2am. See p.236.

Vaudeville, 29 rue Vivienne, 2e. Daily till 2am. See p.201.

Au Virage Lepic, 61 rue Lepic, 18e. Daily except Tues till 2am. See p.228.

LATE-NIGHT PARIS

M° Bastille.
Daily 10am–2am.
A place to be seen in. Decor of trellises, colonial fans and a brushed bronze bar. The clientele studies *recherché* art reviews, and the coffee is excellent.

Le Temps des Cerises

Map 4, D13. 31 rue de la Cerisaie, 4ᵉ. M° Bastille. Mon–Fri till 8pm; food at midday only; closed Aug.
It is hard to say what is so appealing about this café, with its dirty yellow decor, old posters and prints of *vieux Paris*, save that the *patronne* knows most of the clientele, who are young, relaxed and not the dreaded *branchés*. 68F/€10.37 menu.

RESTAURANTS

Blue Elephant

Map 4, F11. 43–45 rue de la Roquette, 11ᵉ Ⓣ01.47.00.42.00. M° Bastille & M° Richard-Lenoir.
Daily except Sat lunchtime till midnight.
Superb Thai restaurant, with a tropical-forest decor. 150F/€22.87 midday menu, otherwise over 270F/€41.16.

Boca Chica

Map 4, G12. 58 rue de Charonne, 11ᵉ. M° Ledru-Rollin.
Daily 8am–2am.
Popular tapas bar/bodega, with colourful arty decor. It's heaving by night and restful in the morning, when you can get coffee and croissant for 10F/€1.52, and a newspaper for an extra 5F/€0.76. Tapas are 28–78F/€4.27–11.89.

Bofinger

Map 4, E12. 7 rue de la Bastille, 3ᵉ Ⓣ01.42.72.87.82. M° Bastille.
Daily until 1am.
A popular *fin-de-siècle* brasserie with its original decor, serving sauerkraut and seafood. Weekday lunchtime menu at 119F/€18.14, evening 178F/€27.13, both including wine; otherwise over 200F/€30.49.

La Canaille

Map 4, D14. 4 rue Crillon, 4ᵉ Ⓣ01.42.78.09.71. M° Sully-

BASTILLE

Morland & Mº Bastille.
Daily till midnight; closed Sat &
Sun lunchtime.
Bar in front, restaurant
behind. Simple, traditional
and well-cooked food in a
friendly atmosphere. There
are 79F/€12.04 and
89F/€13.56 lunch menus –
130F/€19.82 in the evening
– and *à la carte* at
140F/€21.34.

SanZSanS
Map 4, F13. 49 rue du
Faubourg-St-Antoine, 11ᵉ.
Mº Bastille.
Daily 9am–2am.
Features a Gothic decor of
red velvet, oil paintings and
chandeliers, with a young
clientele in the evening.
Drinks reasonably priced;
main courses for around
48–65F/€7.32–9.91, and
there's always a vegetarian
dish on offer.

QUARTIER LATIN

CAFÉS AND BARS

Café de la Mosquée
Map 2, I13. 39 rue Geoffroy-St-
Hilaire, 5ᵉ. Mº Monge.
Daily 8am–midnight.
You can drink mint tea and
eat sweet cakes beside a
fountain and assorted fig trees
in the courtyard of this Paris
mosque – a delightful haven
of calm. The salon has a
beautiful Arabic interior.
Meals are served in the
adjoining restaurant.

Couscous from 55F/€6.38,
tagines from 70F/€10.67.

Cyber Café Latino
Map 2, G11. 13 rue de l'École-
Polytechnique, 5ᵉ. Mº Maubert-
Mutualité.
Mon–Sat 11am–2am, Sun
4–9pm.
Small, friendly bar with a
Venezuelan owner, Latino
sounds on the stereo and fruit
smoothies and tapas on the
menu; six computers out the
back to surf the Net.

QUARTIER LATIN

211

La Fourmi Ailée

Map 2, G9. 8 rue du Fouarre, on sq Viviani, 5ᵉ. Mº Maubert-Mutualité.

Daily noon–midnight.

Simple, light fare – including weekend brunch (2–6pm; 100F/€15.24) – in this former feminist bookshop, which has been transformed into a *salon de thé*. A high ceiling painted with a lovely mural and a book-filled wall contribute to the rarified atmosphere. Around 69F/€10.52 for a *plat*.

Le Piano Vache

Map 2, G11. 8 rue Laplace, 5ᵉ. Mº Cardinal-Lemoine.

Daily noon–2am.

Venerable student bar with canned music and a relaxed atmosphere.

Les Pipos

Map 2, G11. 2 rue de l'École-Polytechnique, 5ᵉ. Mº Maubert-Mutualité & Mº Cardinal-Lemoine.

Mon–Sat 8am–2am; closed three weeks in Aug.

Old, carved, wooden bar, serving its own wines at

14–25F/€2.13–3.81 a glass. *Plats*, which change every day, from 50F/€7.62 to 75F/€11.43.

Le Violon Dingue

Map 2, G10. 46 rue de la Montagne-Ste-Geneviève, 5ᵉ. Mº Maubert-Mutualité.

Daily 6pm–1.30am; happy hour 6–10pm.

A long, dark, student pub that's also popular with young travellers; noisy and friendly. English-speaking bar staff and cheap drinks.

RESTAURANTS

Bistro de la Sorbonne

Map 2, F11. 4 rue Toullier, 5ᵉ ☏ 01.43.54.41.49. RER Luxembourg.

Open Mon–Sat.

Traditional French and delicious North African food is served here in large portions at reasonable prices. Crowded and attractive student/local ambience. 69F/€10.52 lunch menu; 95F/€14.48 and 140F/€12.34 evening.

Brasserie Balzar

Map 2, F10. 49 rue des Écoles, 5e ℡ 01.43.54.13.67. M° Maubert-Mutualité.
Daily until 1am; closed Aug.
A traditional literary–bourgeois brasserie frequented by the intelligentsia of the quartier Latin. *À la carte* about 180F/€27.44.

au Buisson Ardent

Map 2, I11. 25 rue Jussieu, 5e ℡ .01.43.54.93.02. M° Jussieu.
Open Mon–Fri; closed two weeks in Aug.
Copious helpings of first-class traditional cooking: mussels, duck, warm goat cheese salad, lamb, etc. 70F/€10.67 menu lunch, 160F/€24.39 evenings. Reservations recommended.

Chez Léna et Mimile

Map 2, G13. 32 rue Tournefort, 5e ℡ 01.47.07.72.47. M° Censier-Daubenton.
Mon–Fri until 11pm, Sat evening only.
The high south-facing *terrasse*, overlooking a shady little square, is the main attraction, and the 185F/€28.20 menu with wine and coffee included is excellent. Serves a 98F/€14.94 menu at lunchtime on weekdays.

Chieng-Maï

Map 2, G9. 12 rue Frédéric-Sauton, 5e ℡ 01.43.25.45.45. M° Maubert-Mutualité.
Closed Sun.
Excellent Thai cuisine served in elegant surroundings. Dishes include beef sautéed with fresh basil, fish simmered in coconut milk and lemongrass, and a generous selection of vegetarian choices. Menus 69F/€10.52 at lunchtime; otherwise 122F/€18.60 and 173F/€26.37.

Foyer du Vietnam

Map 2, H13. 80 rue Monge, 5e ℡ 01.45.35.32.54. M° Monge.
Mon–Sat until 10pm.
Casual, authentic Vietnamese with dishes from 30F/€4.57 and menus for 56F/€8.54 and 67F/€10.21.

Le Grenier de Notre-Dame

Map 2, G9. 18 rue de la

QUARTIER LATIN

Bûcherie, 5ᵉ. Mᵒ Maubert-
Mutualité.
Daily noon–11.30pm.
Some veggies love this tiny
place, which has been
operating since 1978. Others
dislike it and its posh candle-
lit atmosphere, cramped
tables and cheesy music.
Substantial fare, including
couscous, fried tofu and
cauliflower cheese. Menus at
75F/€11.43 and 105F/€16.

Koutchi
Map 2, H11. 40 rue du
Cardinal-Lemoine, 5ᵉ
☎ 01.44.07.20.56. Mᵒ Cardinal-
Lemoine.
Closed Sun.
A well-regarded Afghan
restaurant, with a congenial
atmosphere, tasty food and
pretty good prices. Menu
55F/€8.38 at lunchtime,
98F/€14.93 in the evening.

Mavrommatis
Map 5, F4. 42 rue Daubenton,
5ᵉ ☎ 01.43.31.17.17.
Mᵒ Censier-Daubenton.
Closed Mon.
A sophisticated Greek
restaurant, quite expensive
(lunchtime menu

120F/€18.29), but you are
definitely tasting Greek food
at its best.

La Petite Légume
Map 2, H11. 36 rue
Boulangers, 5ᵉ. Mᵒ Jussieu.
Mon–Sat noon–2.30pm &
7.30–10pm.
This is a health-food grocery
that doubles as a vegetarian
restaurant, serving quality
ingredients in a variety of
plats for around 58F/€8.84.

Les Quatre et Une
Saveurs
Map 2, H12. 72 rue du
Cardinal-Lemoine, 5ᵉ
☎ 01.43.26.88.80. Mᵒ Cardinal-
Lemoine.
Tues–Sat till 10pm.
Inventive, high-class
macrobiotic vegetarian food.
The 120F/€18.29 and
130F/€19.82 menus include
coffee.

Tashi Delek
Map 5, D2. 4 rue des Fossés-
St-Jacques, 5ᵉ
☎ 01.43.26.55.55. RER
Luxembourg.
Mon–Sat noon & eve until
10.30pm; closed Aug.

An enjoyable Tibetan restaurant run by refugees. Prices are as low as 52F/€7.93 at lunchtime and 64F/€9.76 in the evening.

ST-GERMAIN

CAFÉS AND BARS

- - - - - - - - - - - - - - - - - - - -

Le 10
Map 2, E9. 10 rue de l'Odéon, 6ᵉ. Mº Odéon.
Daily 6.30pm–2am.
The beer here is very cheap, which is why it attracts young people, particularly foreigners. Small dark bar with old posters, a jukebox, and a lot of chatting up.

L'Assignat
Map 2, E7. 7 rue Guénégaud, 6ᵉ. Mº Pont-Neuf.
Mon–Sat 7.30am–8.30pm, food noon–3.30pm; closed July.
Zinc counter, bar stools, bar football and young regulars from the nearby art school in an untouristy café close to quai des Augustins.
27F/€4.12 for a sandwich and a glass of wine.

Chez Georges
Map 2, D9. 11 rue des Canettes, 6ᵉ. Mº Mabillon.
Tues–Sat noon–2am; closed July 14–Aug 15.
An attractive wine bar in the spit-on-the-floor mode, with its old shop front still intact, situated in a narrow street off place St-Sulpice.

Les Deux Magots
Map 2, D8. 170 bd St-Germain, 6ᵉ. Mº St-Germain-des-Prés.
Daily 6.30am–1.30am; closed one week in Jan.
Right on the corner of place St-Germain-des-Prés, this café owes its reputation to the intellos of the Left Bank, past and present. In summertime, it picks up a lot of foreigners seeking the exact location of the spirit of French culture, and buskers galore play to the packed terrace. Come early

for an expensive but satisfying 75F/€11.43 breakfast.

Le Flore

Map 2, D8. 172 bd St-Germain, 6e. M° St-Germain-des-Prés. Daily 7am–1.30am.

The great rival and immediate neighbour of *Les Deux Magots*, with a very similar clientele. Sartre, De Beauvoir, Camus and Marcel Carné used to hang out here. Best enjoyed during a late-afternoon coffee or after-dinner drink.

Le Mazet

Map 2, E8. 60 rue St-André-des-Arts, 6e. M° Odéon. Mon–Thurs 10am–2am, Fri & Sat till 3.30am; happy hour 5–8pm; closed Sun.

Historically, a well-known hang-out for buskers and heavy drinkers. For an evil concoction, try a *bière brûlée* – it's flambéed with gin. Small glass beer 20F/€3.05, cocktails 49F/€7.47.

La Paillote

Map 2, E10. 45 rue Monsieur-le-Prince, 6e. RER Luxembourg & M° Odéon.

Mon–Sat 9pm–dawn; closed Aug.

The late-night bar for jazz fans, with one of the best collections of recorded jazz in the city. Soft drinks start from 30F/€4.57.

La Palette

Map 2, D7. 43 rue de Seine, 6e. M° Odéon. Mon–Sat 8am–2am.

Once-famous Beaux-Arts student hang-out, now more frequented by art dealers and their customers. The service can be uncivil, but the murals and every detail of the decor are superb, including, of course, a large selection of colourful, used palettes.

Pub Saint-Germain

Map 2, E8. 17 rue de l'Ancienne-Comédie, 6e. M° Odéon.

Open 24hr.

Stocks 26 draught beers and hundreds of bottles. Huge, crowded and expensive. Hot food at mealtimes, otherwise cold snacks. For a taste of "real" French beer, try *ch'ti* (patois for "northerner"), a *bière de garde* from the Pas-de-

ST-GERMAIN

Calais. Live music nightly from 10pm.

La Taverne de Nesle
Map 2, E8. 32 rue Dauphine, 6e. Mo Odéon.
Daily 9pm–4am, Fri & Sat till 5am.
Vast selection of beers. Full of local night birds. Cocktails from 45F/€6.86.

RESTAURANTS
- - - - - - - - - - - - - - - - - - - -

aux Charpentiers
Map 2, D9. 10 rue Mabillon, 6e
℡ 01.43.26.30.05. Mo Mabillon.
Daily until 11pm; closed hols.
A friendly, old-fashioned place belonging to the *Compagnons des Charpentiers* (Carpenters' Guild), with appropriate decor of roof-trees and tie beams. Traditional *plats du jour* are their forte – tripe sausage, calf's head and the like – for about 75F/€11.43. Around 200F/€30.49 *à la carte*; lunch menu at 120F/€18.29.

Cosi
Map 2, E8. 54 rue de Seine, 6e
℡ 01.46.33.35.36. Mo St-Germain-des-Prés.
Daily noon–midnight.
Fantastic sandwiches (30–48F/€4.57–7.32) made on home-made focaccia bread. Mix and match your own ingredients, including roast beef, tomatoes stewed with coriander, cucumbers with chèvre, ricotta with nuts, roasted vegetables, smoked salmon, and on it goes. Wine by the glass (18F/€2.74), rich desserts (22F/€3.35). The opera-loving owner has a different opera on the CD player each day.

Lipp
Map 2, D8. 151 bd St-Germain, 6e. Mo St-Germain-des-Prés.
Daily until 12.30am; closed mid-July to mid-Aug.
A 1900s brasserie, and one of the best known establishments on the Left Bank; haunt of the very successful and very famous. *Plat du jour* 100–115F/€15.24–17.53; no reservations, so be prepared to wait.

Le Muniche
Map 2, D8. 7 rue St-Benoît, 6e

ST-GERMAIN

217

℡01.42.61.12.70.
Mº St-Germain-des-Prés.
Daily noon–2am.
A crowded old-style brasserie with an oyster bar, mirrors and theatre posters on the walls, serving classic French brasserie fare: seafood, *choucroute*, leg of lamb. Menus at 98F/€14.94 and 149F/€27.44; *carte* 180F/€27.44.

Orestias

Map 2, E8. 4 rue Grégoire-de-Tours, 6ᵉ ℡01.43.54.62.01.
Mº Odéon.
Mon–Sat lunchtime & evening till 11.30pm.
A mixture of Greek and French cuisine. Good helpings and very cheap – with a menu at 46F/€7.01 available weekdays until 8pm.

Le Petit St-Benoît

Map 2, D8. 4 rue St-Benoît, 6ᵉ
℡01.42.60.27.92. Mº St-Germain-des-Prés.
Mon–Fri noon–2.30pm & 7–10.30pm.
A simple and genuine local, popular with the neighbourhood's chattering classes. Serves solid, traditional fare

in a brown-stained, aproned atmosphere. Menu at 130F/€19.82.

Le Petit Zinc

Map 2, D8. 11 rue St-Benoît, 6ᵉ
℡01.42.61.20.60.
Mº St-Germain-des-Prés.
Daily noon–2am.
Excellent traditional dishes, especially seafood, in stunning Art-Nouveau style premises (built thirty years ago). Not cheap – menu 188F/€28, seafood platter 450F/€68.60 for two.

Polidor

Map 2, E10. 41 rue Monsieur-le-Prince, 6ᵉ ℡01.43.26.95.34.
Mº Odéon.
Mon–Sat till 12.30am, Sun till 11pm.
A traditional bistro, open since 1845, whose visitors' book, they say, boasts more of history's big names than all the glittering palaces put together. Not as cheap as it was in James Joyce's day, but good food and great atmosphere. Lunches at 55F/€8.38 during the week, and an excellent 165F/€25.15 evening menu.

Le Procope

Map 2, E8. 13 rue de
l'Ancienne-Comédie, 6ᵉ
℡ 01.40.46.79.00. Mº Odéon.
Daily noon–1am.

The first establishment to
serve coffee in Paris, opened
in 1686, *Le Procope* is still a
great place to enjoy a cup and
bask in the knowledge that
over the years, Voltaire,
Benjamin Franklin,
Rousseau, Marat and
Robespierre, among others,
have done the very same
thing. Fairly good
130F/€19.82 menu (up to
8pm) and 178F/€27.13
menu with wine included
after 11pm, though some say
it caters too much to tourists'
weary tastebuds.

Restaurant des Beaux-Arts

Map 2, D7. 11 rue Bonaparte,
6ᵉ ℡ 01.43.26.92.64. Mº St-
Germain-des-Prés.
Daily lunchtime & evening till
10.45pm.

The traditional hang-out of
Beaux-Arts students. The
choice is wide, portions are
generous and queues are long
in high season. The
atmosphere is generally good,
though the waitresses can get
pretty tetchy. Menu at
79F/€12.04, including wine.

TROCADÉRO, THE EIFFEL TOWER AND LES INVALIDES

CAFÉS AND BARS

Café du Museé d'Orsay

Map 7, N7–N8. 1 rue
Bellechasse, 7ᵉ. RER Musée-
d'Orsay & Mº Solférino.
Tues–Sun 11am–5pm.

Superb views over the Seine
in the museum's magnificent
rooftop café. Snacks and
drinks. Quick and friendly
service.

Le Poch'tron

Map 7, N8. 25 rue de

Bellechasse, 7e. Mo Solférino.
Mon–Fri 9am–10.30pm.
With a fine selection of
wines by the glass, this is an
excellent place to revive
yourself after visiting the
museums in the arrondissement. Also serves lunch and
dinner; main dishes at around
70F/€10.67.

Totem

**Map 7, B7. Southern wing of
the Palais de Chaillot, place du
Trocadéro, 16e. Mo Trocadéro.
Daily noon–2am.**
Native American-themed
restaurant, but with French
traditional dishes thrown in.
The 134F/€20.43 lunch
menu isn't bad, but the views
from the terrace are magnificent.

RESTAURANTS

au Babylone

**Map 6, G6. 13 rue de Babylone,
7e ☎ 01.45.48.72.13 Mo Sèvres-
Babylone.
Mon–Sat lunch only; closed
Aug.**

Lots of old-fashioned charm
and culinary basics like *rôti de
veau* and steak, plus wine on
the 100F/€15.24 menu.

Le Bourdonnais

**Map 6, B4. 113 av de la
Bourdonnais ☎ 01.47.05.47.06.
Mo École-Militaire.
Daily noon–2.30pm & 8–11pm.**
A gem of a restaurant and a
high-class one at that. *À la
carte* costs upwards of
400F/€60.98, but there's a
superb midday menu including wine for 240F/€36.59,
and an evening menu at
340F/€51.83.

Chez Germaine

**Map 6, F7. 30 rue Pierre-Leroux
☎ 01.42.73.28.34. Mo Duroc &
Mo Vaneau.
Mon–Fri noon–2.30pm &
7–9.30pm, Sat noon–2.30pm;
closed Sun & Aug.**
A simple, tiny and unbelievably cheap restaurant, with a
midday 50F/€7.62 menu
and evening 65F/€9.91
menu, including wine; the
carte costs up to about
90F/€13.72.

MONTPARNASSE AND THE 14ᵉ

CAFÉS AND BARS

La Closerie des Lilas

Map 2, D14. 171 bd du Montparnasse, 6ᵉ. RER Port-Royal.
Daily noon–1.30am.
The smartest, artiest, classiest Montparnasse café, with excellent cocktails for around 60F/€9.15 and a resident pianist. The tables are name-plated after celebrated former habitués (Verlaine, Mallarmé, Lenin, Modigliani, Léger, Strindberg). Very expensive restaurant; brasserie main courses for under 100F/€15.24.

L'Entrepôt

Map 6, E14. 7–9 rue Francis-de-Pressensé, 14ᵉ. Mº Pernety.
Mon–Sat noon–midnight.
Spacious arty café within an excellent arthouse cinema; 77F/€11.74 midday menu, 150F/€22.87 *à la carte* in the evening.

Le Rallye

Map 6, I14. 6 rue Daguerre, 14ᵉ. Mº Denfert-Rochereau.
Tues–Sat until 8pm; closed Aug.
A good place to recover from the Catacombs or Montparnasse cemetery. The *patron* offers a bottle of wine for tasting; gulping the lot would be considered bad form. Good cheese and *saucisson*.

La Pause Gourmande

Map 6, I12. 27 rue Campagne-Première, 14ᵉ. Mº Raspail.
Mon–Fri 8.30am–7pm, Sat 8.30am–3pm.
No imagination spared on the decor of this small café, but it does serve up delicious salads and savoury and sweet *tartes* from 28F/€4.27.

RESTAURANTS

Aquarius 2

Map 6, E14. 40 rue Gergovie, 14ᵉ ☎01.45.41.36.88.
Mº Pernety.

Mon–Sat noon–2.15pm & 7–10.30pm.
Imaginative vegetarian meals served with proper Parisian bustle. 65F/€9.91 menu midday.

Le Berbère

Map 6, E14. 50 rue de Gergovie, 14e ℡ 01.45.42.10.29. Mº Pernety. Daily lunchtime & evening till 10pm.
Very unprepossessing decor-wise, but serves wholesome, unfussy and cheap North African food. Couscous from 50F/€7.62.

La Coupole

Map 6, H10. 102 bd du Montparnasse, 14e ℡ 01.43.20.14.20. Mº Vavin. Daily 8.30–1am.
The largest and perhaps most famous and enduring arty-chic Parisian hang-out for dining, dancing and debate. After 11pm, menu at 138F/€21.04 including wine, or *carte* from 170F/€25.92. Dancing Tues 9.30pm–4am, Fri & Sat 9.30pm–5am (100F/€15.24 and Sun 3–9pm (Sun 80F/€12.20).

au Rendez-Vous des Camionneurs

Map 6, off G14. 34 rue des Plantes, 14e ℡ 01.45.40.43.36. Mº Alésia.
Mon–Fri lunchtime & 6–9.30pm; closed Aug.
No lorry drivers any more, but good food for under 100F/€15.24; menu at 72F/€10.98 and a quarter of wine for under 20F/€3.05. Wise to book.

Restaurant Bleu

Map 6, F14. 46 rue Didot, 14e ℡ 01.45.43.70.56. Mº Plaisance.
Tues–Sat lunchtime & evening until 11pm.
Excellent, high-class cooking in a small and well-tended restaurant. The three-course *menu du marché* is 130F/€19.82, or else you can choose the speciality truffade (mashed potato and sausage) amongst others from the *à la carte* menu for 175F/€26.86.

Student restaurants

at 13/17 rue Dareau, 14e (map See box opposite for information on student restaurants.

STUDENT RESTAURANTS

Students of any age are eligible to apply for tickets for the **university restaurants** under the direction of CROUS de Paris. A list of addresses, which includes numerous cafeterias and brasseries, is available from their offices at 39 av Georges-Bernanos, 5ᵉ (☎01.40.51.36.00; Mon–Fri 9am–5pm; RER Port-Royal). We also list a handful in this chapter. The tickets, however, have to be obtained from the particular restaurant of your choice (opening hours generally 11.30am–2pm & 6–8pm). Not all serve both midday and evening meals, and times change with each term. Though the food is less than wonderful, it's certainly filling, and you can't complain for the **price**. Some are less fussy than others about student credentials, and will sell tickets to anyone for 28.20F/€4.30. They will cost you 13.70F/€2.09 if you're studying at a French university, 23F/€3.51 if you can produce an International Student Card.

5, B7; Mᵒ St-Jacques) and in the Cité Universitaire, 14ᵉ (map 1, E7; RER Cité Universitaire).

N'Zadette M'Foua
Map 6, G14. 152 rue du Château, 14ᵉ ☎01.43.22.00.16. Mᵒ Pernety.

Daily 7pm–2am.
A small Congolese restaurant, with tasty dishes such as *maboké* (meat or fish baked in banana leaves). Reservations required at weekends. Menu at 85F/€12.96, *à la carte* around 120F/€18.29.

THE 15ᵉ ARRONDISSEMENT

CAFÉS AND BARS
----

au Bon Coin
Map 1, D6. 85 rue Brancion,

15ᵉ. Mᵒ Porte-de-Vanves.
Daily till 9pm.
Located next to the Parc Georges-Brassens this well-

established bar with original zinc counter attracts a well-read clientele looking for somewhere to have a drink and flick through their latest find at the secondhand book market over the road.

au Roi du Café

Map 6, C10. 59 rue Lecourbe, 15e. Mo Volontaires & Mo Sèvres-Lecourbe.
Daily till 2am.
Traditional café with a decor that hasn't changed much this century and a pleasant terrace, albeit on a busy road.

RESTAURANTS

Da Attilio

Map 1, D6. 21 rue Cronstadt, 15e ⊤01.40.43.91.90.
Mo Convention & Mo Porte-de-Vanves.
Mon–Sat till 9.30pm.
Close to the Parc Georges Brassens. Unprepossessing decor and run-of-the-mill food, but very friendly service and a great atmosphere. Different Italian specialities each day; *plats du jour* 50F/€7.62.

Le Bistrot d'André

Map 1, C6. 232 rue St-Charles, 15e ⊤01.45.57.89.14.
Mo Balard.
Mon–Sat noon–2.45pm & 7.45–10.30pm.
A reminder of the old Citroën works before the Parc André-Citroën was created, with pictures and models of the classic French car. Great puds: midday menu 65F/€9.91, otherwise around 140F/€21.34.

Le Café du Commerce

Map 1, C5. 51 rue du Commerce, 15e ⊤01.45.75.03.27. Mo Émile-Zola.
Daily noon–midnight.
A two-storey restaurant that's been catering for *le petit peuple* for over a hundred years. Still varied, nourishing and cheap fare. *Formules* 87F/€13.26 and 115F/€17.53; *carte* around 145F/€22.11.

Sampieru Corsu

Map 6, A9. 12 rue de l'Amiral-Roussin, 15e. Mo Cambronne.
Mon–Fri lunchtime & 7–9.30pm.
Decorated with the posters

and passionate declarations of international socialism, this restaurant provides meals for the homeless, unemployed and low-paid. The principle is that you pay what you can and it is left to your conscience how you settle the bill. The minimum requested is 45F/€6.86 for a three-course meal with wine. However poor you might feel, as a tourist in Paris you should be able to pay more. The restaurant only survives on the generosity of its supporters, and it's a wonderful place.

Student restaurant
Map 6, E10. 156 rue Vaugirard, 15e. Mo Pasteur.
See box on p.223 for information on student restaurants.

THE 13e ARRONDISSMENT

CAFÉS AND BARS
- - - - - - - - - - - - - - - - - - - -

La Folie en Tête
Map 5, F9. 33 rue Butte-aux-Cailles, 13e. Mo Place-d'Italie & Mo Corvisart.
Mon–Sat 5pm–2am.
A very warm and laid-back address, where you can get cheap beer, sandwiches and midday *plat du jour*.
Occasional concerts and solidarity events.

Le Merle Moqueur
Map 5, F9. 11 rue Butte-aux-Cailles, 13e. Mo Place-d'Italie & Mo Corvisart.
Daily 9pm–1am.
Old-time co-op still going strong, with live rock some nights.

RESTAURANTS
- - - - - - - - - - - - - - - - - - - -

Auberge Etchegorry
Map 5, F7. 41 rue Croulebarbe, 13e ☎01.44.08.83.51.

M° Gobelins.
Mon–Sat till 10.30pm.
A former *guinguette* on the banks of the Bièvre, this Basque restaurant has preserved an old-fashioned atmosphere of relaxed conviviality, and the food's good too. Menus from 130F/€19.82.

Chez Gladines

Map 5, F9. 30 rue des Cinq-Diamants, 13e
℡ 01.45.80.70.10. M° Corvisart.
Daily 9am–2am.
This small corner bistro is always welcoming. Excellent wines and dishes from the southwest; the mashed/fried potato is a must and goes best with *magret de canard*. Around 120F/€18.29 for a full meal.

Lao-Thai

Map 5, H9. 128 rue de Tolbiac, 13e ℡ 01.44.24.28.10.
M° Tolbiac.
Daily except Wed
11.30am–2.30pm & 7–11pm.
Big glass-fronted resto on a busy interchange. Finely spiced Thai and Lao food, with coconut, ginger and lemongrass flavours. Midday

menu at 46.50F/€7.09, otherwise, around 120F/€18.29.

Phuong Hoang

Map 5, K9. Terrasse des Olympiades, 52 rue du Javelot, 13e ℡ 01.45.84.75.07. M° Tolbiac; take the escalator up from rue de Tolbiac.
Mon–Fri noon–3pm & 7–11.30pm.
Vietnamese, Thai and Singapore specialities, with menus at 50F/€7.62, 70F/€10.67 and 80F/€12.20. If it's full, try *Le Le Lai* or *New Chinatown* nearby.

Student restaurant

Map 5, I4. 105 bd de l'Hôpital, 13e. M° St-Marcel.
See box on p.223 for information on student restaurants.

Le Temps des Cerises

Map 5, F9. 18–20 rue Butte-aux-Cailles, 13e
℡ 01.45.89.69.48. M° Place-d'Italie & M° Corvisart.
Mon–Fri noon–2pm & 7.30–11pm, Sat 7.30–11pm.
A well-established workers'

co-op with elbow-to-elbow seating and a different daily choice of imaginative dishes.

Lunch menu at 58F/€8.84 and evening menus starting at 118F/€17.99.

MONTMARTRE

CAFÉS AND BARS

La Petite Charlotte
Map 3, F3. 24 rue des Abbesses, 18e. Mº Abbesses. Tues–Sun till 8pm.
Crêpes, pâtisseries and 58F/€8.84 *formule* on sunny tables.

Le Refuge
Map 3, G1. cnr rue Lamarck & the steps of rue de la Fontaine-du-But, 18e. Mº Lamarck-Caulaincourt.
Mon–Sat till 8.30pm.
A gentle café stop, with a long view west down rue Lamarck, offering standard café fare and attracting a friendly local clientele.

Le Sancerre
Map 3, F3. 35 rue des Abbesses, 18e. Mº Abbesses.

Daily 7am–2am.
A fashionable hang-out for the young and trendy of all nationalities on the southern slopes of Montmartre.

RESTAURANTS

L'Assiette
Map 3, I1. 78 rue Labat, 18e ☎ 01.42.59.06.63. Mº Château-Rouge.
Closed Wed evening & Sun.
A bit out of the way, but very friendly, with delicious *champignons forestières, chocolate charlotte* and a surprising beetroot sorbet starter. An extraordinarily good-value 98F/€14.94 menu.

Fouta Toro
Map 3, off J1. 3 rue du Nord, 18e ☎ 01.42.55.42.73.
Mº Marcadet-Poissonniers.

Daily except Tues 7.30pm–1am.
A tiny, crowded, welcoming
Senegalese diner in a very
scruffy alley northeast of
Montmartre. No more than
70F/€10.67 all-in. Be
prepared for a wait unless you
come at 8pm or after
10.30pm.

au Grain de Folie

Map 3, H3. 24 rue La Vieuville,
18ᵉ ☎01.42.58.15.57.
Mº Abbesses.
Daily 12.30–2.30pm &
7–11.30pm.
A simple, cheap and friendly
vegetarian restaurant, with
just the sort of traditional
atmosphere that you would
hope for from Montmartre.
Gratin and fruit compote for
55F/€8.38, menu
100F/€15.24.

Marie-Louise

Map 1, F2. 52 rue
Championnet, 18ᵉ
☎01.46.06.86.55. Mº Simplon.
Tues–Sat lunchtime & evening
until 10pm; closed Aug.
A bit of a trek north, but the
excellent traditional French
cuisine at this renowned

restaurant is definitely worth
the journey. Menu at
130F/€19.82, otherwise
around 180F/€27.44.

au Port de Pidjiguiti

Map 3, D1. 28 rue Étex, 18ᵉ
☎01.42.26.71.77. Mº Guy-
Môquet.
Tues–Sun lunchtime & eve until
11pm; closed Jan.
Very pleasant atmosphere and
excellent food. It is run by a
village in Guinea-Bissau,
whose inhabitants take turns
to staff the restaurant; the
proceeds go to the village.
Good-value wine list. Menu
100F/€15.24; *à la carte*
around 120F/€18.29.

au Virage Lepic

Map 3, E2. 61 rue Lepic, 18ᵉ
☎01.42.52.46.79. Mº Blanche
& Mº Abbesses.
Daily except Tues 7pm–2am.
Simple, traditional fare in a
noisy, friendly atmosphere
created by the singers – in the
French/Parisian idiom. Small,
smoky and very enjoyable.
Around 100F/€15.24.

PIGALLE AND SOUTH OF PIGALLE

CAFÉS AND BARS

Le Dépanneur
Map 3, E4. 27 rue Fontaine, 9ᵉ
☎01.40.16.40.20. Mᵒ Pigalle.
Open 24hr.
Relaxed and fashionable all-night bar.

aux Deux-Théâtres
Map 3, E5. 18 rue Blanche, cnr
rue Pigalle, 9ᵉ
☎01.45.26.41.43. Mᵒ Trinité.
Daily 11.30am–2.30pm &
7–midnight.
A distinctly bourgeois but
welcoming and friendly
place, whose 179F/€27.29
menu includes an aperitif.
The entrées and desserts are
particularly good.

au Général Lafayette
Map 3, H6. 52 rue Lafayette,
9ᵉ. Mᵒ Le Peletier & Mᵒ Cadet.
Daily noon–4am.
Old-time brasserie where all
sorts rub shoulders trying the
large variety of beers and
wines on offer.

RESTAURANTS

Le Relais Savoyard
Map 3, H5. 13 rue Rodier, cnr rue
Agent-Bailly, 9ᵉ ☎01.45.26.17.18.
Mᵒ Notre-Dame-de-Lorette, Mᵒ
Anver & Mᵒ Cadet.
Mon–Sat until 9.30pm; closed
Aug.
At the back of a very
ordinary local bar; very good
three-course meal for
115F/€17.53.

La Table d'Anvers
Map 3, I4. 2 place d'Anvers, 9ᵉ
☎01.48.78.35.21. Mᵒ Anvers.
Mon–Fri noon–2.30pm &
7.30–11.30pm, Sat
7.30–11.30pm.
This is one of the city's best
restaurants, whose chef is
renowned for his original
combinations. The menu at
250F/€38.11 gives a good
taste of his skills; the full
experience of four *plats*,
cheese and two desserts will
cost you 650F/€99.09.

PIGALLE AND SOUTH OF PIGALLE

EASTERN PARIS

CAFÉS AND BARS

L'Atmosphère

Map 4, C3. 49 rue Lucien-Sampaix, 10 e. M° Gare-de-l'Est.
Tues–Fri 11am–2am, Sat & Sun 5.30pm–2am.
Next to the Canal St-Martin, this is a lively bar with food and occasional live music. The *Hôtel du Nord* on the opposite bank was the setting for the eponymous film of 1938, and the name of this bar comes from a quote in the film.

Le Baratin

Map 4, H3. 3 rue Jouye-Rouve, 20e. M° Pyrénées.
Tues–Fri 11am–1am, Sat 6pm–1am.
Friendly, unpretentious *bistrot à vins* in a run-down area with a good mix of people. Fine selection of lesser-known wines and whiskies. Midday menu 65F/€9.91.

Le Baron Aligre

Map 4, G14. 1 rue Théophile-Roussel, cnr place d'Aligre market, 12e. M° Ledru-Rollin.
Tues–Sat 10am–2pm & 5–9.30pm, Sun 10am–2pm.
Popular local bar. As well as the wines – around 16F/€2.44 per litre from the barrel to take away – it serves a few snacks of cheese, *foie gras* and *charcuterie*.

Bistrot Cave des Envierges

Map 4, off I4. 11 rue des Envierges, 20e. M° Pyrénées.
Wed–Fri noon–midnight, Sat & Sun noon–8pm.
Another *bistrot à vins* purveying good-quality, lesser-known wines to connoisseurs. An attractive bar – though more a place to taste and buy wine than eat – in a great location above the Parc de Belleville. From rue Belleville, follow rue Piat south, which becomes rue des Envierges.

Café Charbon

Map 4, G7. 109 rue Oberkampf, 11ᵉ. Mᵒ Parmentier. Daily 9am–2am.

A very successful and attractive resuscitation of a *fin-de-siècle* café, drawing a young and trendy clientele. Nice *plats du jour* for 50–60F/€7.62–9.15 at lunchtime; lots of salads and vegetarian dishes. DJ Thurs, Fri & Sat 10pm–2am, and live music on Sun from 8.30pm.

Café de la Musique

Map 4, off E1. 213 av Jean-Jaures, 19ᵉ. Mᵒ Porte-de-Pantin. Daily till 2am.

Part of the Cité de la Musique, this café, with a popular terrace, was designed by the Cité architect Portzamparc and exudes sophistication, discretion and comfort, but be prepared to pay over the odds for a coffee.

Cithea

Map 4, G7. 112 rue Oberkampf, 11ᵉ. Mᵒ Parmentier. Daily 5pm–2am.

Bar and venue next door to the *Café Charbon* for Afro funk, funk reggae, world beat, jazz fusion, etc on Thurs, Fri & Sat nights. Cocktails 45F/€6.86. No admission charge for the music, but busy.

La Flèche d'Or

Map 4, off I11. 102bis rue de Bagnolet, cnr rue des Pyrénées, 20ᵉ. Mᵒ Alexandre-Dumas. Daily 10am–2am.

A large, lively café attracting the biker, arty, post-punkish Parisian young. The decor is *très destroy* – ie railway sleepers and a sawn-off bus front hanging from the ceiling – and the building itself is the old Bagnolet station on the *petite ceinture* railway that encircled the city until around thirty years ago. It's a nightly venue for live world music, pop, punk, ska, fusion and *chanson*, and the reasonably priced food also has a multicultural slant.

Jacques-Mélac

Map 4, off I12. 42 rue Léon-Frot, 11ᵉ. Mᵒ Charonne. Mon–Fri 9am–10.30pm; closed weekends & Aug.

Some way off the beaten track (between Père-Lachaise and place Léon-Blum) but a highly respected and very popular *bistrot à vins*, whose *patron* even makes his own wine – the solitary vine winds round the front of the shop. The food (*plats* around 70F/€10.67, menu 130F/€19.82), wines and atmosphere are great; no bookings.

Le Penty Bar
Map 4, G14. cnr place d'Aligre & rue Emilio-Castelar, 12ᵉ. Mᵒ Ledru-Rollin.
Small, old-fashioned café making no concessions to modern standards of sanitation, and still charging only 7F/€1.07 for a sit-down cup of coffee.

Le Réveil du Dixième
Map 4, B4. 35 rue du Château-d'Eau, 10ᵉ ☎01.42.41.77.59. Mᵒ Château-d'Eau.
Mon–Sat 7.15am–9pm.
A welcoming, unpretentious wine bar serving glasses of wine and regional *plats* or a menu at 150F/€22.87 including wine.

La Ville de Jagannath
Map 4, I10. 10 rue St Maur, 11ᵉ. Mᵒ St-Maur.
Closed Mon lunch and Sun. Authentic vegetarian Indian food served in thalis. Lunch menu 50F/€7.62. For a small corkage fee you can bring your own wine.

RESTAURANTS

Les Amognes
Map 4, I14. 243 rue du Faubourg-St-Antoine, 11ᵉ ☎01.43.72.73.05. Mᵒ Faidherbe-Chaligny.
Mon–Sat noon–2.30pm & 7.30–10.30pm; closed Mon lunch, Sun & two weeks in Aug. Excellent, interesting food in a very popular place. Booking essential. Menu at 190F/€28.96, otherwise well over 250F/€38.11.

Astier
Map 4, F6. 44 rue Jean-Pierre-Timbaud, 11ᵉ ☎01.43.57.16.35. Mᵒ Parmentier.
Mon–Fri until 10pm; closed Aug, two weeks in May & two weeks at Christmas.

Very successful, popular restaurant, with simple decor, unstuffy atmosphere and fresh, refined food. Booking essential. Menu at 140F/€21.34.

Bistrot du Peintre
Map 4, G12. 116 av Ledru-Rollin, 11ᵉ ⊤01.47.00.34.39. Mº Ledru-Rollin. Mon–Sat 7am–2am, Sun 10am–8pm. Small tables jammed together beneath Art-Nouveau frescoes and wood panelling. Traditional Parisian bistro food, with *plats du jour* from 62F/€9.45.

de Bourgogne
Map 4, C3. 26 rue des Vinaigriers, 10ᵉ ⊤01.46.07.07.91 Mº Jacques-Bonsergent. Mon–Fri lunchtime & evening till 10pm, Sat lunchtime only; closed Aug. Homely, old-fashioned restaurant; dinner around 80F/€12.19.

Chez Prune
Map 4, D4. 36 rue Beaurepaire, 10ᵉ ⊤01.42.41.30.47. Mº Jacques-Bonsergent. Mon–Sat 7.30am–1.45am, Sun 10am–1.45am. Lovely location for casual canal-side dining. Creative *assiettes* (starting at 40F/€6.10) guaranteed to tempt both meat-eaters and vegetarians, and a romantic place to sip a glass of wine or indulge in a dessert. *Plats* in the 55F/€8.38 to 80F/€12.20 range.

Les Cinq Points Cardinaux
Map 4, I12. 14 rue Jean-Macé, 11ᵉ ⊤01.43.71.47.22. Mº Faidherbe-Chaligny & Mº Charonne. Mon–Fri noon–2pm & 7–10pm; closed Aug. An excellent, simple, old-time bistro, still mainly frequented by locals. Prices under 60F/€9.15 for lunch, and under 100F/€15.24 in the evening.

L'Ébauchoir
Map 4, H14. 43–45 rue de Cîteaux, 12ᵉ ⊤01.43.42.49.31. Mº Faidherbe-Chaligny. Mon–Sat until 11pm. Good bistro fare in a

sympathetic atmosphere. Best to book for the evening. Midday menu for 66F/€10.06; *carte* 150F/€22.87 upwards.

Flo

Map 4, A3. 7 cours des Petites-Écuries, 10ᵉ ⓣ 01.47.70.13.59. Mᵒ Château-d'Eau.
Daily until 1.30am.
Handsome old-time brasserie where you eat elbow-to-elbow at long tables, served by waiters in ankle-length aprons. Excellent food and atmosphere; good-value menus, including wine, at 138F/€21.04 and 179F/€27.29.

La Fontaine aux Roses

Map 4, off I8. 27 av Gambetta, 20ᵉ ⓣ 01.46.36.74.75. Mᵒ Père-Lachaise.
Tues–Sat till 10pm; closed Sun evening, Mon & Aug.
Small, beautiful restaurant with first-rate menus: midday 120F/€18.29 and evenings 170F/€25.91, both including *kir royale*, wine and coffee.

L'Homme Bleu

Map 4, F6. 57 rue Jean-Pierre-Timbaud, 11ᵉ. Mᵒ Parmentier.
Mon–Sat evenings only till 10pm.
Very affordable and pleasant Berber restaurant, popular with students.

Julien

Map 4, A4. 16 rue du Faubourg-St-Denis, 10ᵉ ⓣ 01.47.70.12.06. Mᵒ Strasbourg-St-Denis.
Daily till 1.30am.
Part of the same enterprise as *Flo*, with an even more splendid decor. Same good traditional French cuisine at the same prices, and it's just as crowded.

Lao Siam

Map 4, H3. 49 rue de Belleville, 19ᵉ ⓣ 01.40.40.09.68. Mᵒ Belleville.
Daily till 11pm.
Extremely good Thai and Lao food make this folksy restaurant popular with locals. Dishes 42–60F/€6.40–9.15.

La Mansouria

Map 4, I13. 11 rue Faidherbe, 11ᵉ ⓣ 01.43.71.00.16. Mᵒ Faidherbe-Chaligny.
Tues–Sat lunchtime & evening

EASTERN PARIS

till 11.30pm; closed two weeks in Aug.

An excellent, elegant Moroccan restaurant, serving superb couscous and *tagines*. Menu at 170F/€25.61.

Le Pacifique

Map 4, H3. 35 rue de Belleville, 20ᵉ ☎01.42.49.66.80.
Mᵒ Belleville.
Daily 11am–1am.

A huge Chinese eating house with variable culinary standards but low prices. Main courses from 50F/€7.62, 85F/€12.96 or 100F/€15.24 menu.

Pho-Dong-Huong

Map 4, G4. 14 rue Louis-Bonnet, 11ᵉ ☎01.43.57.18.88.
Mᵒ Belleville.
Daily except Tues noon–10.30pm.

Spotlessly clean Vietnamese resto, where all dishes are under 50F/€7.62 and come with piles of fresh green leaves. Spicy soups, crispy pancakes, but slow service.

Pooja

Map 4, A4. 91 passage Brady, 10ᵉ ☎01.48.24.00.83.
Mᵒ Strasbourg-St-Denis & Mᵒ Château-d'Eau.
Daily noon–2.30pm & 5–11pm; closed Mon lunchtime.

Located in a passage that is Paris's own slice of the Indian subcontinent; authentic, good-value Indian cuisine. *Formules* at 45F/€6.86 lunch and 89F/€13.57 evening.

aux Rendez-Vous des Amis

Map 4, off I8. 10 av Père-Lachaise, 20ᵉ
☎01.47.97.72.16.
Mᵒ Gambetta.
Mon–Sat noon–2.30pm; closed last week July to mid-Aug.

Unprepossessing surroundings for very good, simple and satisfying family cooking. Main courses 45–78F/€6.86–11.89; menu at 65F/€9.91.

Le Rendez-vous des Quais

Map 4, off E1. 10 quai de la Seine, 19ᵉ. Mᵒ Jaurès & Mᵒ Stalingrad.
Daily 11.30am–12.30am.

Attached to the MK2 art-house cinema, the outside tables of this café/brasserie sit right on the banks of the Bassin de la Villette providing a relaxing spot for a refreshment before or after the canal cruises which depart opposite.

Rittal et Courts
Map 4, off I4. 1 rue des Envierges, 20ᵉ
℡ 01.47.97.08.40. Mº Pyrénées. Tues–Sat noon–2am, Sun noon–7pm.
Mellow bar/café/trattoria which specializes in showing "Courts Métrages" – short films (Tues–Sun 3.30–7pm, Sat midnight–2am). It's in an unbeatable situation overlooking the Parc de Belleville: get a pavement table on a summer evening and you'll have the best restaurant view in Paris. The Italian food is tasty and affordable, with a large pasta selection, including numerous vegetarian options; 50–90F/€7.62–13.72.

aux Saveurs du Liban
Map 4, off D1. 11 rue Eugène-Jumin, 19ᵉ. Mº Porte-de-Pantin. Mon–Sat 11am–11pm.
Excellent authentic Lebanese food at this tiny restaurant in a lively local street not far from the Parc de la Villette. Very good value with *plats* for 30F/€4.57 and wine for 9F/€1.37 a glass; sandwiches from 18F/€2.74 to take away; 40F/€6.10 lunchtime formula.

Taï Yen
Map 4, G3. 5 rue de Belleville, 20ᵉ ℡ 01.42.41.44.16.
Mº Belleville.
Daily 10am–2am.
Admire the koi carps idling round their aquarium like embroidered satin cushions while you wait for the generous soups and steamed specialities of this Chinese restaurant. 65F/€9.91 menu, dishes from 49F/€7.47.

Au Trou Normand
Map 4, D7. 9 rue Jean-Pierre-Timbaud, 11ᵉ
℡ 01.48.05.80.23. Mº Filles-du-Calvaire, Mº Oberkampf & Mº République.
Mon–Fri lunchtime & evenings till 9.30pm, Sat evenings only; closed Aug.
A small, totally unpretentious and very attractive local

bistro, serving good traditional food at knock-down prices. *Plat du jour* from 30F/€4.57.

Le Zéphyr

Map 4, off I3. 1 rue Jourdain, 20ᵉ ⊤01.46.36.65.81. Mᵒ Jourdain.

Mon–Sat till 11.30pm.

A rather trendy but relaxed 1930s-style bistro with menus at 69F/€10.52 and 130F/€19.82.

RESTAURANTS OF PARIS

As you would expect, there are some really spectacular restaurants in Paris. One of the best is *Alain Ducasse* at 59 av Raymond Poincaré, 16ᵉ (⊤01.47.27.12.27) which has been awarded three Michelin stars. It's run by the enterprising Alain Ducasse, who has also been awarded three stars for another of his restaurants, *Le Louis XV*, in Monte Carlo, making him the only chef to have been awarded six Michelin stars. At midday during the week, the menu at his Paris restaurant is around 300–395F/€45.73–60.21; *prixe fixe* menus range from 480F/€73.17 to 1500F/€228.66; and there's no limit to the amount you can pay for beautiful wines. Ducasse has also recently opened a smaller, less fussy establishment, *Spoon, Food & Wine*, at 14 rue de Marignan, 8ᵉ (⊤01.40.76.34.44), with cheaper, though no less superb cuisine.

The other greats include: *Lucas Carton*, 9 place de la Madeleine, 8ᵉ (⊤01.42.65.22.90), with splendid Art-Nouveau decor, run by chef Alain Senderens; *Taillevent*, 15 rue Lamennais, 8ᵉ (⊤01.45.61.12.90); *Les Ambassadeurs*, in the *Hôtel Crillon*, 10 place de la Concorde, 8ᵉ (⊤01.44.71.16.16); *Ledoyen*, 1 av Dutuit, 8ᵉ (⊤01.47.42.35.98), headed by a Flemish woman chef, Ghislaine Arabian; and *Guy Savoy*, 18 rue Troyon, 17ᵉ (⊤01.43.80.40.61).

GOURMET RESTAURANTS OF PARIS

Music and nightlife

The strength of the Paris **music** scene is its diversity, largely a result of its absorption of immigrant and exile populations. The city has no rivals in Europe for the variety of **world music** to be found: African, Caribbean and Latin American sounds are represented in force both by city-based groups and touring bands.

Jazz fans, too, are in for a treat. Paris has long been home to new jazz styles and old-time musicians. Standards are high and the line-ups varied, and the ancient cellars housing many of the clubs make for great acoustics and atmosphere.

One of France's own popular musical traditions, the **chanson**, closely associated with Édith Piaf and taken to its greatest heights by Georges Brassens and the Belgian Jacques Brel, has been experiencing something of a revival recently. *Chanson* evenings in restaurants and brasseries can be great fun and a very "French" experience. Also alive and well is ballroom dancing, held at the old music halls or sur-burban eating-and-drinking venues known as **guinguettes**.

Although a lot of commercial French **popular music** is best avoided, the French rock, pop and techno scene is taken much more seriously than it used to be. Much French electronic music has gained international success, while on a national level, some exciting new sounds are emerging in the rock and pop scene, drawing on multicultural influences.

Classical music, as you might expect in this Neoclassical city, is alive and well and takes up twice the space of "jazz-pop-folk-rock" in the listings magazines. The Paris Opéra, with its two homes – the Palais Garnier and Opéra Bastille – puts on a fine selection of ballet as well as opera. The choice of concerts is enormous, ranging from free recitals in the city's atmospheric churches to concerts by international names and orchestras, staged in prestigious venues such as the Salle Pleyel and Théâtre des Champs-Élysées. The capital's two main orchestras are the Orchestre de Paris and the Orchestre National. If you're interested in the **contemporary** scene of Systems composition and the like, check out the state-sponsored experiments of Laurent Bayle at the Pompidou Centre, and L'Ensemble InterContemporain at La Villette's Cité de la Musique.

TICKETS AND INFORMATION

The best place to get **tickets** for most musical events is FNAC Forum des Halles (see p.283). Other FNAC *musique* branches and the Virgin Megastores (see p.291) are also a good bet.

To find out **what's on**, consult the listings magazines *Pariscope* and *L'Officiel des Spectacles*, available at *tabacs* and métro stations. Keep an eye out also for *Lylo*, published every three weeks, the most comprehensive listings magazine for rock, world, jazz and *chansons*, which can be picked up free from many bars and other venues. The best way to find out about the latest club nights is to pick up flyers at the various specialized record shops detailed in the "Shopping" chapter (see p.290).

TICKETS AND INFORMATION

WORLD MUSIC, ROCK AND TECHNO

The last few years have seen considerable diversification in the Paris clubs and rock venues. They now concentrate more on international sounds, leaving the big Western rock bands to play the major arenas. Almost every club features **Latin and African** dance music, and at least one night per week is usually devoted to **techno**. Big names in world music are almost always in town, especially **zouk** musicians from the French Caribbean, and musicians from **West Africa**. Algerian **raï** is flourishing, with singers like Khaled and Cheb Mami enjoying megastar status.

As the divisions between world sounds blur, more and more bands have produced their own rewarding hybrids: **Les Négresses Vertes** are still going strong and were perhaps the first group to experiment with different sounds and to gain international recognition. The Paris-based **Orchestre National de Barbès** has a distinctly African flavour and is made up of ten members, each bringing something of their own musical heritage with them. **Manu Chau**, former member of Mano Negra, combines Latin American, reggae and rock influences to create his own inimitable style, while the group **Zebda** parades a strong Maghrebi influence.

The "marginale" culture of the *banlieue*, the dispossessed immigrant suburbs, has found musical expression in **rap** and **hip-hop**, appreciation of which has become more mainstream. Names to look out for are NTM, IAM and MC Solaar, who moves beyond traditional rap to something a good deal more melodic and musical, with superb words that you need to be pretty fluent, however, to appreciate.

France's only rock'n'roll megastar still rocks on, now in his mid-fifties and packing out stadiums, but fortunately, Johnny Halliday is not the only face of contemporary French **rock**. More representative are the soloists Miossec

THE BIG PERFORMANCE HALLS

Events at any of the performance spaces listed below will be well advertised on billboards and posters throughout the city. Tickets can be obtained at the halls themselves or through agents like FNAC or Virgin Megastore (see pp.283 & 291).

Le Bataclan, 50 bd Voltaire, 11e; ℡01.47.00.39.12 (map 4, E7; Mo Oberkampf). One of the best places for visiting and native rock bands.

Olympia, 28 bd des Capucines, 9e; ℡ 01.47.42.25.49 (map 3, D8; Mo Madeleine & Mo Opéra). An old, recently refurbished, music hall hosting occasional well-known rock groups and large popular concert performers.

Palais Omnisports de Bercy, 8 bd de Bercy, 12e; ℡01.43.46.12.21 (map 5, N4–N5; Mo Bercy). Opera, cycle racing, Bruce Springsteen, ice hockey, and Citroën launches – a multipurpose stadium with seats to make even the most level-headed dizzy, but an excellent space when used in the round.

Stade de France, St-Denis ℡01.55.93.00.00, Ⓦ*www.stadefrance.fr* (map 9, E2; RER D Stade-de-France-St-Denis & RER B La-Plaine-Stade-de-France). Purpose-built for France's hosting of the 1998 Football World Cup. Major football and rugby events, as well as Johnny Halliday, Tina Turner and the like. Seats 100,000.

Zénith, Parc de la Villette, 211 av Jean-Jaurès, 20e; ℡01.42.08.60.00 or 01.42.40.60.00 (map 1, G1; Mo Porte-de-Pantin). Seating for 6500 people in an inflatable stadium, designed exclusively for rock and pop concerts.

THE BIG PERFORMANCE HALLS

●

and Jean-Louis Murat, and the groups Rita Mitsouko and Louise Attaque, whose chart-topping style combines rock and gallic elements.

Increasingly, however, the rage is for professionally produced **techno**, now firmly established in the annals of Parisian music, with a yearly Techno Parade and freqeunt DJ nights in bars and clubs. The techno group Daftpunk scored success abroad, as well as in France, on the release of their first album in 1997, while groups such as Air and St-Germain are known for their mellow sound, mixing electronic sounds with jazz and pop.

CONCERT VENUES

Most of the venues listed below are primarily **concert venues**, though some double up as clubs. A few of them will have live music all week, but the majority host bands on just a couple of nights. Admission prices vary, depending on who's playing, but usually range from 30F/€4.57 to 120F/€18.29.

Batofar

Map 5, N6. Quai de la Gare, 13e ℡ 01.56.29.10.00. Mº Quai-de-la-Gare & Mº Bibliothèque-Tolbiac.

Daily 7pm–1am.

One of a bunch of barges moored at the foot of the Bibliothèque Nationale Tolbiac. Live world concerts, as well as a brilliant line-up of DJs from all over the world spinning mostly techno.

Café de la Danse

Map 4, F12. 5 passage Louis-Philippe, 11e ℡ 01.47.00.57.59. Mº Bastille.

Good, friendly venue playing rock, pop, world and folk music in an intimate and attractive space. Note that there's no bar, though. Open nights of concerts only; check local press, or ring for details and prices.

La Cigale

Map 3, G4. 120 bd de Rochechouart, 18ᵉ ⓣ01.49.25.89.99. Mᵒ Pigalle. An eclectic programming policy, embracing punk and indie, in an old-fashioned converted theatre, long a fixture on the Pigalle scene.

Le Divan du Monde

Map 3, G4. 75 rue des Martyrs, 18ᵉ ⓣ01.44.92.77.66. Mᵒ Pigalle. Daily 7pm–5am. A youthful venue in a one-time café whose regulars included Toulouse-Lautrec. An eclectic and exciting programming policy that includes a round-the-world theme – the country chosen is represented by food, music and events.

Élysée Montmartre

Map 3, H4. 72 bd de Rochechouart, 18ᵉ ⓣ 01.44.92.45.45, ⓦ www.elyseemontmartre.com Mᵒ Anvers. An historic Montmartre nightspot, now dedicated to rock. Inexpensive and fun, it pulls in a young and excitable crowd.

Le Grand Rex

Map 3, I8. 1 bd Poissonnière, 2ᵉ ⓣ01.45.08.93.89. Mᵒ Grands-Boulevards. Mythical rococo-style cinema that doubles up as a concert venue with 2750 places. Varied programming with well-known names.

La Guinguette Pirate

Map 5, N6. Quai de la Gare, 13ᵉ ⓣ 01.44.24.89.89. Mᵒ Quai-de-la-Gare & Mᵒ Bibliothèque-Tolbiac. Tues–Sat 7pm–2am. Beautiful Chinese barge, moored alongside the quay in front of the Bibliothèque Nationale, hosting funk, reggae, rock and folk concerts.

Maroquinerie

Map 1, H3. 23 rue Boyer, 20ᵉ ⓣ01.40.33.30.60. Mᵒ Gambetta. The concert venue is downstairs in part of an arts centre. Smallish room with some seating. The line-up is

WORLD MUSIC, ROCK AND TECHNO

rock, pop and folk with a particularly good selection of French musicians.

Trabendo
Map 1, H1. Parc de la Villette, 19ᵉ ⓣ01.49.25.81.75.
Mº Porte-de-Pantin.

A wide range of programming – world, jazz and rock, with big French names such as Les Négresses Vertes. Open nights of concerts only; check local press, or ring for details.

CLUBS

The venues listed below are essentially places where you can go to **dance** – from afternoon tea-dances, through to storming techno **clubs** that stay open till dawn. A few have the odd live group which people go to watch, but groups are generally there to get the crowd dancing. In most cases, the admission price includes your first drink.

Arapaho
Map 5, H8. 30 av de l'Italie, 13ᵉ ⓣ01.45.89.65.05. Mº Place-de-l'Italie.
Fri & Sat 11pm–3am.
80F/€12.20, free on Fri for women.
Friday is the famous Asia Folly theme night, with extravagant decoration and costumes. Changing themes on Saturdays and occasional live bands during the week.

Les Bains
Map 2, H4. 7 rue du Bourg-l'Abbé, 3ᵉ ⓣ01.48.87.01.80. Mº Étienne-Marcel.
Midnight to dawn every day.
100F/€15.24 weekdays, 120F/€18.29 at the weekend.
This is as posey as they come – an old Turkish bathhouse where the Stones filmed part of their *Under Cover of the Night* video, now redone in the anti-perspirant, passionless style pioneered for the *Café Costes*. The music is house, rap

and funk, with occasional live (usually dross) bands. It's not a place where a 500F/€76.22 note has much life expectancy. The decor features a plunging pool by the dance floor in which the punters are wont to ruin their non-colour-fast designer creations. Whether you can partake in this spectacle depends on the bouncers, who have fixed ideas. Drinks are expensive.

L'Escale

Map 2, E9. 15 rue Monsieur-le-Prince, 6e ℡ 01.40.51.80.49. Mo Odéon.
Tues–Sat 10.30pm–5am.
80F/€12.20.
More Latin American musicians must have passed through here than any other club. The dancing sounds, salsa mostly, are in the basement, while on the ground floor, every variety of South American music is given an outlet.

Le Gibus

Map 4, D5. 18 rue du Faubourg-du-Temple, 11e ℡ 01.47.00.78.88.

Mo République.
Tues–Sat 11pm–5am; Sat only in Aug. 50–100F/€7.62–15.24, free on Wed.
For twenty years, English rock bands on their way up played their first Paris gig at *Le Gibus* – the Clash and Police among them. These days the sounds have turned to house, garage and Latin with occasional live bands, but it's still hot, loud and hopping.

La Java

Map 4, F4. 105 rue du Faubourg-du-Temple, 10e ℡ 01.42.02.20.52. Mo Goncourt & Mo Belleville.
Thurs–Sat 11pm till dawn.
100F/€15.24.
The oldest disco in town has welcomed Édith Piaf in its time. These days it's renowned for its Cuban jam sessions featuring live bands and DJs. Free salsa lesson on a Thurs (10pm). Reasonably priced drinks.

La Locomotive

Map 3, E3. 90 bd de Clichy, 18e ℡ 08.36.69.69.28. Mo Blanche.

WORLD MUSIC, ROCK AND TECHNO

Daily 11pm till dawn. 60F/€9.15 weekdays, 100F/€15.24 weekends.

Enormous high-tech nightclub boasting three dance floors: one for house; one for rock, heavy metal and concerts; and one for rap and funk. Also one of the most crowded, popular and democratic clubs in the city, and you're sure of a good time.

Le Queen

Map 7, F3. 102 av des Champs-Élysées, 8e ⓣ 01.53.89.08.90, ⓦ *www.queen.fr* Mº George-V. Daily 11pm till dawn. 30F/€4.57 Sun–Tues, 50F/€7.62 Wed & Thurs, 100F/€15.24 Fri & Sat. Legendary gay club whose success draws a heterosexual clientele as well. These days, everyone is welcome, except on Thurs, when the club is strictly gay. "Disco Inferno" on Mon, otherwise mainly house music and top-name DJs.

Rex Club

Map 3, I8. 5 bd Poissonnière, 2e ⓣ 01.42.36.10.96.

Mº Grands-Boulevards. Thurs–Sat and occasionally Wed 11.30pm–6am; closed Aug. 50–80F/€7.62–12.20. A happening club in the same building (but different entrance) as the mythical cinema-cum-concert venue, with strictly electronic music – house, drum'n'bass, etc.

Zed Club

Map 2, G9. 2 rue des Anglais, 5e ⓣ 01.43.54.93.78. Mº Maubert-Mutualité. Wed–Sat 11pm–5.30am. 50F/€7.62 Wed & Thurs, 100F/€15.24 Fri & Sat. *The* rock'n'roll club.

BALS MUSETTES AND GUINGUETTES

Balajo

Map 4, F12. 9 rue de Lappe, 11e ⓣ 01.47.00.07.87. Mº Bastille. Mon–Sun 10.30pm–5am. 100F/€15.24. The last and greatest survivor of the old-style dance halls of working-class and slightly louche Paris. The *Balajo*

WORLD MUSIC, ROCK AND TECHNO

dates from the 1930s and has kept its extravagant contemporary decor, with a balcony for the orchestra above the vast dance floor. The clientele is very mixed now, and attracts all ages, though recently the bouncers have started to show a preference for a younger generation. The music encompasses everything from mazurka to tango, cha-cha, twist, and the slurpy inter-war *chansons*.

Chez Gégène

Map 9, G5. 162bis quai de Polangis, Joinville-le-Pont ℡01.48.83.29.43. RER Joinville-le-Pont.
Mid-March to mid-Oct only, Fri & Sat 9.30pm–2am, Sun 3–7pm.
Just the other side of the Bois de Vincennes, this is a genuine *guinguette* established in the 1900s. You don't have to dine to dance. Non-diners pay around 70F/€10.67.

JAZZ, BLUES AND CHANSONS

Jazz has long enjoyed an appreciative audience in France, especially since the end of World War II, when the intellectual rigour and agonized musings of bebop struck an immediate chord of sympathy in the existentialist hearts of the *après-guerre*. Charlie Parker, Dizzy Gillespie and Miles Davis were household names in France in the 1950s, while in Britain they were hardly known at all.

Home-grown talents, gypsy guitarist Django Reinhardt and his partner, violinist Stéphane Grappelli, helped to popularize the genre. It was also greatly enhanced by the presence of many front-rank black American musicians, for whom Paris was a haven of freedom and culture after the racial prejudice and philistinism of the States. Among them was the soprano sax player Sidney Bechet, who set up in

A NOTE ON PRICES

For virtually all of the **jazz clubs** listed, expense is a real drawback to enjoyment. Admission charges are generally high and, when they're not levied, there's usually a whacking charge for your first drink. Subsequent drinks, too, are absurdly priced – about twice what you'd pay in a similar club in London, and more than double what you'd pay in New York.

legendary partnership with French clarinettist Claude Luter. Another prominent figure was Bud Powell, whose turbulent exile partly inspired the tenor man played by Dexter Gordon (himself a veteran of the *Montana* club) in the film *Round Midnight*.

Jazz is still alive and well in the city, with a good selection of clubs playing all styles, from New Orleans to current experimental. Frequent festivals are also a good source of concerts, particularly in the summer (see "Festivals", p.267). Bistros and bars are a good place to catch musicians carrying on the tradition of Django Reinhardt – Romane and the Ferre brothers are just a couple of musicians doing the rounds.

Performances of French traditional **chansons** have made a comeback recently. These aren't usually advertised in the press, but you'll see hand-made posters in the bistros, or if you have access to the internet, you could check out the site Ⓦ *www.zingueures.com*

MAINLY JAZZ

Le Baiser Salé
Map 2, H6. 58 rue des Lombards, 1er

Ⓣ 01.42.33.37.71. Mº Châtelet. Mon–Sat 8pm–5am. 30–90F/€4.57–13.72. A bar downstairs and a small, crowded upstairs room with live music every night from

11pm – usually jazz, rhythm and blues, Latino-rock, reggae or Brazilian.

Caveau de la Huchette

Map 2, G8. 5 rue de la Huchette, 5e ⓣ 01.43.26.65.05. Mº St-Michel.
Daily 9.30pm–2am or later.
Sun–Thurs 60F/€9.15 (students 55F/€8.38) Fri & Sat 75F/€11.43; Fri–Sun 5–9pm free.

A wonderful slice of old Parisian life in an otherwise horribly touristy area. Live jazz, usually trad, to dance to on a floor surrounded by tiers of benches, and a bar decorated with caricatures of the barman drawn on any material to hand. Drinks cost from 26F/€3.96.

Au Duc des Lombards

Map 2, H6. 42 rue des Lombards, 1er ⓣ 01.42.33.22.88, ⓦ www.jazzvalley-com/duc Mº Châtelet-Les Halles.
Daily until 3am. 100F/€15.24. Small, unpretentious bar with performances every night from 10pm – jazz piano, blues, ballads, fusion.

Sometimes big names. Drinks from 28F/€4.27.

Instants Chavirés

Map 1, I4. 7 rue Richard-Lenoir, Montreuil ⓣ 01.42.87.25.91. Mº Robespierre.
Tues–Sat 8pm–1am; concerts at 8.30pm.
40–80F/€6.10–12.20.

Avant-garde jazz joint – no comforts – on the eastern edge of the city, close to the Porte de Montreuil. A place where musicians go to hear each other play, its reputation has attracted subsidies from both state and local authorities.

Maxwell Café

Map 1, B1. 17 bd Vital-Bouhot, Île de la Jatte, Neuilly ⓣ 01.46.24.22.00. Mº Pont-de-Levallois, then down the steps from the bridge.
Thurs–Sat, music at 10.45pm & midnight.
80–100F/€12.20–15.24.
Not the most central of places to get to, but worth the hike if you're a blues fan. Mainly blues, R&B, gospel – American musicians.

JAZZ, BLUES AND CHANSONS

New Morning

Map 3, K7. 7–9 rue des Petites-Écuries, 10ᵉ
ⓉolⓉ01.45.23.51.41. Mº Château-d'Eau.
Daily 9pm–1.30am (concerts start around 9.30pm).
110F/€16.77.
This is the place where the big international names in jazz come to play. Blues and Latin, too.

Le Petit Journal

Map 2, E11. 71 bd St-Michel, 5ᵉ Ⓣ01.43.26.28.59. RER Luxembourg.
Mon–Sat 10pm–2am; closed Aug. First drink 100–150F/€15.24–22.87, 50F/€7.62 thereafter.
Small, smoky bar, long frequented by Left Bank student-types, with good, mainly French, traditional and mainstream sounds. These days rather middle-aged and tourist-prone.

Le Petit Journal Montparnasse

Map 6, F12. 13 rue du Commandant-Mouchotte, 14ᵉ
Ⓣ01.43.21.56.70. Mº Montparnasse-Bienvenue.

Mon–Sat 9pm–2am. First drink 100F/€15.24, 50F/€7.62 thereafter.
Under the *Hôtel Montparnasse*, and sister establishment to the above, with bigger visiting names, both French and international.

Le Petit Opportun

Map 2, G6. 15 rue des Lavandières-Ste-Opportune, 1ᵉʳ
Ⓣ01.42.36.01.36. Mº Châtelet-Les Halles.
Tues–Sat 9pm–2.30am. Music from 11pm.
50–80F/€7.62–12.20.
It's worth arriving early to get a seat for the live music in the dungeon-like cellar, where the acoustics play strange tricks and you can't always see the musicians. Fairly eclectic policy and a crowd of genuine connoisseurs.

Les 7 Lézards

Map 4, C11. 10 rue des Rosiers, 4ᵉ Ⓣ01.48.87.08.97. Mº St-Paul.
Wed–Sat 9.30pm–2am.
40–70F/€6.10–10.67.
This new jazz club is already making a name for itself, attracting local and

JAZZ, BLUES AND CHANSONS

international acts alike.
There's also a restaurant.

Le Sunset

Map 2, H6. 60 rue des
Lombards, 1er
℡ 01.40.26.46.20. Mº Châtelet-
Les Halles.
Mon–Sat 9pm–2am.
50–120F/€7.62–18.29.
Restaurant upstairs, jazz club
in the basement, featuring the
best musicians – the likes of
Alain Jeanmarie and Turk
Mauro.

MAINLY CHANSONS

Casino de Paris

Map 3, D5. 19 rue de Clichy, 9e
℡ 01.49.95.99.99. Mº Trinité.
120F/€18.29–180F/€27.44.
This decaying, once-plush
casino in one of the seediest

streets in Paris is a venue for
all sorts of performances –
chansons, poetry combined
with flamenco guitar, cabaret.
Check the listings magazines
under "*Variétés*" and
"*Chansons*".

Le Lapin Agile

Map 3, G2. 22 rue des Saules,
18e ℡ 01.46.06.85.87.
Mº Lamarck-Caulaincourt.
Tues–Sun 9pm–2am.
130F/€19.82 including drink,
students 90F/€13.72.
Old haunt of Apollinaire,
Utrillo and other
Montmartre artists, some of
whose pictures adorn the
walls. Cabaret, poetry and
chansons; you may be lucky
enough to catch singer-
composer Arlette Denis, who
carries Jacques Brel's flame.

CLASSICAL AND CONTEMPORARY MUSIC

Paris is a stimulating environment for **classical music**,
both established and contemporary. The former is well represented with a choice of ten to twenty concerts every day
of the week. Many take place in the city's churches and are
often free. More unusual venues include the Musée du
Louvre and Musée d'Orsay. **Contemporary** and experi-

mental computer-based work flourishes, too; leading exponents are Paul Mefano and Pierre Boulez, founder of the Pompidou Centre's IRCAM centre.

The **Cité de la Musique**, at La Villette in the 19ᵉ, is an important venue. Regular classical, early- and contemporary-music concerts are held at the Cité's Conservatoire, the museum amphitheatre and the fabulously designed Salle des Concerts – the hall's so-called "modular" construction means its size can be adjusted to suit the performance.

The city hosts a good number of **music festivals** (see p.267), many of which vary from year to year. For details, pick up the current year's festival schedule from the tourist office or the Hôtel de Ville.

Tickets for classical concerts in the auditoriums and theatres listed below are best bought at the box offices, though for big names you may find overnight queues, and a large number of seats are always booked by subscribers. The price range is very reasonable. The listings magazines and daily newspapers will have details of concerts in these venues, in the churches and in the suburbs.

Admission-free concerts are held at the Maison de la Radio, 166 av du Président-Kennedy, 16ᵉ; ☎01.56.40.15.16 (map 1, C5; Mᵒ Passy). All you have to do is turn up half an hour in advance at the Salle Olivier Messiaen to secure a yellow *carton d'invitation*.

CLASSICAL AND CONTEMPORARY MUSIC

CONCERT VENUES

Cité de la Musique
Map 1, H2. 221 av Jean-Jaurès, 19ᵉ ☎01.44.84.44.84 for the Salle des Concerts,

🌐 www.cite-musique.fr
Mᵒ Porte-de-Pantin.
Ticket prices 90F/€13.72–200F/€30.49.
The Cité de la Musique's main concert hall, the Salle des Concerts, has seating for

800–1200 listeners, depending on the programme, which can cover anything from traditional Korean music to the contemporary sounds of the centre's own Ensemble InterContemporain. Performances also take place in the museum amphitheatre.

Conservatoire National Supérieur de Musique et de Danse de Paris

Map 1, G2. 209 av Jean Jaurès, 19ᵉ ⓣ 01.40.40.46.46, Ⓦ *www.cite-musique.fr* Mᵒ Porte-de-Pantin. Debates, masterclasses and free perfomances from the Conservatoire's students.

Musée du Louvre

Map 2, D5. Palais du Louvre, 1ᵉʳ ⓣ 01.40.20.84.00. Mᵒ Louvre-Rivoli & Mᵒ Palais-Royal-Musée-du-Louvre. 40F/€6.10–135F/€20.58. Midday and evening concerts of chamber music in the auditorium.

Musée d'Orsay

Map 2, B5. 1 rue de Bellechasse, 7ᵉ ⓣ 01.40.49.47.17. Mᵒ Solférino & RER Musée-d'Orsay. 40F/€6.10–80F/€12.20. Varied programme of midday and evening concerts in the auditorium.

Salle Gaveau

Map 7, J2. 45 rue de la Boétie, 8ᵉ ⓣ 01.49.53.05.07. Mᵒ Miromesnil. 60F/€9.15–200F/€30.49. The Salle Gaveau was recently restored in order to improve the acoustics for its solo recitals and baroque and chamber music concerts. Seats 1000.

Salle Pleyel

Map 7, G1. 252 rue du Faubourg-St-Honoré, 8ᵉ ⓣ 01.45.61.53.00. Mᵒ Ternes. 60F/€9.15–380F/€57.93. The Orchestre de Paris performs here most frequently, along with visiting international orchestras.

St-Julien-le-Pauvre

Map 2, G9. 23 quai de Montebello, 5ᵉ ⓣ 01.42.08.49.00. Mᵒ St-Michel.

CLASSICAL AND CONTEMPORARY MUSIC

80–150F/€12.20–22.87.
Varied programmes.

St-Séverin

Map 2, G9. 1 rue des Prêtres
St-Séverin, 5ᵉ ☎01.48.24.16.97.
Mᵒ St-Michel.
Varied programmes. Entrance
free.

Ste-Chapelle

Map 2, F7. 4 bd du Palais, 1ᵉʳ
☎01.42.77.65.65. Mᵒ Cité.
100–150F/€15.24–22.87.
Mainly chamber music.

Théâtre des Champs-Élysées

Map 7, G5. 15 av Montaigne,
8ᵉ ☎01.49.52.50.50. Mᵒ Alma-Marceau.

50F/€7.62–250F/€38.11.
2000-seat capacity in this
historic theatre built in 1913.
Home to the Orchestre
National de France and the
Orchestre Lamoureux, but
also welcomes international
superstar conductors, ballet
troupes and opera companies.

Théâtre Musical de Paris

Map 2, G6. Théâtre du
Châtelet, 1 place du Châtelet,
1ᵉʳ ☎01.40.28.28.00,
ⓦ www.chatelet-theatre.com
Mᵒ Châtelet.
30F/€4.57–670F/€102.14.
The recently restored Théâtre
Musical puts on concerts,
solo recitals, ballet and
operas.

OPERA

The **Opéra National** de Paris has two homes, the original
Palais Garnier and the newer **Opéra Bastille**,
Mitterrand's most extravagant legacy to the city. In addition
to these main venues, occasional operas and concerts by
solo singers are hosted by the **Théâtre des Champs
Élysées** (see p.265) and the **Théâtre Musical de Paris**
(see above). The **Opéra Comique** (see p.263) gives a platform to solo singers and also puts on opéra bouffe and
operettas.

CLASSICAL AND CONTEMPORARY MUSIC

TICKETS FOR THE OPÉRA NATIONAL

Tickets (60–670F/€9.15–102.14) for operas at both the Palais Garnier and Opéra Bastille can be booked at least four weeks in advance Monday to Saturday 9am to 7pm on ☏08.36.69.78.68, or via the internet at Ⓦ*www.opera-de-paris.fr* Alternatively, they can be bought in person at the ticket offices up to two weeks before the performance (Mon–Sat 11am–6.30pm). The cheapest seats are only available to personal callers; unfilled seats are sold at a discount to students five minutes before the curtain goes up. For programme details, phone ☏08.36.69.78.68 or visit the website.

Palais Garnier

Map 3, E8. Place de l'Opéra, 9e. Mo Opéra.

With the arrival of the Bastille opera house, only smaller operatic productions are now performed at the lavishly refurbished old Palais Garnier.

Opéra Bastille

Map 4, E13–F14. 120 rue de Lyon, 12e. Mo Bastille.

Opened in 1989, Paris's latest addition to the opera scene, the Opéra Bastille has been plagued by controversy, including the dismissal of several musical directors and an accident at the Seville Expo 92, when a chorus singer was killed and many others injured. Nevertheless, the place is packed every night and despite the inevitable discussion about the acoustics, the Bastille orchestra is considered the best. The current musical director, James Conlon, keeps opera-goers happy scheduling both classic as well as more obscure operatic works.

CLASSICAL AND CONTEMPORARY MUSIC

CONTEMPORARY MUSIC

One of the few disadvantages of the high esteem in which the French hold their intellectual and artistic life is that it encourages, at the extremes, a tendency to sterile *intellectualisme*, as the French themselves call it. In the eyes of many music lovers and musicians, this has been nowhere more evident than in **contemporary music**, where the avant-garde is split into post-serialist and spectral music factions. Doyen of the former is composer Pierre Boulez; of the latter, Paul Mefano, director of the 2E2M ensemble.

Boulez's experiments for many years received massive public funding in the form of a vast laboratory of acoustics and "digital signal processing" – a complex known as **IRCAM** (Ⓦ *www.ircam.fr*) – housed next to the Pompidou Centre, on place Igor-Stravinsky. Boulez's Ensemble InterContemporain is now based in the Cité de la Musique under the direction of David Robertson, but IRCAM occasionally opens its doors to the public. Concerts are advertised in *Pariscope* and the like.

Film, theatre and dance

Movie-goers have a choice of around three hundred **films** showing in Paris in any one week, covering every place and period. Moreover, new works, with the exception of British movies, arrive here long before they reach London and New York.

The city also has a vibrant **theatre** scene and several superstar directors have chosen to base themselves here, including Peter Brook and Ariane Mnouchkine, known for their highly visual and explosive productions. In addition, there are numerous venues given over to the exciting developments in **dance** and multi-genre stage performances, some of it incorporating **mime**.

Listings for all films and stage productions are detailed in *Pariscope* and other weekly listing magazines (see p.239).

FILM

In recent years, several of the tiny little *salles* in obscure corners of the city, where you could find yourself the sole audience for an afternoon showing of *Hiroshima Mon Amour* or *The Maltese Falcon*, have closed and the big cinema chains, UGC and Gaumont, have opened new multiscreen cinemas. But Paris remains one of the few cities in the world in which it's possible to get not only serious entertainment but a serious film education from the programmes of regular – never mind the specialist – cinemas.

Aside from new and recent film releases, the repertoires of outstanding directors from the world over are regularly shown as part of **retrospective seasons**. These will be listed along with other cinema-clubs and museum screenings under "*Séances exceptionnelles*" or "*Ciné-clubs*", and are usually cheaper than ordinary cinemas.

Foreign films will be shown at some cinemas in the original language (with subtitles in French) – *version originale* or *v.o.* in the listings – as opposed to *version française* or *v.f.*, which means it's dubbed into French.

For the seriously committed film-freak, the best movie venues in Paris are the **cinémathèques**. The Cinémathèque Française, temporarily housed in the Salle du Palais Chaillot, 7 av Albert–de–Mun, 16ᵉ (Mᵒ Trocadéro; ℡01.56.26.01.01) and the Salle Grands Boulevards, 42 bd Bonne Nouvelle, 10ᵉ (Mᵒ Bonne-Nouvelle; closed Mon; ℡01.56.26.01.01) until a new home is confirmed, gives you a choice of more than fifty different films a week, many of which would never be shown commercially, and tickets are only 29F/€4.42 (18F/€2.74 for students and members). The Forum des Images (℡01.44.76.62.00), in the Forum des Halles (see p.52), is another excellent-value venue for the bizarre or obscure on screen.

FILM

NOTEWORTHY CINEMAS

L'Arlequin

Map 2, C9. 76 rue de Rennes, 6ᵉ. Mᵒ St-Sulpice.

Owned by Jacques Tati in the 1950s, then by the Soviet Union as the cosmos cinema until 1990, L'Arlequin has now been renovated and is once again *the* cinephile's palace in the Latin Quarter. There are special screenings of classics every Sunday at 11am, followed by debates in the café opposite.

Cinema **tickets** rarely need to be purchased in advance, and they're cheap by European standards. The average price is 40–45F/€6.10–6.86; and some cinemas have lower rates on Monday or Wednesday, as well as reductions for students from Monday to Thursday. Some matinée *séances* also have discounts.

L'Entrepôt

Map 6, E14. 7–9 rue Francis-de-Pressensé, 14ᵉ. Mᵒ Pernety.

One of the best alternative Paris movie houses, which has been keeping ciné-addicts happy for years with its three screens dedicated to the obscure, the subversive and the brilliant – among those categories many Arab and African films. It also shows videos, satellite and cable TV, and has a bookshop (Mon–Sat 2–8pm) and a restaurant (daily noon–midnight).

La Géode

Map 1, G1. 26 av Corentin-Carlou, 19ᵉ. Mᵒ Porte-de-la-Villette.

Tues–Sun 10am–8pm; tickets 57F/€8.69 or 92F/€14.03 for combined ticket with Cité des Sciences; programme details on ☎ 01.40.05.12.12.

Part of the Cité des Sciences at La Villette (see p.123), La Géode is an Omnimax cinema; a 180-degree projection system which works with a special camera and a 70mm horizontally progressing – rolling loop – film giving the

FILM

259

viewer the sensation of being amidst the action. Brilliant plots are not to be expected. What you get is a Readers' Digest view of natural and man-made wonders and breathtaking shots taken from the front of moving trains, bobsleighs, cars and so on. However trite the film, it's a cinematic experience that can be recommended.

Grand Action & Action Écoles

Map 2, G10. 5 & 23 rue des Écoles, 5ᵉ. Mᵒ Cardinal-Lemoine & Mᵒ Maubert-Mutualité.

The Action chain specializes in new prints of ancient classics and screens collections of contemporary films from different countries. More

screens at Action Christine Odéon, 4 rue Christine, 6ᵉ (Mᵒ Odéon & Mᵒ St-Michel).

Max Linder Panorama

Map 3, I8. 24 bd Poissonnière, 9ᵉ. Mᵒ Bonne-Nouvelle.

Opposite Le Grand Rex, this always shows films in the original, and has almost as big a screen, state-of-the-art sound, and Art Deco decor.

Le Studio des Ursulines

Map 2, F13. 10 rue des Ursulines, 5ᵉ. Mᵒ Censier-Daubenton & RER Luxembourg.

This was where *The Blue Angel* had its world première. Avant-garde movies are still premièred here, often followed by in-house debates with the directors and actors.

THEATRE

Certain directors in France do extraordinary things with the medium of **theatre**. Classic texts are shuffled into theatrical moments, where spectacular and dazzling sensation takes precedence over speech. Their shows can be overwhelming: huge casts, vast sets, exotic lighting effects, original music scores. It adds up to a unique experience, even if you haven't understood a word.

THEATRE

Ariane Mnouchkine, whose **Théâtre du Soleil** is based at the Cartoucherie in Vincennes, is the director par excellence of this form. **Peter Brook**, the English director based at the Bouffes du Nord theatre, is another great magician of the all-embracing show. Any show by these two should not be missed, and there are often other weird and wonderful productions by younger directors, such as **Jérôme Savary**, who is artistic director at the Opéra Comique.

At the same time, bourgeois farces, postwar classics, Shakespeare, Racine and the like, are staged with the same range of talent, or lack of it, that you'd find in London or New York. The great generation of French or Francophone dramatists, which included Anouilh, Genet, Camus, Sartre, Adamov, Ionesco and Cocteau, came to an end with the death of **Samuel Beckett** in 1989 and Ionesco in 1994. Their plays, however, are still frequently performed and can now be included alongside Corneille and Shakespeare in the programme of the **Comédie Française**, the national theatre for the classics.

Parisian suburbs are a great source of excellent theatre productions, thanks to the ubiquitous **Maisons de Culture**. Ironically, however, although they were designed to bring culture to the masses, their productions are often among the most "difficult" and intellectually inaccessible.

Another plus is the Parisian theatre's openness to **foreign influence** and foreign work. Argentinian Jorge Lavelli and Catalan Lluis Pasqual direct at the Théâtre National de la Colline and at the Odéon, and foreign artists are as welcome as they've always been.

The best time of all for theatre lovers to come to Paris is for the **Festival d'Automne**, from the end of September to December (see p.271), an international celebration of all the performing arts, which attracts stage directors of high calibre.

THEATRE

BUYING THEATRE TICKETS

The easiest places to get **tickets** to see a stage performance in Paris are one of the FNAC shops or Virgin Megastores (see pp.283 and 291), or alternatively, the ticket kiosks on **place de la Madeleine**, 8ᵉ, opposite no. 15 and on the parvis of the **Gare du Montparnasse**, 14ᵉ (Tues–Sat 12.30–8pm, Sun 12.30–4pm). These last two sell same-day tickets at half price and 16F/€2.44 commission, but queues can be very long.

Booking well in advance is essential for new productions and all shows by the superstar directors, tickets for which are usually quite expensive. **Prices** for the theatre vary between 30F/€4.57 (up in the gods) and 170F/€25.92 for state theatres, 60F/€9.15 and 260F/€39.64 for privately owned ones, and around 130F/€19.82 for the suburban venues. There are weekday discounts for students. Most theatres are closed on Sunday and Monday, and during August.

NOTEWORTHY VENUES

Bouffes du Nord
Map 3, M3. 37bis bd de la Chapelle, 10ᵉ.
℡01.46.07.34.50.
Mᵒ La Chapelle.
Peter Brook's Paris base, where he occasionally produces epic events. He shares the directorship with Stéphane Lissner who is responsible for classical–music events.

Cartoucherie
Map 1, I6. Rte du Champ-de-Manoeuvre, 12ᵉ. Mᵒ Château-de-Vincennes.
Notable as home to the Théâtre du Soleil (see p.261; ℡01.43.74.24.08), the Cartoucherie is also the base for other good theatre companies.

Comédie Française (national theatre)
Map 2, D4. 2 rue de Richelieu, 1ᵉʳ ℡01.44.58.15.15. Mᵒ Palais-Royal.

THEATRE

The national theatre for the classics. However, the trend now seems to be to cut down on traditional productions, with the exception of Molière and Feydeau, in favour of more contemporary work and modernized versions of the classics.

Odéon Théâtre de l'Europe (national theatre)

Map 2, E10. 1 place Paul-Claudel (off place de l'Odéon), 6ᵉ ⓣ 01.44.41.36.36.
Mᵒ Odéon.

Contemporary plays, as well as *version originale* productions by well-known foreign companies. During May 1968, this theatre was occupied by students and became an open parliament with the backing of its directors, Jean-Louis Barrault (of Baptiste fame in *Les Enfants du Paradis* and who died in 1994) and Madeleine Renaud, one of the great French stage actresses.

Opéra Comique

Map 3, G8. Rue Favart, 2ᵉ ⓣ 01.42.44.45.46.

Mᵒ Richelieu-Drouot.
New artistic director Jérôme Savary (ex-Théâtre National de Chaillot) blends all forms of stage arts: modern and classical opera, musicals, comedy, dance and pop music, creating a bold and exciting programme.

Théâtre de la Colline (national theatre)

Map 1, H4. 15 rue Malte-Brun, 20ᵉ. ⓣ 01.44.62.52.52.
Mᵒ Gambetta.

Most of the work put on by Jorge Lavelli is twentieth-century and innovative, and nearly always worth seeing.

Théâtre de Gennevilliers

Map 9, E3. Centre Dramatique National, 41 av des Grésillons, Gennevilliers
ⓣ 01.41.32.26.26. Mᵒ Gabriel-Péri.

Several stimulating productions by Bernard Sobel have brought acclaim – and audiences – to this suburban venue in recent years.

THEATRE

Théâtre National de Chaillot (national theatre)

Map 7, B7. Palais de Chaillot, place du Trocadéro, 16e
℡01.53.65.30.00. M°
Trocadéro.

With the departure of Jérôme Savary to the Opéra Comique, the role of artistic director here is to be taken by Ariel Goldenberg (ex-Maison de la Culture de Bobigny). An innovative individual translation system makes performances here accessible to foreign audiences.

DANCE AND MIME

Aside from incomparable performances by **Marcel Marceau**, the famous mime practitioner now in his 70s, pure mime is rarely seen these days in Paris. The trend is to incorporate mime skills into dance, comedy routines and improvisation, creating an interesting cross-fertilization of genres and giving rise to new standards in performing arts.

French **dance** has benefitted, in recent years, from state subsidies which have gone to regional companies expressly to decentralize the arts. But all the best contemporary practitioners come to the capital regularly. Names to look out for are Maguy Marin's from Rilleux-le-Pape, and Joëlle Bouvier and Régis Obadia's from Angers. Creative choreographers based in or around Paris include José Montalvo, Karine Saporta and the Californian Carolyn Carlson.

Many of the **theatres** listed above (see pp.262–264) include both mime and dance in their programmes. Plenty of space and critical attention are also given to **tango**, **folk** and to visiting **traditional dance** troupes from all over the world.

As for **ballet**, the principal stage is at the Palais Garnier, home to the Ballet de l'Opéra National de Paris. Ballet fans can also be sure of masterly performances at the Bastille opera house, the Théâtre des Champs-Élysées and the Théâtre Musical de Paris.

Festivals combining theatre, dance, mime and classical music include the Festival Exit in Créteil, the Paris Quartier d'Été from mid-July to mid-August and the Festival d'Automne from mid-September to mid-December (see "Festivals", p.267).

VENUES

Centre Mandapa
Map 5, D9. 6 rue Wurtz, 13ᵉ
℡01.45.89.01.60. Mᵒ Glacière.
Paris's only theatre dedicated to traditional dances from around the world.

Opéra de Bastille
Map 4, E13. Place de la Bastille, 12ᵉ ℡08.36.69.78.68,
Ⓦ www.opera-de-paris.fr
Mᵒ Bastille.
Stages some productions – usually contemporary and avant-garde – by the Ballet de l'Opéra National de Paris,.

Palais Garnier
Map 3, E8. Place de l'Opéra, 9ᵉ

℡08.36.69.78.68,
Ⓦ www.opera-de-paris.fr
Mᵒ Opéra.
Main home of the Ballet de l'Opéra National de Paris and the place to see ballet classics.

Théâtre des Champs-Élysées
Map 7, G5. 15 av Montaigne, 8ᵉ ℡01.49.52.50.50.
Mᵒ Alma-Marceau.
Forever aiming to outdo the Opéra with even grander and more expensive ballet productions. The Ballet National de Marseille was welcomed here most recently.

Théâtre de la Ville
Map 2, G6. 2 place du Châtelet, 4ᵉ ℡01.42.74.22.77.

DANCE AND MIME

Mº Châtelet.
The height of success for contemporary dance productions is to end up here. Karine Saporta's work is regularly featured, as is Maguy Marin and Pina Bausch. Look out also for slightly more off-beat performances at the Théâtre de la Ville's sister company, Théâtre des Abbesses, 31 rue des Abbesses, 18ᵉ; Mº Abbesses (map 3, F3).

Festivals

With all that's going on in Paris, **festivals** – in the traditional "popular" sense – are no big deal. But there is an impressive array of arts events and an inspired internationalist jamboree at the Fête de l'Humanité.

The tourist office produces a biannual *Saisons de Paris – Calendrier des Manifestations*, which gives details of all the mainstream events; otherwise, check the listings and other Paris magazines (see p.239).

Many Parisian quartiers like Belleville and Montmartre have *portes ouvertes* (open doors) weeks, when artists' studios are open to the public and some festivities are laid on – keep an eye open for posters and flyers.

JANUARY

La Grande Parade
New Year's Day parade on January 1 from Porte St-Martin to Madeleine.

FEBRUARY

Chinese New Year
Paris's Chinese community brings in the New Year in the 13e around Avenue d'Ivry.

MARCH

Festival Exit

International festival of contemporary dance, performance and theatre at Créteil; information from Maison des Arts, place Salvador-Allende, 9400 Créteil (℡ 01.45.13.19.19).

Printemps des Rues

Free street performances at the end of March in the areas of La Villette, Gambetta, Nation and République.

END OF MARCH/ BEGINNING OF APRIL

Banlieues Bleus

International jazz festival in the towns of Seine-Saint-Denis (Blanc-Mesnil, Drancy, Aubervilliers, Pantin, St-Ouen, Bobigny); info on ℡ 01.49.22.10.10, ⓦ *www.banlieusbleues.org*

Festival de Films des Femmes

Women's film festival at Créteil; information from Maison des Arts, place Salvador-Allende, 9400 Créteil (℡ 01.49.80.38.98, ⓦ *www.gdebussac.fr/filmfem*).

Festival du Film de Paris

Films on preview at the Cinéma Gaumont Marignan, 27–33 av des Champs-Élysées, 8e (℡ 08.36.68.75.55).

APRIL

Poisson d'Avril

April Fools' Day, on April 1, with spoofs in the media and people sticking paper fishes on the backs of unsuspecting fools.

END APRIL/ BEGINNING OF MAY

Foire de Paris

Food and wine fair at the Parc des Expositions, Porte de Versailles (℡ 01.49.09.60.00).

MAY

Fête du Travail
May Day (May 1) with marches and festivities in eastern Paris and around place de la Bastille.

MAY TO JULY

Jazz in the Parc Floral
Big jazz names give free concerts in the Parc Floral at the Bois de Vincennes (entrance to park 10F/€1.52, ℡01.43.43.92.95).

JUNE

Festival Agora
Contemporary theatre/dance/music festival organized by IRCAM and the Pompidou Centre (℡01.44.78.48.16, Ⓦ *www.ircam.fr*).

Festival de St-Denis
Classical and world-music festival the last two weeks in June, with opportunities to hear music in the Gothic St-

Denis basilica (℡01.48.13.06.07, Ⓦ *www.festival-saint-denis.fr*).

Fête de la Musique
On June 21, live bands and free concerts throughout the city. (℡01.40.03.94.70, Ⓦ *www.fetedelamusique.culture .fr*).

Feux de la Saint-Jean
Around June 21, fireworks for St-Jean's Day at the Parc de la Villette and quai St-Bernard.

Gay Pride
Gay and Lesbian Pride march (℡01.43.57.21.47).

JUNE TO JULY

Foire St-Germain
Concerts, antique fairs, poetry and exhibitions in the 6e (℡01.40.46.75.12, Ⓦ *www.foirestgermain.org*).

Villette Jazz Festival
Jazz festival at in the park and Grande Halle at la Villette (℡01.40.03.75.75, Ⓦ *www.la-villette.com*).

MAY–JULY

●

269

JULY

Arrivée du Tour de France Cyclistes

On the third or fourth Sunday of July, the Tour de France cyclists cross the finishing line in the avenue des Champs-Élysées.

Bastille Day

On July 14 and the evening before, the 1789 surrender of the Bastille is celebrated with official pomp: tanks parade down the Champs-Élysées, firework displays and concerts are put on. At night there is dancing in the streets around place de la Bastille to good French bands.

La Goutte d'Or en Fête

Held in the first week of July, a music festival of rap, reggae and raï with local and international performers (℡ 01.53.09.99.22).

Paris Quartier d'Été

Music, cinema, dance and theatre events around the city (℡ 01.44.94.98.00, Ⓦ *www.quartierdete.com*).

JULY 15 TO AUGUST 15

Festival de Cinéma en Plein Air

Open-air cinema for free at Parc de la Villette (℡ 01.40.03.76.92, Ⓦ *www.la-villette.com*).

SEPTEMBER

Fête de l'Humanité

Mº La Courneuve, then bus #177 or special shuttle from RER.

Held in the second weekend of September and sponsored by the French Communist Party and *L'Humanité* newspaper, this annual three-day event just north of Paris at La Courneuve attracts people in their tens of thousands and of every political persuasion. Food and drink (all very cheap), and music and crafts from every corner of the globe, are the predominant features, rather than political platforms. Info on ℡ 01.49.22.72.72.

Journées du Patrimoine

On a weekend in mid-September, a France-wide event where normally off-limits buildings – like the Palais de l'Élysée – are opened to a curious public. Details in local press.

Techno Parade

Held in mid-September. Floats and sound systems parade from Place de la République to Pelouse de Reuilly and celebrations culminate in a big party (℡ 08.36.68.94.94, Ⓦ *www.technoparade.org*).

END OF SEPTEMBER TO END OF DECEMBER

Festival d'Automne

Theatre and music festival including companies from Eastern Europe, America and Japan; multilingual productions; lots of avant-garde and multimedia stuff, most of it very exciting (℡ 01.53.45.17.17).

OCTOBER

Fête des Vendanges

On the first or second Saturday in October, the grape harvest festival takes place in the Montmartre vineyard, at the corner of rue des Saules and rue St-Vincent (℡ 01.53.41.18.18).

Foire Internationale d'Art Contemporain (FIAC)

International contemporary art fair held at Paris Expo, Porte de Versailles (℡ 01.41.90.47.80).

NOVEMBER

Festival FNAC-Inrockuptibles

Dubbed *Les Inrocks*, a rock festival in early November, featuring lots of new names at various venues around town, put on by the book and record chain-store FNAC (see pp.283 & 291 for addresses).

SEPTEMBER–NOVEMBER

Lancement des Illuminations des Champs-Élysées

At the end of November, jazz bands, the Republican Guard and an international star turning on the Christmas lights on the Champs-Élysées.

Marjolaine

Environmental/ecological festival in early November, with more than 400 stalls in the Parc Floral, Bois de Vincennes. Everything from organic produce to Greenpeace stands (℡01.45.56.09.09).

Mois de la Photo

A biennial event (even years). Photographic exhibitions are held in museums, galleries and cultural centres throughout the city (℡01.44.78.75.00).

END OF NOVEMBER TO MID-DECEMBER

Festival d'Art Sacré de la Ville de Paris

Concerts and recitals of church music in Paris's churches and concert halls (℡01.44.70.64.10).

DECEMBER

Le Nouvel An

New Year's Eve, December 31, means fireworks, drinking and kissing, notably on the Champs-Élysées.

Gay and lesbian Paris

Paris is one of Europe's major centres for **gay** men. There are numerous gay bars, clubs, restaurants, saunas and shops, concentrated especially in the **Marais**. While less visible, the **lesbian** community is strong and well organized, with networks of feminist groups and a number of publications.

The high spots of the calendar are the annual Gay Pride parade and festival, and the Bastille Day Ball. **Gay Pride** is normally held on the Saturday closest to the summer solstice, and is a major carnival for both lesbians and gays. The **Bastille Day Ball** (July 13, 10pm–dawn), a wild open-air dance on the quai de la Tournelle, 5e (Mº Pont Marie), is free for all to join in.

HELPLINES AND INFORMATION

Act Up Paris
Map 4, F11. 45 rue Sedaine, 11e ℡ 01.48.06.13.89, Ⓦ www.actupp.org Mº Bréguet-Sabin.

The Paris branch of the

273

international organization against AIDS in the homosexual community. They hold weekly meetings and two-monthly information/discussion groups.

ARCL (Les Archives, Recherches et Cultures Lesbiennes)

Map 5, N1. Maison des Femmes (see p.275).
ARCL publish a biannual directory of lesbian, gay and feminist addresses in France, called *L'Annuaire* (70F/€10.67), and organize frequent meetings around campaigning, artistic and intellectual issues. In addition, they produce a regular newsletter, and run a feminist/lesbian archive–library at the Maison des Femmes which you can consult Fri 7–10pm.

Association des Médecins Gais (AMG; gay doctors' organization)

Map 4, F11. 45 rue Sedaine, 11e ℡01.48.05.81.71, Ⓦ*www.gaipied.fr/associations/*

amg M° Bréguet-Sabin.
Wed 6–8pm, Sat 2–4pm.
Provides help with all health concerns relative to the gay community.

Centre Gai et Lesbienne

Map 4, G12. 3 rue Keller, 11e
℡01.43.57.21.47,
Ⓕ01.43.57.27.93,
Ⓦ*www.cglparis.org* M° Ledru-Rollin.
Mon–Sat 4–8pm; gay family afternoon Sun 2–7pm.
The main information centre for the gay, lesbian, bisexual and transexual community in Paris. It's also the meeting place for numerous campaigning, identity, health, arts and intellectual groups.

Écoute Gaie

℡01.44.93.01.02,
Ⓦ*www.gai-ecoute.qc.ca*
Mon, Wed & Thurs 8–10pm,
Tues & Fri 6–10pm.
Helpline in French with information on the gay community and advice on problems related to being gay.

FACTS-Line

℡01.44.93.16.69.
Wed 6–10pm.

Helpline in English for AIDS-related concerns.

Lesbian and Gay Pride

ⓣ 08.36.68.11.31,
ⓦ www.gaypride.fr
Organizes the annual Gay Pride march in Paris.

Maison des Femmes

Map 5, N1. 163 rue de Charenton, 12ᵉ
ⓣ 01.43.43.41.13,
ⓕ 01.43.43.42.13. Mᵒ Reuilly-Diderot & Mᵒ Gare-de-Lyon.
A women's meeting place, which also organizes a range of events and actions.

MEDIA

FG (Fréquence Gaie) 98.2 FM

24hr gay and lesbian radio station with music, news, chats and information on groups and events.

Gai Pied

ⓦ www.gaipied.fr
Publishes the annual *Guide Gai/Gay Guide*, which is the most comprehensive gay guide to France, carrying a good selection of lesbian and gay addresses, in both French and English; 79F/€12.04 from newsagents and bookshops.

Lesbia

A monthly lesbian publication, available from most newsagents, featuring a wide range of articles, listings, reviews, lonely hearts and contacts.

Minitel

3615 GAY is the Minitel number to dial for information on groups and contacts.

Les Mots à la Bouche

Map 4, B10. 6 rue Ste-Croix-de-la-Bretonnerie, 4ᵉ
ⓣ 01.42.78.88.30,
ⓦ www.motalabouche.com
Mᵒ Hôtel-de-Ville.
Mon–Thurs 11am–11pm, Fri & Sat 11am–midnight, Sun 2–8pm.

MEDIA

●

The main gay and lesbian bookshop, with exhibition space and meeting rooms; a selection of literature in English, too. Lots of free listings mags and club flyers.

ⓦ **www.attirentdelles.org**
Magazine-style internet site in French with information and articles on all aspects of lesbian life.

ⓦ **www.phospho.com**
Internet site with all the usual chat-rooms, shopping, forum, etc. Good for up-to-date news and events and a few links.

BARS, CLUBS AND DISCOS

Lesbian clubs in Paris are less of a rarity than they were ten years ago, but are still relatively few and far between. The pleasures of **gay men** are far better catered for. While the selection of gay male-oriented establishments listed in this chapter only scratches the surface, for gay women our listings more or less cover all that's available. Lesbians, however, are welcome in some of the predominantly male clubs.

Gay clubs' reputation for wild hedonism attracts a fair number of heterosexuals in search of a good time. Many hetorosexuals are indeed welcome in some gay establishments if accompanied, while some clubs have all but abandoned a gay policy; the legendary gay club *Le Queen*, for example, is only gay on a Thursday now. Equally, some of the more mainstream clubs have started doing gay nights. For a complete rundown of events, consult *Em@le* (free in gay bars) which has a comprehensive weekly listing of gay nights, or Gai Pied's *Guide Gai* (published annually) for venues. Alternatively, tune into Paris's gay radio station RadioFG (98.2 FM), and keep an eye out for flyers.

WOMEN

- - - - - - - - - - - - - - - - - - -

L'Alcantara

Map 4, B11. 30 rue du Roi-de-Sicile, 4ᵉ. Mº St-Paul.
Daily 5–11pm.
This ex-boulangerie with its relaxed café-style area on the ground floor and bar area downstairs is a welcome addition to the lesbian scene in Paris. The crowd is young, trendy and outgoing. Drinks start at 18F/€2.74.

La Champmeslé

Map 2, D2. 4 rue Chabanais, 2ᵉ ℡01.42.96.85.20. Mº Opéra & Mº Pyramides.
Mon–Wed 7pm–2am, Thurs–Sat 7pm–4am. Closed Sun.
Enduring lesbian bar with back room reserved for women, front room for mixed company. Cabaret on Thurs. Drinks 30–50F/€4.57–7.62.

Le Pulp

Map 3, I8. 25 bd Poissonnière, 2ᵉ ℡01.40.26.01.93. Mº Grands-Boulevards.
Thurs–Sun from 11.30pm, Fri & Sat 50F/€7.62 entrance from midnight.
Diverse music – from techno to Madonna. Happy hour 11pm–1.30am. Drinks 40F/€6.10.

Les Scandaleuses

Map 4, B11. 8 rue des Écouffes, 4ᵉ ℡01.48.87.39.26. Mº Hôtel-de-Ville.
Daily 5pm–2am.
Trendy and high-profile women-only bar in the Marais. Lively atmosphere guaranteed.

Unity Bar

Map 2, H4. 176–178 rue St-Martin, 3ᵉ ℡01.42.72.70.59. Mº Rambuteau & Mº Les Halles.
Daily 4pm–2am.
Popular women-only bar with billiards and a happy hour 4–8pm.

L'Utopia

Map 2, I4. 15 rue Michel le Comte, 3ᵉ ℡01.42.71.63.43. Mº Rambuteau.
Mon–Sat 7pm–2pm.
Bar on two levels, with billiards and chess downstairs. Themed nights, varied music and friendly atmosphere. Predominantly women.

BARS, CLUBS AND DISCOS

MEN

Banana Café

Map 2, G5. 13 rue de la Ferronnerie, 1er ℡ 01.42.33.35.31. M° Chatelet-Les Halles.
Daily 4.30pm–dawn.
Popular, expensive and very trendy. Try and catch the cabaret and go-go dancing.

Le Central

Map 4, B10. 33 rue Vieille-du-Temple, 4e ℡ 01.48.87.99.33. M° Hôtel-de-Ville.
Daily 2pm–2am.
The oldest gay local in the quarter. Small, friendly and always crowded. Drinks 20–60F/€3.05–9.15.

Le Dépôt

Map 2, H4. 10 rue aux Ours, 3e ℡ 01.44.54.96.96. M° Étienne-Marcel.
Mon–Sat from 11pm.
Two floors of music in this hardcore club, popular for cruising. On Sun there's a tea-dance from 5pm; ladies welcome on a Wed. Admission 45–60F/€6.86–9.15.

Folies Pigalle

Map 3, F4. 11 place Pigalle, 18e ℡ 01.48.78.25.26. M° Pigalle.
One-time famous cabaret that has turned its hand to club-nights. Sundays host two celebrated events; afternoon tea-dance "Black, Blanc, Beur" (6pm–midnight; 40F/€6.10), and a transvestite night based on the New York Escualita, open also to a non-transvestite but tolerant public (midnight–dawn; 60F/€9.15). Also open Wed–Sat for a mixed crowd midnight–dawn; 100F/€15.24.

Le Keller

Map 4, G12. 14 rue Keller, 11e ℡ 01.47.00.05.39. M° Bastille.
Daily 10pm–2am.
Cruising bar where leather, latex and uniform is the requisite dress-code.

La Luna

Map 4, G12. 28 rue Keller, 11e ℡ 01.40.21.09.91. M° Bastille.
Wed–Sun 11pm–6am.
The latest high-tech rendezvous for the gay

BARS, CLUBS AND DISCOS

Bastille crowd, complete with mirrors to dance in front of. Fri & Sat lesbian nights. Weekend entry 50F/€7.62; drinks from 35F/€5.34.

Mixer Bar

Map 4, A10. 23 rue Ste-Croix de la Bretonnerie, 4ᵉ ⓣ01.42.78.26.20. Mº Hôtel-de-Ville.
Daily 4pm–2am.
Another popular and crowded Marais bar. Women also welcome.

Open Café

Map 4, A10. 17 rue des Archives, 4ᵉ. Mº Hôtel-de-Ville.
Daily 10am–2am.
The first gay bar/café to have tables out on the pavement.

Le Quetzal

Map 4, A10. 10 rue de la Verrerie, 4ᵉ ⓣ01.48.87.99.07. Mº Hôtel-de-Ville.
Daily noon–5am, happy hours 5–9pm & 11pm–midnight.
Lots of beautiful bodies cram into this popular nightspot.

Le Tango

Map 4, B7. 13 rue au-Maire, 3ᵉ ⓣ01.42.72.17.78. Mº Arts-et-Métiers.
Fri, Sat & the eve of public hols 10.30pm–dawn, Sun 6–10pm.
Gay & lesbian dance-hall with a traditional *bal* until midnight, then all other types of music except techno. Admission 40F/€6.10 Fri & Sat, 30F/€4.57 Sun.

ACCOMMODATION AND EATING

Although gays and lesbians shouldn't come across any anti-social behaviour in restaurants and hotels, there is a choice of gay-oriented **places to stay and eat**. You don't need to look any further than the Marais; restaurants are plentiful, and even if they aren't exclusively gay, the location can guarantee a mainly gay clientele. Although there's only one hotel, *Hôtel Central Marais*, that caters exclusively to gays and lesbians, there are a few where the majority of customers are gay.

RESTAURANTS

Amadéo

Map 4, B11. 19 rue François-Miron, 4e ℡01.48.87.01.02.
M° St-Paul.
Closed Sun and Mon lunch.
Baroque decor and opera music accompany your meal of French modern cuisine. Thursdays are the evenings to go for the live opera recital and 285F/€43.45 three-course meal that includes coffee and a glass of champagne.

Krokodil

Map 2, H5. 20 rue de La-Reynie, 4e ℡01.48.87.55.67,
Ⓦ *www.krokodil.fr* M° Châtelet.
Daily 7pm–2am.
Lively restaurant with a terrace, themed *soirées* and traditional French food.

Le Rude

Map 4, A10. 23 rue du Temple, 4e ℡01.42.72.17.78. M° Hôtel-de-Ville.
Daily noon–12.30am.
Posey, but not snobbish, bar/restaurant. The food is good and reasonably priced, with an American slant.

HOTELS

The accommodation **price codes** used below are explained on p.167 in the "Accommodation" chapter.

Hôtel des Acacias

Map 2, I6. 20 rue du Temple, 4e
℡01.48.87.07.70,
Ⓕ01.48.87.17.20. M° Hôtel-de-Ville.
Small and pleasant hotel in a refurbished eighteenth-century mansion sandwiched between the Pompidou, the Marais and bustling rue de Rivoli. Provides all expected amenities and is particularly gay-friendly. ❻.

Hôtel Beaumarchais

Map 4, E8. 3 rue Oberkampf, 11e ℡01.43.38.16.16,
Ⓕ01.43.38.32.86,
Ⓦ *www.hotelbeaumarchais.com* M° Filles-de-Calvaire & M° Oberkampf.
Fashionable, funky and gay-

friendly hotel with personal service and colourful Fifties-inspired decor; all rooms en suite with air conditioning, safes and cable TV. ⑤–⑥.

Hôtel Central Marais
Map 4, B10. 33 rue Vieille-du-Temple, 4e ⓣ 01.48.87.56.08, ⓕ 01.42.77.06.27. Mº Hôtel-de-Ville.

The only self-proclaimed gay hotel in Paris, with a relaxed bar downstairs. Seven small rooms with shared bathrooms. Also lets an apartment that sleeps four. The entrance is on Rue Sainte-Croix-de-la-Bretonnerie. ⑥.

ACCOMMODATION AND EATING

Shopping

E ven if you don't plan – or can't afford – to buy, browsing in Paris's **shops and markets** is one of the city's chief delights. Flair for style and design is as evident here as it is in other aspects of Paris life. Parisians' epicurean tendencies and fierce attachment to their small local traders have kept alive a wonderful variety of speciality shops, despite the pressures to concentrate consumption in gargantuan underground and multistorey complexes. One of the best shopping areas is the square kilometre around **place St-Germain-des-Prés**, packed with books, antiques, gorgeous garments, artworks and playthings. But in every *quartier* you'll find enticing displays of all manner of consumables.

OPENING HOURS

Most businesses **open** Monday to Saturday, often with two hours off at midday, and generally close at around 7pm. In addition, the larger department stores tend to stay open until 9pm or 10pm on Thursday nights. Almost all shops close on Sunday and some stay closed on Monday as well, though there is often a corner shop open in each neighbourhood to fill in the gap.

BOOKSHOPS

The best areas for **books** are the narrow streets of the quartier Latin and along the Seine, where rows of **stalls** are perched against the river parapet. Here we've listed a few specialists and favourites. For books in English, head for Abbey Bookshop, Shakespeare & Co or W H Smith.

Abbey Bookshop/La Librairie Canadienne
Map 2, F9. 29 rue de la Parcheminerie, 5e. Mo St-Michel.
Mon–Sat 10am–7pm.
A Canadian bookshop round the corner from Shakespeare & Co (see below), with lots of secondhand British and North American fiction, good social science sections, plus knowledgeable and helpful staff – and free coffee.

Artcurial
Map 7, J3. 9 av Matignon, 8e. Mo Franklin-D-Roosevelt.
Tues–Sun 10am–7.15pm; closed two weeks in Aug.
The best art bookshop in Paris.

FNAC
Map 2, F5. Forum des Halles, niveau 2, Porte Pierre-Lescot, 1er. Mo/RER Châtelet-Les Halles.
Mon–Sat 10am–7.30pm.
Not the most congenial of bookshops, but it's the biggest and covers everything; there are numerous other branches throughout the city.

Galerie Maeght
Map 2, B7. 42 rue du Bac, 7e. Mo Rue-du-Bac.
Tues–Sat 9.30am–7pm.
Famous art gallery which makes its own beautifully printed art books.

Présence Africaine
Map 2, G10. 25bis rue des Écoles, 5e. Mo Maubert-Mutualité. Mon–Sat 10am–7pm.
Specialist black African bookshop, with titles ranging from literature to economics and philosophy by Caribbean and North American, as well as African writers.

BOOKSHOPS

283

Parallèles

Map 2, F5. 47 rue St-Honoré, 1er. Mo Châtelet-Les Halles. Mon–Sat 10am–7pm.

An alternative bookshop, with everything from anarchism to New Age. Good for info on current events and gigs.

Shakespeare & Co

Map 2, G9. 37 rue de la Bûcherie, 5e. Mo Maubert-Mutualité. Daily noon–midnight.

A cosy, famous literary haunt, American-run, with the biggest selection of secondhand English books in town. Also poetry readings and the like.

W H Smith

Map 2, B3. 248 rue de Rivoli, 1er. Mo Concorde. Mon–Sat 9.30am–7pm.

Paris outlet of the British chain. Wide range of books and newspapers.

CLOTHES

The haute couture shows may be well out-of-bounds, but there's nothing to prevent you trying on fabulously expensive creations by famous **couturiers** in rue du Faubourg-St-Honoré, avenue François-1er and avenue Victor-Hugo – apart from the intimidating air of the assistants and the awesome chill of the marble portals. Likewise, you can treat the **younger designers** round place des Victoires and in the Marais and St-Germain areas as stops on your sightseeing itinerary. The long-time darlings of the glitterati are Jean-Paul Gaultier and Azzedine Alaïa, who, in 1991, were prevailed upon to design some gear for the city's **cheapest department store** – Tati (whose main branch is at 13 place de la République, 11e; Mo République). Of the more recent star designers three are British – John Galliano at Dior, Stella McCartney at Chloé and the controversial Alexander McQueen at Givenchy. For **smart clothes**

DESIGNER FASHION

The addresses below are those of the main or most conveniently located shops for designer clothes.

Agnès B, 6 rue du Jour, 1er (map 2, F4; Mº Châtelet-Les Halles).

Azzedine Alaïa, 7 rue de Moussy, 4e (map 4, A10; Mº Hôtel-de-Ville).

Chanel, 31 rue Cambon, 1er (map 3, C9; Mº Madeleine).

Christian Lacroix, 73 rue du Faubourg-St-Honoré, 8e (map 7, L3; Mº Concorde).

Gianni Versace, 62 rue du Faubourg-St-Honoré, 8e (map 7, L3; Mº Concorde).

Giorgio Armani, 25 place Vendôme, 1er (map 2, C2; Mº Opéra).

Inès de la Fressange, 14 av Montaigne, 8e (map 7, G5; Mº Alma-Marceau).

Issey Miyake, 3 place des Vosges, 4e (map 4, D11; Mº St-Paul).

Jean-Paul Gaultier, 30 rue du Faubourg St-Antoine, 12e (map 4, E12; Mº Bastille).

Jil Sander, 52 av Montaigne, 8e (map 7, I4; Mº Franklin-D-Roosevelt).

Junko Shimada, 54 rue Étienne-Marcel, 2e (map 2, F3; Mº Châtelet-Les Halles).

Kenzo, 3 place des Victoires, 1er (map 2, E3–F3; Mº Bourse).

Sonia Rykiel, 175 bd St-Germain, 6e (map 7, D8; Mº St-Germain-des-Prés).

Thierry Mugler, 49 av Montaigne, 8e (map 7, H5; Mº Alma-Marceau).

Yves Saint-Laurent, 6 place St-Sulpice, 6e (map 2, D9; Mº St-Sulpice & Mº Mabillon).

DESIGNER FASHION

without the fancy labels the best areas are rue St-Placide and rue St-Dominique in the 6e and 7e. The department stores Galeries Lafayette and Au Printemps have good selections of designer prêt-à-porter; and the Forum des Halles is choc-a-bloc with clothes shops at less competitive prices. The **sales** take place in January and July, with reductions of up to forty percent on designer clothes. Designer ends of lines and old stock are sold year-round in **discount shops** concentrated in rue d'Alésia in the 14e and rue St-Placide in the 6e. For **shoes**, take a wander down rue Meslay in the 3e.

DEPARTMENT STORES

Au Bon Marché
Map 6, G6. 38 rue de Sèvres, 7e. Mo Sèvres-Babylone.
Mon–Fri 9.30am–7pm, Sat till 8pm.
Paris's oldest department store, founded in 1852. Prices are lower on average than at the more upmarket Galeries Lafayette and Printemps. Excellent kids' department and a legendary food hall.

Galeries Lafayette
Map 3, E7. 40 bd Haussmann, 9e. Mo Havre-Caumartin.
Mon–Sat 9.30am–6.45pm, Thurs till 9pm.
The store's forte is, above all,

high fashion. Two complete floors are given over to the latest creations by leading designers for men, women and children. Then there's household stuff, tableware, furniture, a huge *parfumerie*, and much else – all under a superb 1900 dome.

Au Printemps
Map 3, C7. 64 bd Haussmann, 9e. Mo Havre-Caumartin.
Mon–Sat 9.30am–7pm, Thurs till 10pm.
Books, records, a *parfumerie* even bigger than that of rival Galeries Lafayette, excellent fashion for women – less so for men.

La Samaritaine
Map 2, F5–F6. 75 rue de Rivoli,

1er. Mº Louvre-Rivoli, Mº Châtelet & Mº Pont-Neuf. Mon–Sat 9.30am–7pm, Thurs till 10pm.
The largest of the department stores, spread over three buildings, boasts that it can provide anything you could possibly want. You get a superb view of Paris from the eleventh-floor rooftop, and from the inexpensive tenth-floor terrace café (closed Oct–March).

FOOD AND DRINK

Sumptuous food stores are to be found all over Paris: the listings below are for the **specialist places**, many of them palaces of gluttony, with prices to match. Everyday food shopping is best done at the **street markets** or **supermarkets**, though save your bread-buying at least for the local *boulangerie*. The cheapest supermarket chain is Ed Discount. Food markets are listed on pp.293–295.

Le Baron Aligre

Map 4, G14. 1 rue Théophile-Roussel, 12e. Mº Ledru-Rollin. Tues–Fri 10am–2pm & 5–9.30pm, Sat 10am–9.30pm, Sun 10.30am–1pm.
Stocks a good selection of dependable lower-range French wines; 7F/€1.07 for a small tasting glass. Very drinkable Merlot at 16F/€2.44 a litre, if you bring your own containers.

Barthélémy

Map 2, B8. 51 rue de Grenelle, 7e. Mº Bac.
Tues–Sat 8.30am–1pm & 4–7.30pm; closed Aug.
Purveyors of cheeses to the rich and powerful.

Carmès et Fils

Map 3, off A4. 24 rue de Lévis, 17e. Mº Villiers.
Tues–Sat 8.30am–1pm & 4–7.30pm, Sun am; closed Aug.
Run by a family of experts who mature many of the cheeses sold here in their own cellars.

Caves Michel Renaud

Map 4, off I19. 12 place de la

Nation, 12e. Mo Nation.
9.30am–1pm & 2–8.30pm;
closed Sun pm and Mon am.
Established in 1870, this
wine shop purveys superb-
value French and Spanish
wines, champagnes and
Armagnac.

Comptoir du Saumon
Map 4, B11. 60 rue François-
Miron, 4e. Mo St-Paul.
Mon–Sat 10am–10pm.
Specializes in salmon, but
sells eels, trout and all things
fishy as well – there's also a
delightful little restaurant in
which to taste the fare.

Debauve and Gallais
Map 2, D7. 30 rue des Sts-
Pères, 6e. Mo St-Germain-des-
Prés. Mon–Sat 9am–7pm;
closed Aug.
A beautiful, ancient shop
specializing in chocolate and
elaborate sweets.

Diététique DJ Fayer
Map 4, C12. 45 rue St-Paul, 4e.
Mo St-Paul.
Mon–Sat 9.30am–1.30pm &
2.30–8.45pm.
One of the city's oldest

specialists in dietary,
macrobiotic and vegetarian
fare.

Divay
Map 7, off E1. 4 rue Bayen,
17e. Mo Ternes.
Tues–Sun 8am–1.30pm &
3.30–7.30pm; closed Wed pm,
Sun pm & Aug.
Purveyor of *foie gras*,
choucroute, *saucisson* and
suchlike.

Fauchon
Map 7, N4. 26 place de la
Madeleine, 8e. Mo Madeleine.
Mon–Sat 9.40am–7pm.
Carries an amazing range of
super-plus groceries and
wine, all at exorbitant prices;
there's a self-service counter
for pâtisseries and *plats du
jour*, and a *traiteur* which stays
open a little later, until
8.30pm.

Goldenberg's
Map 4, C11. 7 rue des Rosiers,
4e. Mo St-Paul.
Daily 9am–2am.
Superlative Jewish deli and
restaurant, specializing in
charcuterie.

FOOD AND DRINK

Hédiard

Map 7, N4. 21 place de la Madeleine, 8ᵉ. Mᵒ Madeleine. Mon–Sat 8am–10pm.
Since 1850 the aristocrat's grocer. Several other branches throughout the city.

La Maison de l'Escargot

Map 6, off A9. 79 rue Fondary, 15ᵉ. Mᵒ Dupleix.
Tues–Sat 9am–7.30pm, Sun 9am–1pm; closed mid-July to Sept.
As the name suggests, this place specializes in snails: they even sauce them and re-shell them while you wait.

Mariage Frères

Map 4, B10. 30 rue du Bourg-Tibourg, 4ᵉ. Mᵒ Hôtel de Ville. Daily 10.30am–7.30pm.
Hundreds of teas, neatly packed in tins, line the floor-to-ceiling shelves of this 100-year-old tea emporium. There is a *salon de thé* in the back with exquisite pastries (daily noon–7pm).

À la Mère de Famille

Map 3, H7. 35 rue du Faubourg-Montmartre, 9ᵉ. Mᵒ Le Peletier.
Tues–Sat 8.30am–1.30pm & 3–7pm.
An eighteenth-century confiserie serving *marrons glacés*, prunes from Agen, dried fruit, sweets, chocolates and even some wines.

Poilâne

Map 2, C9. 8 rue du Cherche-Midi, 6ᵉ. Mᵒ Sèvres-Babylone. Mon–Sat 7.15am–8.15pm.
Bakes bread to ancient and secret family recipes; there is always a queue.

Rendez-Vous de la Nature

Map 2, H13. 96 rue Mouffetard, 5ᵉ. Mᵒ Cardinal Lemoine.
Tues–Sat 9.30am–7.30pm, Sun 9.30am–noon.
One of the city's most comprehensive health-food stores, with everything from organic produce to herbal teas.

FOOD AND DRINK

MUSIC

New **cassettes and CDs** are not particularly cheap in
Paris, but there are plenty of secondhand bargains, and you
may come across selections that are novel enough to tempt
you. Like the live music scene, there are albums of
Brazilian, Caribbean, Antillais, African and Arab sounds
that would be specialist rarities in London or the States, and
there's every kind of jazz.

Afric' Music
Map 6, off I14. 3 rue des
Plantes, 14e. Mo Mouton-
Duvernet.
Mon–Sat 10am–7pm.
A small shop with an
original selection of
African, Caribbean and
reggae discs.

BPM Records
Map 4, G12. 1 rue Keller, 11e.
Mo Bastille.
Mon–Sat noon–8pm.
Specialists in house, including
acid, hip-hop, rap, techno
and dub. A good place to
pick up club flyers.

Camara
Map 3, off J1. 45 rue
Marcadet, 18e. Mo Marcadet-
Poissonnière. Mon–Sat
noon–8pm.

The best selection of West
African music on cassette and
video in town.

Crocodisc
Map 2, G10. 40–42 rue des
Écoles, 5e. Mo Maubert-
Mutualité.
Tues–Sat 11am–7pm.
Folk, Oriental, Afro-Antillais,
funk, reggae, salsa, rap, soul,
country, new and
secondhand. Some of the best
prices in town.

Crocojazz
Map 2, G10. 64 rue de la
Montagne-Ste-Geneviève, 5e;
40 & 42 rue des Ecoles, 5e (all
Mo Maubert-Mutualité).
Tues–Sat 11am–1pm & 2–7pm.
Mainly new imports: jazz,
blues, gospel and country.

Dream Store

Map 2, F8. 4 place St-Michel, 6ᵉ. Mᵒ St-Michel.
Mon 1.30pm–7.15pm, Tues–Sat 9.30am–7.15pm.
Good discounts on jazz and classical in particular but also rock and folk.

FNAC Musique

Map 4, E12. 4 place de la Bastille, 12ᵉ, next to opera house. Mᵒ Bastille.
Mon–Sat 10am–8pm, Wed till 10pm.
Extremely stylish shop in black, grey and chrome, with computerized catalogues, books, every variety of music, and a concert booking agency. The other many branches of FNAC also sell music and hi-fi; the branch at 24 bd des Italiens, 9ᵉ, has a greater emphasis on rock and popular music, and stays open till midnight.

Paul Beuscher

Map 4, E11–12. 15–29 bd Beaumarchais, 4ᵉ. Mᵒ Bastille.
Mon–Fri 9.45am–12.30pm & 2–7pm, Sat 9.45am–7pm.
A music department store that's been going strong for over a hundred years.
Instruments, scores, books, recording equipment, etc.

Virgin Megastore

Map 7, H3. 56–60 av des Champs-Élysées, 8ᵉ (Mᵒ Franklin-D-Roosevelt); and Carrousel du Louvre, 1ᵉʳ (Mᵒ Louvre–Rivoli).
Mon–Sat 10am–midnight, Sun noon–midnight.
The biggest and trendiest of all Paris's music shops. Concert booking agency and expensive internet connection.

SPORT AND OUTDOOR PURSUITS

- -

Le Ciel Est à Tout le Monde

Map 2, F12. 10 rue Gay-Lussac, 5ᵉ. RER Luxembourg.
Mon–Sat 10am–7pm; closed Mon in Aug.
The best kite shop in Europe. It also sells frisbees, boomerangs, etc, plus books and traditional toys.

Nomades

Map 4, D–E13. 37 bd Bourdon,

4ᵉ. Mᵒ Bastille.
Mon–Fri 11am–7pm, Sat & Sun
10am–7pm.
The place to buy and rent
rollerblades and equipment,
with its own bar out back
where you can find out about
the scene.

Au Vieux Campeur
Map 2, F10. 48 rue des Écoles,
5ᵉ. Mᵒ Maubert-Mutualité.
Mon–Fri 10.30am–7.30pm, Wed
till 9pm, Sat 9.30am–8pm.
Maps, guides, climbing,
hiking, camping, ski gear,
plus a kids' climbing wall.

For more information on bicycle and rollerblade rentals, see
p.311.

MARKETS

Paris's **markets**, like its shops, are grand spectacles.
Mouthwatering arrays of **food** from half the countries of
the globe, captivating in colour, shape and smell, assail the
senses in even the drabbest parts of town. In addition, there
are street markets of **secondhand goods** (the flea markets,
or *marchés aux puces*), **clothes** and **textiles**, **flowers**, **birds**,
books and **stamps**. Though all have semi-official opening
and closing hours, many begin business in advance and drag
on till dusk.

SECONDHAND AND FLEA MARKETS

Marché aux Livres
Map 1, D6. Pavillon Baltard,
Parc Georges-Brassens, rue
Brancion, 15ᵉ. Mᵒ Porte-de-
Vanves. Sat & Sun 9am–6pm.
Secondhand and antiquarian
books.

Marché aux Timbres
Map 7, K4. Junction of avs
Marigny and Gabriel, 8ᵉ. Mᵒ
Champs-Élysées–Clemenceau.

Thurs, Sat, Sun & hols
10am–dusk.
Paris's best stamp market.

Porte de Montreuil
Map 1, H5. 20ᵉ. Mᵒ Porte-de-Montreuil.
Sat, Sun & Mon 7am–5pm.
Best of the flea markets for secondhand clothes – cheapest on Mon when leftovers from the weekend are sold off. Also good for old furniture, household goods and assorted junk.

Porte de Vanves
Map 1, D6. Av Georges-Lafenestre/av Marc-Sangnier, 14ᵉ. Mᵒ Porte-de-Vanves.
Sat & Sun 7am–1.30pm.
The best choice for bric-a-brac.

St-Ouen
Map 1, E1. 18ᵉ. Mᵒ Porte-de-Clignancourt.
Sat, Sun & Mon 7.30am–7pm.
The biggest and most touristy flea market, with stalls selling new and secondhand clothes, shoes, records, books and junk of all sorts, as well as expensive antiques.

For more information on the St-Ouen flea market, see p.116.

FOOD MARKETS

Food markets usually start between 7am and 8am and tail off around 1pm. Details of locations and days of operation are given below. The covered markets have specific opening hours, which are also detailed below.

Belleville
Map 4, G4–H5. Bd de Belleville, 20ᵉ. Mᵒ Belleville & Mᵒ Ménilmontant. Tues & Fri.

Buci
Map 2, E8. Rue de Buci & rue de Seine, 6ᵉ. Mᵒ Mabillon.
Tues–Sun.

FOOD MARKETS

Carmes

Map 2, G10–H10. Place Maubert, 5ᵉ. Mᵒ Maubert-Mutualité.
Tues, Thurs & Sat.

Convention

Map 6, off A12. Rue de la Convention, 15ᵉ. Mᵒ Convention.
Tues, Thurs & Sun.

Dejean

Map 3, J2. Place du Château-Rouge, 18ᵉ. Mᵒ Château-Rouge. Tues–Sun.

Edgar-Quinet

Map 6, H11. Bd Edgar-Quinet, 14ᵉ. Mᵒ Edgar-Quinet.
Wed & Sat.

Enfants-Rouges

Map 4, C7–8. 39 rue de Bretagne, 3ᵉ. Mᵒ Filles-du-Calvaire.
Tues–Sat 8am–1pm & 4–7pm, Sun 9am–1pm.

Monge

Map 2, H13. Place Monge, 5ᵉ. Mᵒ Monge.
Wed, Fri & Sun.

Montorgueil

Map 2, G4. Rue Montorgueil & rue Montmartre, 1er. Mᵒ Châtelet-Les Halles & Mᵒ Sentier.
Tues–Sat 8am–1pm & 4pm–7pm, Sun 9am–1pm.

Mouffetard

Map 2, H13–14. Rue Mouffetard, 5ᵉ. Mᵒ Censier-Daubenton.
Tues–Sun.

Place d'Aligre

Map 4, G14. 12ᵉ. Mᵒ Ledru-Rollin.
Tues–Sun until 1pm.

Port-Royal

Map 2, D14. Bd Port-Royal, nr Val-de-Grâce, 5ᵉ. RER Port-Royal. Tues, Thurs & Sat.

Porte-St-Martin

Map 3, L8. Rue du Château-d'Eau, 10ᵉ. Mᵒ Château-d'Eau.
Tues–Sat 8am–1pm & 4–7.30pm, Sun 8am–1pm.

Raspail

Map 2, B10. Bd Raspail, between rue du Cherche-Midi & rue de Rennes, 6ᵉ. Mᵒ Rennes.
Tues & Fri. Organic on Sun.

FOOD MARKETS

Rue Cler
Map 6, B3–C4. 7e. Mo École-Militaire.
Tues–Sat.

Rue de Lévis
Map 3, off A4. 17e. Mo Villiers.
Tues–Sun.

Rue du Poteau
Map 3, off G1. 18e. Mo Jules-Joffrin.
Tues–Sat.

Saint-Germain
Map 2, D9. rue Mabillon, 6e. Mo Mabillon.
Tues–Sat 8am–1pm & 4–7.30pm, Sun 8am–1pm.

Secrétan
Map 4, off F1. av Secrétan/rue Riquet, 19e. Mo Bolivar.
Tues–Sat 8am–1pm & 4–7.30pm, Sun 8am–1pm.

Tang Frères
Map 5, I8. 48 av d'Ivry, 13e. Mo Porte-d'Ivry.
Tues–Sun 9am–7.30pm.
Not really a market, but a vast emporium of all things oriental.

Ternes
Map 7, off E1. Rue Lemercier, 17e. Mo Ternes.
Tues–Sat 8am–1pm & 4–7.30pm, Sun 8am–1pm.

FOOD MARKETS

Kids' Paris

With its vibrant street atmosphere, buskers and lively pavement cafés, Paris holds an immediate appeal for many **children**. The most popular tourist attractions such as the Eiffel Tower and boat trips on the Seine are also sure to delight the young. Don't necessarily rule out museums – some, such as the Musée des Arts et Métiers, Pompidou Centre and Parc de la Villette, have interactive displays and hands-on activities, designed to appeal to all ages. When your children get fed up of trawling the streets you can recharge batteries in one of the city's many parks and gardens. And if you really want to give the kiddies a treat, Disneyland Paris is just outside the city, and there's also the home-grown theme park to the north, Parc Astérix.

The French are extremely welcoming to children on the whole. Many **restaurants** and cafés offer a special menu *enfant* or are willing to cook simpler food on request. **Hotels** tack on only a small supplement to the regular room rate for an additional bed or cot.

PARKS AND GARDENS

Children are well catered for by the **parks and gardens** within the city. There's even a park designed especially for kids, the **Jardin d'Acclimatation**, in the Bois de Boulogne, with an impressive array of activities and attractions. On the other side of the city in the Bois de Vincennes, the **Parc Floral** also offers a host of treats, and the high-tech **Parc de la Villette** (described on p.123), in the northeast of the city, will keep children entertained for hours. Most of the city's other parks have some activities for children, usually an enclosed playground with swings, climbing frames and often a sandpit. Many also have **guignol** (puppet) shows, the French equivalent of Punch and Judy.

THE JARDIN D'ACCLIMATATION

Map 1, B3–4. Bois de Boulogne. Daily: Oct–May 10am–6pm; June–Sept 10am–7pm; special attractions Wed, Sat, Sun & all week during school hols. Admission 13F/€1.98, children 6.5F/€1, under-3s free; rides from 10F/€1.52. Mº Les Sablons & Mº Porte-Maillot.

The **Jardin d'Acclimatation**, within the Bois de Boulogne, is a cross between a funfair, zoo and amusement park. The fun starts at the Porte-Maillot métro stop: a little train runs from near here, behind *L'Orée du Bois* restaurant, to the *jardin* (every 10min, 11am–6pm; 25F/€3.81 ticket combines return ride and entry to park). The park's attractions range from bumper cars, go-karts, pony and camel rides, sea lions, birds, bears and monkeys, to a magical mini-canal ride (*la rivière enchantée*; 11F/€1.68), distorting mirrors, a huge trampoline, scaled-down farm buildings and a puppet theatre with free shows at 3 & 4pm daily. There are also two museums: the brand-new high-tech **Exploradôme** is designed to help children discover science, the five human senses and art through interactive computer-based exhibits and the usual array of hands-on activities. The **Musée en Herbe** (Mon–Fri & Sun 10am–6pm, Sat 2–6pm; 16F/€2.44, 4–18s 13F/€1.98, under-4s free) aims to bring alive art history through workshops and games. The park also has its own theatre, the **Théâtre du Jardin pour l'Enfance et la Jeunesse**, which puts on musicals, ballets and poetry readings. Outside the *jardin*, in the **Bois de Boulogne** (see p.140), older children can amuse themselves with mini-golf and bowling, boating on the Lac Inférieur or roaming the wood's 14km of cycle trails (rentals near the entrance to the *jardin*).

Guignol puppet shows in the Jardin d'Acclimatation take place on Wednesday and weekend afternoons (and more frequently in the summer holidays), last about 45 minutes and cost 13–24F/€1.98–3.66; see the "Enfants" section of *Pariscope* for more details.

PARC FLORAL

Map 1, H–I6. Bois de Vincennes, on route de la Pyramide (Mº Château-de-Vincennes, then bus #112 or a 10-min walk past the Château Vincennes). Daily: March–Sept 9.30am–8pm; Oct–Feb 9.30am–5pm. Admission 10F/€1.52, 6- to 10-year-olds 5F/€.76 plus supplements for some activities, under-6s free.
Ⓦ *www.parcfloraldeparis.com*

To the delight of kids, the **Parc Floral** has much more than just flowers. It's known for its excellent playground, with slides, swings, ping-pong (racket and ball 30F/€4.57) and pedal carts (from 2pm; 42–60F/€6.40–€9.15 per half-hour), mini-golf (from 2pm; 30F/€4.57, children under 12 18F/€2.74), an electric car circuit, and a little train touring all the gardens (April–Oct daily 10.30am–5pm; 6F/€0.91). Tickets for the paying activities are sold at the playground between 1.45pm and 5.30pm weekdays and until 7pm on weekends; activities stop fifteen minutes afterwards. At 2.30pm on Wednesdays from May to September, there are free puppet shows and performances by clowns and magicians. A further programme of mime and other shows is put on at the **Théâtre Astral** (Wed & school hols 3pm, Sat 3.30pm, Sun & public hols April–Oct 4.30pm, Nov–March 3.30pm; 34F/€5.18; ☎01.43.71.31.10). Another hit with kids is the wonderful **butterfly garden** (mid-May to mid-Oct Mon–Fri 1.30–5.15pm, Sat & Sun 1.30pm–6pm).

JARDIN DES ENFANTS AUX HALLES

Map 2, F–G4. 105 rue Rambuteau, 1er ☎01.45.08.07.18. Mo/RER Châtelet-Les Halles. 7–11-year-olds only except Sat am; summer Tues–Thurs & Sat 10am–7pm, Fri 2–5pm, Sun 1–7pm; winter till 4pm; closed Mon & during bad weather; 2.50F/€.38 per hour. Right in the centre of town, just west of the Forum des Halles, the **Jardin des Enfants aux Halles** is a series of cleverly designed fantasy landscapes supervised by professional child-carers. In order to drop off your child, you have to reserve a place an hour or so in advance. Under-7s are allowed in on Saturday mornings (10am–2pm) only, provided they are accompanied by an adult. Several languages are spoken, including English. Opening times vary a little in the middle of the day, so it might be best to phone ahead.

FUNFAIRS

Three big **funfairs** (*fête foraines*) take place in Paris each year. The season kicks off in late March with the Fête du Trône in the Bois de Vincennes (running until late May), followed by the funfair in the Tuileries gardens in mid-June to late August, with more than forty rides including a giant ferris wheel, and ending up with the Fête à Neu Neu, held near the Bois de Boulogne from early September to the beginning of October. Look up "Fêtes Populaires" under "Agendas" in *Pariscope* for details if you're in town at these times.

Out of season, rue de Rivoli around St-Paul métro stop occasionally hosts a mini-fairground, and there's usually a merry-go-round at the Forum des Halles and beneath Tour St-Jacques at Châtelet. Merry-go-rounds for smaller children are to be found on place de la République, at the Rond-Point des Champs-Élysées by avenue Matignon, at place de la Nation, and at the base of the Montmartre funicular in place St-Pierre. The going rate for a ride is 10F/€1.53.

CIRCUSES

Circuses (*cirques*) are taken seriously in France and come under the heading of culture as performance art (and there are no qualms about performing animals). As circuses tend to travel, you'll find details of the seasonal ones under "Cirques" in the "Jeunes" section of *L'Officiel des Spectacles* and under the same heading in the "Enfants" section of *Pariscope*. The Cirque Diana Moreno Bormann, Grands Sablons, at the Jardin d'Acclimatation, 16ᵉ (℡01.45.00.23.01; Mº Sablons) is a perennial favorite; admission prices start at 70F/€10.67.

MUSEUMS

One of the city's best treats for children of every age from three upwards is the **Cité des Sciences** (described on p.123) in the Parc de la Villette. A number of other museums may also appeal to children, for example the under-touristed **Musée des Arts Africains et Océaniens** (see p.134), with its masks, tropical fish and live crocodiles; the **Grande Galerie de l'Évolution** (see p.78) offers a children's discovery room on the first floor with child-level microscopes, glass cases with live caterpillars and moths and a burrow of Mongolian rodents. Doll-lovers should enjoy the **Musée de la Poupée** (see p.58). The **Pompidou Centre** (see p.55) has a children's *espace*, consisting of a room filled with hands-on exhibits. Paris has two excellent **planetariums**, in the Palais de la Découverte (see p.41) and the Cité des Sciences (p.123).

For a more earthy experience, you could visit **les égouts** – the sewers – at place de la Résistance, in the 7ᵉ. Dank, damp, dripping, claustrophobic and filled with echoes, this is just the sort of place pre-teens love. For further details, see p.91. Another underground experience popular with youngsters is the **catacombs** at 1 place Denfert-Rochereau, 14ᵉ, described on p.102.

SHOPS

The fact that Paris is filled with beautiful, enticing, delicious and expensive things all artfully displayed is not lost on most modern youngsters. Toys, gadgets and clothing are all bright, colourful and very appealing, while the sheer amount of ice cream, chocolate, candy, and sweets of all shapes and sizes is almost overwhelming. Below is a small selection of shops to seek out, be dragged into or to avoid at all costs.

BOOKS

The following stock a good selection of English books, though prices are not cheap.

Brentano's
Map 3, E9. 37 av de l'Opéra, 2ᵉ
℡ 01.42.61.52.50
Ⓦ *www.brentanos.fr* Mᵒ Opéra.
Mon–Sat 10am–7pm.

Storytelling sessions, singing and crafts on Wednesday afternoons and Saturday mornings. Call first to check.

SHOPS

Chantelivre
Map 2, B9.13 rue de Sèvres, 6ᵉ
ⓣ 01.45.48.87.90. Mᵒ Sèvres-
Babylone.
Mon 1–6.50pm, Tues–Sat
10am–6.50pm; closed
mid–Aug.

A huge selection of
everything to do with and for
children, including good
picture books for the younger
ones, an English section, and
a play area.

TOYS AND GAMES

In addition to the shops listed below, department stores,
such as **Galeries Lafayette** (see p.286), large speciality
stores like **FNAC Junior** at 19 rue Vavin, 6ᵉ (Mᵒ Vavin)
and museum boutiques, particularly the **Cité des
Sciences**, have an enormous selection of books, models,
games and toys covering a wide price range.

**Le Ciel Est à Tout le
Monde**
Map 2, F12. 10 rue Gay-
Lussac, 5ᵉ ⓣ 01.46.33.21.50
(RER Luxembourg); 7 av
Trudaine, 9ᵉ ⓣ 01.48.78.93.40
(Mᵒ Anvers).
Mon–Sat 10.30am–7pm.
The best kite shop in Europe
also sells frisbees,
boomerangs, etc, and, next
door, books, slippers, mobiles
and traditional wooden toys.

Au Nain Bleu
Map 7, N4. 406–410 rue St-
Honoré, 8ᵉ ⓣ 01.42.60.39.01.

Mᵒ Madeleine.
Mon–Sat 9.45am–6.30pm;
closed Mon in Aug.
Since opening in the 1830s,
Au Nain Bleu have become
experts at delighting children
with wooden toys, dolls and
faux china tea sets galore.

Puzzles Michèle Wilson
Map 6, F14.116 rue du
Château, 14ᵉ ⓣ 01.43.22.18.47.
Mᵒ Pernety.
Mon–Fri 8.30am–8pm, Sat
10am–8pm.
Puzzles galore; with
workshop on the premises.

SHOPS

Si Tu Veux
Map 2, 1E. 68 galerie Vivienne,
2ᵉ ⓣ 01.42.60.59.97.
Mᵒ Bourse.

Mon–Sat 10.30am–7pm.
Well-made traditional toys,
plus do-it-yourself and ready-
made costumes.

CLOTHES

Besides the specialist shops listed here, most of the big
department stores and the discount shops have children's
sections.

Dipaki
Map 2, B6. 46 rue de
l'Université, 7ᵉ
ⓣ 01.42.97.49.89. Mᵒ Rue de
Bac. Also at 23 other
addresses.
Mon–Sat 10am–7pm.
Dependable, hard-wearing
and reasonably priced clothes
for up to 14-year-olds.

Lara et les Garçons
Map 2, B11. 60 rue St-Placide,
6ᵉ ⓣ 01.45.44.01.89. Mᵒ St-
Placide.
Mon noon–7pm, Tues–Sat
10am–7pm.
One of several samples and
seconds clothes shops for
children on this street. Cute
little "Marin" blue-and-
white sailors' caps from

20F/€3.05 to make your
baby look very French.

Du Pareil au Même
Map 4, G13. 122 rue du
Faubourg-St-Antoine, 12ᵉ
ⓣ 01.43.44.47.66. Mᵒ Ledru-
Rollin.
Mon–Sat 10am–7pm.
Beautiful kids' clothing at
very good prices. Gorgeous
inexpensive floral dresses,
cute jogging suits, and
bright-coloured basics.
Branches all over Paris.

Pom d'Api
Map 2, F4. 13 rue du Jour, 1ᵉʳ
ⓣ 01.42.36.08.87. Mᵒ/RER
Châtelet-Les Halles.
Mon–Sat 10.30am–7pm.
The most colourful,

imaginative and well-made shoes for kids in Paris (up to size 40/UK7, and from 250F/€38.11).

Unishop

Map 2, I5. 4 rue Rambuteau, 3ᵉ ⓣ01.42.78.07.81. Mᵒ Rambuteau.
Very cheap and cheerful kids' clothes: vibrant selection of zebra leggings, teeny hooded sweatshirts and floral dresses.

Au Vieux Campeur

Map 2, F10. 48 rue des Écoles, 5ᵉ ⓣ01.53.10.48.48. Mᵒ Cluny-La Sorbonne.
Mon 2–7pm, Tues, Thurs & Fri 10.30am–7.30pm, Wed 10.30am–9pm, Sat 10am–7.30pm.
The best camping and sporting equipment range in Paris, spread over several shops in the quartier. The special attraction for kids is a climbing wall.

See Chapter 20 for listings of department stores and other clothes shops.

THEME PARKS

Disneyland Paris has put all Paris's other **theme parks** in the shade and is one of the country's top visitor attractions. The enchanted kingdom certainly works its magic on most children, though if you're prepared to make the effort to get there, **Parc Astérix** theme park, north of Paris, is better mind-fodder and cheaper than Disney.

DISNEYLAND PARIS

There are no two ways about it, children will love **Disneyland Paris**, 25km east of the capital. What their minders will think of it is another matter. It is expensive, crowded and sugar-coated. The best time to come is off-season on a weekday, especially Monday & Thursday, when

THEME PARKS

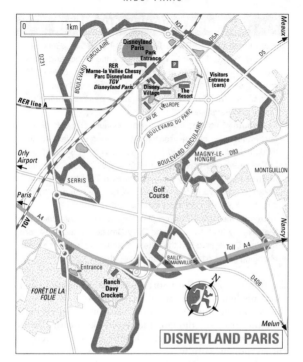

0   1km

DISNEYLAND PARIS

you will probably get round every ride you want. Otherwise, one-hour queues for the popular rides are common in the middle of the day. All told, the enchanted city shines far brighter than the enchanted kingdom.

Information, access and regulations

Information about the day's events is available just inside the entrance in a building called the **City Hall**. You can

THEME PARKS

GETTING TO DISNEYLAND PARIS

From Paris, take **RER line A** (Châtelet-Les Halles, Gare-de-Lyon, Nation) to Marne-la-Vallée/Chessy, the Disneyland Paris stop. The journey takes about 40min, and costs 76F/€11.59 return (38F/€5.79 child, under-3s free). For prices of one-, two- and three-day *Paris Visites* transport passes, including Disneyland Paris, see p.13.

A **shuttle bus** runs from Charles de Gaulle and Orly (times and frequencies change seasonally, but roughly every 45min 8.30am–8pm; for recorded information call ☎01.64.30.66.56; 85F/€12.96 one-way, children 65F/€9.91, under-3s free). Marne-la-Vallée/Chessy also has its own TGV train station, linked to Lille, Lyon and London: Eurostar (see p.9) runs trains direct from London Waterloo and Ashford in Kent.

By **car**, the park is 32km east of Paris along the A4 direction Metz/Nancy (exit 13 for Ranch Davy Crockett and exit 14 for the Parc Disneyland and the hotels); from Calais follow the A26 changing to the A1, the A104 and finally the A4.

also find out about the resort's hotels and evening's entertainments here. Visitors are allowed to smoke in the park, but not in the queues, and may not bring food or drink onto the grounds, though discreet snacks are the norm. When the park first opened, alcohol was not served – a Disney policy worldwide – a rule that was quickly dispensed with by balking Europeans, who reminded the paternalistic corporation that the park is, after all, in France.

The attractions and parades

The park is divided into four "lands": Frontierland, Fantasyland, Adventureland and Discoverland. The starting point is **Main Street USA** which leads to Central Plaza, the hub of the standard radial layout. As the guide you get on entry covers the park in a clockwise direction, you

THEME PARKS

might consider approaching it in the opposite direction to avoid the longest queues – some of which require a wait of up to one hour. A steam train Railroad runs round the park, with stations at each "land" and at the entrance. Apart from some height restrictions, there is little guidance about the suitability of rides for small children, though several stand out as ones to avoid. The *Pirates of the Caribbean* might frighten little ones, *Big Thunder Mountain* is too violent for

ADMISSION FEES FOR THE PARK

	Low season Oct–March excl Christmas hols	High season April–Sept & 3rd week Dec to 1st week Jan
1 day	160/130F/€24.50/19.9	220/170F/€33.70/26
2 days	310/250F/€47.50/38.30	425/330F/€65/50.50
3 days	435/355F/€66.60/54.30	595/460F/€ 91.10/70.40

Reduced tariff: children aged 3–11; under-3s free.

Passes, known as "passports", can be purchased in advance – this is highly advised in order to avoid long queues at the park itself – at the Paris Tourist Office and at all Disney shops, or you can buy admission passes and train tickets in Paris at all RER line A and B stations and in major métro stations. You can come and go during the day – your wrist is stamped with invisible ink when you leave the park, allowing you to return. Multi-day passes don't have to be used on consecutive days.

Opening hours vary greatly depending on the season and whether it's a weekend. Generally, low-season opening hours are Mon–Fri 10am–6pm, Sat & Sun till 8pm; high-season daily 9am–11pm, but check exact hours before you buy your ticket (you can check the internet on Ⓦ *www.disneylandparis.com*).

THEME PARKS

any child under about eight, and *Honey, I Shrunk The Audience* is too intense for most young children. For the tiniest tots, Fantasyland is likely to be the most fun as there are no height restrictions here, rides are generally gentle, and the atmosphere is less manic. Adventureland has the most outlandish sets and its centrepiece, Adventure Isle, provides a low-key place to take a break. Boat trips in canoes, keelboats and a paddle-steamer are to be had in Frontierland. Bone-rattling thrills are to be had on the *Space Mountain* ride or *Indiana Jones and the Temple of Doom* (*Le Temple du Péril*) ride. All rides provide the twists, turns, surprises, and sound effects expected of a theme park.

For small children, almost as exciting as the attractions is **La Parade Disney**, which happens every day at 3pm and also at 6pm in July and August, lasts for half an hour and manages to represent all the top box-office Disney movies. Two good spots for viewing are on the queuing ramp for *It's a Small World*, right by the gates through which the floats appear, and in front of the Fantasyland Castle.

Disney Village and the hotels

When the park gates close it's festival time in the **Disney Village** entertainment and restaurant complex next to the RER station. Numerous theme restaurants await you with live music on summer nights: bluegrass bands, rock'n'roll and the Top 40 hits. And, if you aren't on sensory overload, there's always the new multiplex cinema where you can catch a flick – Disney, of course.

If you haven't had enough enchantment, consider staying in a themed **hotel**. The frilly pastel-pink *Disneyland Hotel* is the most upmarket (1600F/€243.90 off-season to 2590F/€394.82 in peak season), followed by the Art Deco *Hotel New York* (1000–1780F/€152.44–271.34). The more mid-range *Newport Bay Club* (885F/€134.91,

375F/€209.60 peak season) is modelled on a "New England seaside resort circa 1900," while the *Sequoia Lodge* (775F/€118.14 to over 1255F/€191.31) has a distinct "mountain lodge" feel. The *Hotel Cheyenne* (615F/€93.75 to 1050F/€160) makes the most sense for families since all the rooms have bunk beds, and the *Hotel Santa Fe* (515F/€78.51 off-season to 780F/€118.90 in peak season) is New Mexico right down to the junked cars in the yard. All hotels can be reached by hopping in and out of the free bright-yellow shuttle buses. Easily the most economical option is the *Davy Crockett Ranch*, a fifteen-minute drive from the park. Prices range from 350F/€53.35 to 850F/€129.57 for a self-catering log cabin (4–6 people) and 90F/€13.72 for the chance to park your motorcoach or pitch your tent in its gravelly campsite. The nearby *Camping du Parc de la Colline*, Route de Lagny, 77200 Torcy (☏01.60.05.42.32), welcomes campers all year round.

PARC ASTÉRIX

April–June Mon–Fri 10am–6pm, weekends 9.30am–7pm; July & Aug daily 9.30am–7pm; Sept Wed & weekends only 10am–6pm; Oct one Wed & two weekends only 10am–6pm. Closed most of Oct to early April, and for several days in May, June and Sept; check times on ☏03.44.62.34.04. Admission 175F/€26.28, 3–12s 125F/€19.05, under-3s free; at most RER and métro stations you can buy an inclusive transport and admission ticket for 219/149F/€33.38/22.71. ⓦ www.parcasterix.fr

Parc Astérix is a theme park featuring characters from the Asterix comics. It's located in Plailly, 38km north of Paris off the A1 autoroute, and is most easily reached by half-hourly shuttle bus from RER Roissy-Charles-de-Gaulle (line B). Like Disneyland, the park is divided into different areas. A Via Antiqua shopping street, with buildings from every country in the Roman Empire, leads to a Roman town where gladiators

THEME PARKS

play comic battles and dodgem chariots line up for races. There's a legionaries' camp where incompetent soldiers attempt to keep watch, and a wave-manipulated lake which you cross on galleys and longships. In the Gaulish village, Getafix mixes his potions, Obelix slaves over boars, Astérix plots further sorties against the occupiers, and the dreadful bard is exiled up a tree. In another area, street scenes of Paris show the city changing from Roman Lutetia to the present-day capital. All sorts of rides are on offer (with long queues for the best ones); dolphins and sea lions perform tricks for the crowds; there are parades and jugglers; restaurants for every budget; and most of the actors speak English. Information about Parc Astérix is available on ☎01538/702200 in the UK.

City Directory

AIDS/HIV see p.274.

AIRLINES Aer Lingus, 47 av de l'Opéra, 2e (℡ 01.47.42.12.50,
🖝 www.aerlingus.ie); Air Canada, 106 bd Haussmann, 8^e
(℡ 08.20.87.08.71, 🖝 www.aircanada.ca); Air France, 119 av des
Champs-Élysées, 8e (℡ 01.42.99.21.01 or 08.02.80.28.02,
🖝 www.airfrance.fr); British Airways, 12 rue Castiglione, 1er
(℡ 08.25.82.54.00, 🖝 www.british-airways.com); British Midland, 4
pl de Londres, Roissy-en-France 95700 (℡ 01.48.62.55.65,
🖝 www.iflybritishmidland.com); Delta, 4 rue Scribe, 9^e
(℡ 01.47.68.92.92, 🖝 www.delta-air.com); Qantas, 7 rue Scribe, 9^e
(℡ 01.44.55.52.05, 🖝 www.qantas.com.au).

AIRPORT INFORMATION Roissy-Charles de Gaulle
(℡ 01.48.62.22.80 for recording in English; Orly (℡ 01.49.75.15.15);
see p.5 for more details.

AMERICAN EXPRESS, 11 rue Scribe, 9e (℡ 01.47.77.79.50; M°
Opéra). Bureau de change open Mon–Fri 9am–6pm, Sat 9am–5pm,
Sun 10am–4pm, public hols 9am–5pm. In a pinch, there is
Chequepoint, open 24 hours every day, 150 av des Champs-
Élysées, 8e (℡ 01.49.53.02.51; M° Charles-de-Gaulle–Etoile).

BIKE RENTAL Charges start from about 80F/€12.20 a day with a
caution (deposit) of 1000–2500F/€152.44–381.10. If you want a
bike for Sunday, when all of Paris takes to the *quais*, you'll need to

book in advance. Try Paris-Vélo, 2 rue du Fer-à-Moulin, 5ᵉ (Ⓣ01.43.37.59.22; Mᵒ Censier-Daubenton) for 21-speed and mountain bikes; Paris À Vélo C'est Sympa/Vélo Bastille, 37 bd Bourdon, 4ᵉ (01.48.87.60.01; Mᵒ Bastille), which also runs good bicycle tours; Bike N'Roller, 6 rue St-Julien-Le-Pauvre, 5ᵉ (Ⓣ01.44.07.35.89, Ⓦ www.bikenroller.com; Mᵒ/RER St-Michel); or the Maison du Vélo, 11 rue Fénélon, 10ᵉ (Ⓣ01.42.81.24.72; Mᵒ Gare du Nord or Poissonnière), with summer outlets at the Gare-de-l'Est and Gare-du-Montparnasse.

BOAT TRIPS Bateaux-Mouches boat trips on the Seine start from the Embarcadère du Pont de l'Alma, on the Right Bank in the 8ᵉ (reservations Ⓣ01.42.25.96.10, information Ⓣ01.40.76.99.99; Mᵒ Alma-Marceau). The rides, which usually last an hour, depart at 11am, 11.30am, 12.15pm, 1pm and every half hour from 2pm to 10pm most of the year round; departure times are less frequent in winter (50F/€7.62, under-14s 20F/€3.05). There are also lunch and dinner trips, though these are outrageously priced and you'll need to dress smartly. The main competitors to the Bateaux-Mouches are Bateaux Parisiens (Ⓣ01.44.11.33.44; Mᵒ Trocadero), Bateaux-Vedettes de Paris (Ⓣ01.47.05.71.29; Mᵒ Bir-Hakeim) and Bateaux-Vedettes du Pont Neuf (Ⓣ1.46.33.98.38; Mᵒ Pont-Neuf). They're all much the same, and can be found detailed in *Pariscope* under "Croisières" in the "Visites-Promenades" section and in *L'Officiel des Spectacles* under "Promenades" in the "À Travers Paris" section.

An alternative way of riding on the Seine – one in which you are mercifully spared the commentary – is the Batobus (Ⓣ01.44.11.33.99); see p.16 for more details.

CUSTOMS With the Single European Market you can bring in and take out most things as long as you have paid tax on them in an EU country, and they are for personal consumption. Duty-free was abolished on June 30, 1999, for all trips beginning and ending in the EU. However, there are still personal allowance limits on what were once duty-free goods – alcohol, tobacco and perfume. Each person is allowed up to 800 cigarettes, 400 cigarillos, 200 cigars, 1kg of smoking tobacco, 90 litres of wine (no more than 60 litres of which can be sparkling wine), 10 litres of spirits, 20 litres of fortified wine and 110 litres of beer. Limits for non-EU countries are: 200 cigarettes or 250g tobacco or 50 cigars; 1 litre spirits or 2 litres fortified wine, or 2 litres sparkling wine; 2 litres table wine; 50gm perfume and 250ml toilet water.

DISABILITY For publications detailing wheelchair access in Paris, contact ADF (Association des Paralysées de France), 17 bd Auguste-Blanqui, 13ᵉ (☎ 01.40.78.69.00), which publishes *Paris comme sur des Roulettes (Paris on Wheels)* in French for 49F/€7.47; or CNRH (Comité National Français de Liaison pour la Réadaptation des Handicapés), 236bis rue Tolbiac, 13ᵉ (☎ 01.53.80.66.66), whose guide, *Paris-Île de France: Guide Touristique pour les Personnes à Mobilitée Réduite* is available in English for 60F/€9.15. In the UK, RADAR (Royal Association for Disability and Rehabilitation), 12 City Forum, 250 City Rd, London EC1 (☎ 020/7250 3222, 🖷 020/7250 0212, minicom ☎ 020/7250 4119) offers *Access in Paris* by Gordon Couch and Ben Roberts (£6.95, Quiller Press), a guide to accommodation, monuments, museums, restaurants and travel to the city.

DOCTORS see Emergencies, below.

ELECTRICITY 220V out of double, round-pin wall sockets. If you haven't bought the appropriate converter (*adapteur*) or transformer (*transformateur* – for US appliances) before leaving home, head for the electrical section of a department store, where someone is also more likely to speak English; cost is around 60F/€9.15. If you are using an appliance larger than an electric razor or a radio – a laptop computer for example – you will need an adapter capable of transforming a large electrical load. La Samaritaine (see p.286) carries such converters in its hardware section; cost is around 120F/€18.29.

DISABILITY–ELECTRICITY

EMBASSIES/CONSULATES Australia: 4 rue Jean-Rey, 15ᵉ (☏01.40.59.33.00; Mº Bir-Hakeim); Britain: 35 rue du Faubourg-St-Honoré, 8ᵉ (☏01.44.51.31.02; Mº Concorde); Canada: 35 av Montaigne, 8ᵉ (☏01.44.43.29.00; Mº Franklin-D-Roosevelt); Ireland: 4 rue Rude, 16ᵉ (☏01.44.17.67.00; Mº Charles-de-Gaulle–Étoile); New Zealand: 7ter rue Léonardo-de-Vinci, 16ᵉ (☏01.45.00.24.11; Mº Victor-Hugo); USA: rue St-Florentin, 1ᵉʳ (☏01.43.12.22.22; Mº Concorde).

EMERGENCIES Fire brigade (Sapeurs-Pompiers) ☏18; Ambulance (Service d'Aide Médicale Urgente – SAMU) ☏15; Doctor call-out (SOS Médecins) ☏01.47.07.77.77 or 01.43.37.77.77; Rape crisis (SOS Viol; Mon–Fri 10am–6pm) ☏08.00.05.95.95; SOS Help (crisis line/any problem: 3–11pm) in English ☏01.47.23.80.80. For a list of English-speaking hospitals, see below.

EURO France is one of twelve European Union countries which have changed over to a single currency, the euro (€). The transition period, which began on January 1, 1999, is however lengthy: euro notes and coins are not scheduled to be issued until January 1, 2002, with francs remaining in place for cash transactions, at a fixed rate of 1 franc to 6.56 euros, until they are scrapped entirely on February 17, 2002. Even before euro cash appears in 2002, you can opt to pay in euros by credit card and you can get travellers' cheques in euros – you should not be charged commission for changing them in any of the twelve countries in the euro zone (also known as "Euroland"), nor for changing from any of the old Euroland currencies to any other (pesetas to French francs, for example).

All prices in this book are given in francs and the exact equivalent in euros. When the new currency takes over completely, prices are likely to be rounded off – and if decimalization in the UK is anything to go by, rounded up. Euro notes will be issued in denominations of 5, 10, 20, 50, 100, 200 and 500 euros, and coins in denominations of 1, 2, 5, 10, 20 and 50 cents and 1 and 2 euros.

EXCHANGE Some of the more conveniently located bureaux de change are at: Charles-de-Gaulle airport (daily 7am–10pm) and Orly airport (daily 6.30am–11pm); Gare d'Austerlitz (Mon–Fri 7am–9pm), Gare de l'Est (summer 6.45am–10pm; winter 6.45am–7pm), Gare de Lyon (Mon–Sat 8am–8pm), Gare du Nord (8am–8pm), Gare St–Lazare (summer 8am–8pm; winter 8am–6.45pm); Office de Tourisme de Paris (127 av des Champs-Élysées, 8ᵉ; 9am–7.30pm; Mᵒ Charles-de-Gaulle–Étoile).

FILM Camera film is expensive in Paris. Stores like Monoprix will generally be cheaper than shops closer to the tourist sites. Since most museums and monuments will not allow you to use a flash, consider purchasing very high-speed film which is designed to take photos in low light.

HAMMAMS or Turkish baths, are much more luxurious than the standard Swedish sauna. Prices begin at 80F/€12.20 and rise steadily. Some worth trying include: Les Bains du Marais, 31–33 rue des Blancs-Manteaux, 4ᵉ, ☏01.44.61.02.02 (Mᵒ Rambuteau & Mᵒ St-Paul); *women:* Mon 10am–8pm & Tues 10am–11pm, *men:* Thurs 10am–11pm, Fri & Sat 10am–7pm, *mixed*: Wed & Sat 8pm–midnight, Sun 11am–11pm; Cleopatra Club, 53 bd de Belleville, 11ᵉ, ☏01.43.57.34.32 (Mᵒ Belleville),Tues–Sun 10am–6.30pm, closed Aug, women only; Hammam de la Mosquée, 39 rue Geoffroy-St-Hilaire, 5ᵉ, ☏01.43.31.38.20 (Mᵒ Censier-Daubenton), daily 10am–9pm; hours and days for men and women change, so phone first, but generally women on Mon & Wed–Sat and men on Tues & Sun; closed Aug.

HOSPITALS English-speaking hospitals include the American Hospital, 63 bd Victor-Hugo, Neuilly-sur-Seine (☏ 01.46.41.25.25; Mᵒ Porte Maillot then bus #82 to terminus); and the Hertford British Hospital, 3 rue Barbès, Levallois-Perret (☏ 01.46.39.22.22; Mᵒ Anatole-France).

INTERNET ACCESS You can stay online while travelling at the following cybercafés. Expect to pay approximately 1F/€0.15 per minute. *Cybercafé Latino*, 13 rue de l'Ecole-Polytechnique, 5e (see "Eating & Drinking", p.211); *Cyber Cube*, 5 rue Mignon, 6e, Mº Grands-Boulevards (Mon–Sat 10am–10pm); *Phonebook of the World*, 11–15 rue des Halles, 1er, Mº Châtelet (Ⓦ www.phonebookoftheworld.com); *Web 46*, 46 rue de Roi-de-Sicile, 4e, Mº St-Paul (Mon–Fri 11am–midnight, Sat noon–9pm, Sun 1pm–midnight); *Web Bar*, 32 rue de Picardie, 3e (see "Eating & Drinking", p.203). In addition, most post offices now have a computer geared up for public internet access. You need to buy a card first (50F/€7.62, including 1hr connection) which can be recharged at 30F/€4.57 for an hour's connection.

LAUNDRY Self-service laundries have multiplied in Paris over the last few years, and you'll probably find one near where you're staying. If you can't immediately spot one, look in the phone book under "Laveries Automatiques". They're often unattended, so come pre-armed with small change. The smallest machines cost around 22F/€3.35 for a load, though some laundries only have bigger machines and charge around 45F/€6.86. Dryers run about 2F/€0.46 for 5min. Generally, self-service laundry facilities open at 7am and close between 7pm and 9pm. The alternative *blanchisserie*, or pressing services, are likely to be expensive, and hotels in particular charge very high rates. If you're doing your own washing in hotels, keep quantities small as most forbid doing any laundry in your room.

LEFT LUGGAGE Located at all the main train stations. You cannot leave luggage at the airports.

LOST BAGGAGE Airports: Orly (☏ 01.49.75.04.53); Charles de Gaulle (☏ 01.48.62.10.86).

LOST PROPERTY Bureau des Objets Trouvés, Préfecture de Police, 36 rue des Morillons, 15e; ☏ 01.55.76.20.00 (Mº Convention). Mon, Wed & Fri 8.30am–5pm, Tues & Thurs till 8pm. For property lost on public transport, phone the RATP on ☏ 01.40.06.75.27.

PHARMACIES All pharmacies, signalled by an illuminated green cross, are equipped to give first aid on request (for a fee). When closed, as many are on Sundays, they all display the address of the nearest open pharmacy. Pharmacies open at night include Dérhy/Pharmacie des Champs-Élysées, 84 av des Champs-Élysées, 8e ☏ 01.45.62.02.41; 24hr; Mo George-V); Pharmacie Européenne, 6 place de Clichy, 9e (☏ 01.48.74.65.18; 24hr; Mo Place-de-Clichy); Pharmacie des Halles, 10 bd Sébastopol, 4e (☏ 01.42.72.03.23; Mon–Sat 9am–midnight, Sun noon–midnight; Mo Châtelet); Pharmacie Matignon, 2 rue Jean-Mermoz, 8e (☏ 01.43.59.86.55; daily 8.30am–2am; Mo Franklin-D-Roosevelt); Pharmacie Internationale de Paris, 5 pl Pigalle, 9e (☏ 01.48.78.38.12; daily to 1am; Mo Pigalle); Grand Pharmacie de la Nation, 13 place de la Nation, 11e (☏ 01.43.73.24.03; Mon noon–midnight, Tues–Sat 8am–midnight, Sun 8pm–midnight; Mo Nation).

POST OFFICE Main office at 52 rue du Louvre, Paris 75001 (Mo Châtelet-Les Halles) open daily 24hr for letters, poste restante, faxes, telegrams and phone calls; currency exchange Mon–Fri 8am–7pm, Sat 8am–noon. Branch offices are located in every neighbourhood – look for the bright-yellow signs and the words "la Poste" or "le PTT" – and are generally open Mon–Fri 9am–7pm & Sat 9am–noon.

PUBLIC HOLIDAYS January 1, New Year's Day; Easter Sunday; Easter Monday; Ascension Day (40 days after Easter); Pentecost or Whitsun (seventh Sunday after Easter, plus the Monday); May 1, May Day/Labour Day; May 8, Victory in Europe Day; July 14, Bastille Day; August 15, Assumption of the Virgin Mary; November 1, All Saints' Day; November 11, 1918 Armistice Day; December 25, Christmas Day.

PUBLIC TOILETS Ask for *les toilettes* or look for signs for the WC (pronounced "vay say"); when reading the details of facilities outside hotels, don't confuse *lavabo*, which means washbasin, with lavatory. French toilets in bars are still often of the hole-in-the-ground squatting variety, and tend to lack toilet paper. Standards of cleanliness aren't always high. Toilets in railway stations and department stores are commonly staffed by attendants who will expect a bit of spare change. Some have coin-operated locks, so always keep 50 centimes and 1F and 2F pieces handy for these and for the frequent tardis-like public toilets found on the streets. These beige- or brown-coloured boxes have automatic doors which open when you insert coins to the value of two francs, and are cleaned automatically once you exit. Children under ten aren't allowed in on their own.

RADIO The main French news broadcasts are at 7.45pm on Arte and at 8pm on F2 and at TF1. English-language news on the BBC World Service can be found on 648kHz or 198kHz long wave from midnight to 5am (and Radio 4 during the day). The Voice of America transmits on 90.5, 98.8 and 102.4FM. Radio France International (RFI) broadcasts the news in English between 3 and 4pm on 738kHz AM. For radio news in French, there's the state-run France Inter (87.8FM), Europe 1 (104.7FM), or round-the-clock news on France Info (105.5FM).

ROLLERBLADING See "Bike Rental," p.311.

SAFER SEX A warning: Paris has the highest incidence of AIDS of any city in Europe; people who are HIV positive are just as likely to be heterosexual as homosexual. Condoms (*préservatifs*) are readily available at supermarkets, clubs, from dispensers on the street – often outside pharmacies – and in the métro. From pharmacies you can also get spermicidal cream and jelly (*dose contraceptive*), suppositories (*ovules*, *suppositoires*), and (with a prescription) the pill (*la pillule*), a diaphragm or IUD (*le stérilet*). Pregnancy test kits (*tests de grossesse*) are sold at pharmacies; if you need the morning-after pill (the RU624), you will have to go to a hospital.

SALES TAX What is called VAT (Value Added Tax) in Britain is referred to as TVA in France (*taxe sur la valeur ajoutée*). The standard rate in France is 20.6 percent; it's higher for luxury items and lower for essentials, but there are no exemptions (books and children's clothes are therefore more expensive than in the UK). However, non-EU residents who have been in the country for less than six months are entitled to a refund (*détaxe*) of some or all of this amount (but usually around 14 percent) if you spend at least 1200F/€182.93 in a single trip to one shop. The procedure is rather complicated: present your passport to the shop while paying and ask for the three-paged *bordereau de vente a l'exportation* form. They should help you fill it in and provide you with a self-addressed envelope. When you leave the EU, get customs to stamp the filled-in form; you will then need to send two of the pages back to the shop in the envelope within three months; the shop will then transfer the refund through your credit card or bank. The Centre de Renseignements des Douanes (☏ 01.53.24.68.24) can answer any customs-related questions.

SMOKING Laws requiring restaurants to have separate smokers' (*fumeurs*) and non-smokers' (*non-fumeurs*) areas are widely ignored. Non-smokers may well find themselves eating elbow-to-elbow alongside smokers, and waiters are not that likely to be sympathetic. Smoking is not allowed on public transport, including surburban trains, or in cinemas. Most office reception areas are non-smoking. But smoking is still a socially acceptable habit in France, and cigarettes are cheap in comparison with Britain, for example. Note that you can only buy tobacco in *tabacs*.

STUDENT INFORMATION CROUS, 39 av Georges-Bernanos, 5ᵉ (☏ 01.40.51.36.00; Mᵒ Port-Royal).

TELEPHONES You can make international phone calls from any telephone box (*cabine*) and can receive calls where there's a blue logo of a ringing bell. A 50-unit (48.60F/€7.41) and 120-unit (96.70F/€14.74) phonecard (called a *télécarte*) is essential, since coin boxes have been almost phased out. Phonecards are available from *tabacs* and newsagents as well as post offices, tourist offices and some train-station ticket offices; alternatively, you can use a credit or calling card. All calls are timed in France and off-peak charges apply on weekdays between 7pm and 8am, and after noon on Saturday until 8am Monday. For calls within France – local or long-distance – dial all ten digits of the number. For international calls, calling codes are posted in the telephone box; remember to omit the initial 0 of the local area code from the subscriber's number.

TELEVISION French TV has six terrestrial channels: three public (France 2, Arte/La Cinquième and France 3); one subscription (Canal Plus, with some unencrypted programmes); and two commercial open broadcasts (TF1 and M6). In addition, there are the **cable** networks, which include LCI (French news), CNN, the BBC World Service, BBC Prime (*Eastenders*, etc), Planète, which specializes in documentaries, Paris Première (lots of VO – *version originale* – films), and Canal Jimmy (*Friends* and the like in VO). There are several **music channels**: MTV for rock and pop, Mezzo for classical and Muzzik for classical and jazz.

TIME France is one hour ahead of Britain (Greenwich Mean Time), six hours ahead of Eastern Standard Time (eg New York), and nine hours ahead of Pacific Standard Time (eg Los Angeles). Australia is eight to ten hours ahead of France, depending on which part of the continent you're in. Remember also that France uses a 24hr clock, with, for example, 2am written as 2h and 2.30pm written as 14h30. The most confusing are noon and midnight – respectively 12h and 00h. Talking clock ☎ 36.99. Alarm ☎ 36.88, or with a digital phone dial *55* then the time in four figures (eg 0715 for 7.15am) then #. To annul, dial #55* then the time, then # (costs around 3.70F/€0.56).

TOURS The best walking tours of Paris in English are those offered by Paris Walking Tours (☎ 01.48.09.21.40; 1hr 30min; 60F/€9.15), with subjects ranging from "Hemingway's Paris" to "Historic Marais". A full list of times, meeting points and prices can be found in *Pariscope* in the *Time Out Paris* English-language section. The Paris transport authority, RATP, also runs numerous excursions, some to quite far-flung places, which are far less expensive than those offered by commercial operators. Details are available from RATP's Bureau de Tourisme, place de la Madeleine, 1ᵉ (℡ 01.40.06.71.45; Mᵒ Madeleine).

TRAFFIC & ROAD CONDITIONS For Paris's traffic jams listen to 105.1 FM (FIP) on the radio; for the *boulevard périphérique* and main routes in and out of the city, ring ℡ 01.48.99.33.33.

TRAIN INFORMATION SNCF information in English ℡ 01.45.82.08.41. Eurostar ℡ 08.36.35.35.39, Ⓦ *www.eurostar.com*; Hoverspeed SeaTrain Express ℡ 08.00.90.17.77.

TRAVEL AGENCIES Council Travel, 16 rue de Vaugirard, 6ᵉ (℡ 08.00.14.81.48; Mᵒ Odéon), is a dependable student/youth agency as is OTU Voyages, 119 rue St-Martin, 4ᵉ, opposite the Pompidou Centre (℡ 01.40.29.12.12). Access Voyages, 6 rue Pierre-Lescot, 1ᵉʳ (℡ 01.44.76.84.50; Mᵒ Châtelet-Les Halles), has cheap transatlantic and train fares.

WEATHER Paris and Île de France ℡ 08.36.68.02.75; rest of France ℡ 01.36.68.01.01. On the internet at Ⓦ *www.meteo.fr* and Ⓦ *www.weather.com*

WOMEN'S GROUPS The Maison des Femmes, 163 rue de Charenton, 12ᵉ (℡ 01.43.43.41.13, Ⓕ 01.43.43.42.13; Mᵒ Reuilly-Diderot & Mᵒ Gare-de-Lyon), is the meeting place of a myriad of women's organizations. Open Wed & Fri 4–7pm; café Fri 7–10pm. The Bibliothèque Marguerite Durand, 3rd floor, 79 rue Nationale, 13ᵉ (℡ 01.45.70.80.30; Mᵒ Tolbiac), is the first official feminist library in France. Open Tues–Sat 2–6pm.

TOURS—WOMEN'S GROUPS

CONTEXTS

A brief history of Paris

t was **Rome** that put Paris on the map, as it did the rest of western Europe. When Julius Caesar's armies arrived in 52 BC, they found a Celtic settlement confined to an island in the Seine – the Île de la Cité.

Under the name of Lutetia, it remained a **Roman colony** for the next three hundred years, prosperous commercially because of its commanding position on the Seine trade route, but insignificant politically. The Romans established their administrative centre on the Île de la Cité, and their town on the Left Bank on the slopes of the Montagne Ste-Geneviève. Though only two monuments from this period remain today – the baths by the *Hôtel de Cluny* and the amphitheatre in rue Monge – the Roman **street plan**, still evident in the north–south axis of rue St-Martin and rue St-Jacques, determined the future growth of the city.

Although Roman rule disintegrated under the impact of **Germanic invasions** around 275 AD, Paris held out until it fell to **Clovis the Frank** in 486, whose conversion to Christianity hastened the **Christianization** of the whole country. Under his successors, Paris saw the foundation of several rich and influential monasteries, especially on the Left Bank.

With the election of **Hugues Capet**, Comte de Paris, as king in 987, the fate of the city was inextricably identified with that of the **monarchy**. Recurrent political tension between the classes and the crown led to open **rebellion**, such as in 1356, when Étienne Marcel, a wealthy cloth merchant, demanded greater autonomy for the city. Further rebellions, fuelled by the hopeless poverty of the lower classes, led to the king and court abandoning the capital in 1418, not to return for more than a hundred years.

Growth of the city

As the city's livelihood depended from the first on its river-borne trade, commercial activity naturally centred on the place where the goods were landed. This was the **place de Grève** on the **Right Bank**, where the Hôtel de Ville now stands. Marshy ground originally, it was gradually drained to accommodate the business quarter. The Right Bank continues to be associated with commerce and banking today.

The **Left Bank**'s intellectual associations are similarly ancient, dating from the growth of schools and student accommodation round the two great **monasteries** of Ste-Geneviève and St-Germain-des-Prés. In 1215, a papal licence allowed the formation of what gradually became the renowned **University of Paris**, eventually to be known as **the Sorbonne**, after Robert de Sorbon, founder of a college for poor scholars.

To protect this burgeoning city, Philippe Auguste (king from 1180 to 1223) built the Louvre fortress and a defensive wall, which swung south to enclose the Montagne Ste-Geneviève and north and east to encompass the Marais. The administration of the city remained in the hands of the king until 1260, when St Louis ceded a measure of responsibility to the leaders of the Paris watermen's guild, whose power was based on their monopoly control of all river traffic.

Civil wars and foreign occupation

From the mid-thirteenth to mid-fourteenth centuries, Paris shared the same unhappy fate as the rest of France, embroiled in the long and destructive **Hundred Years War** with the English. The country reached its lowest point when the English king, Henry VI, had himself crowned king of France in Notre-Dame in 1430.

It was only when the English were expelled – from Paris in 1437 and from France in 1453 – that the economy had a chance to recover from decades of devastation. It received a further boost when **François I** decided to re-establish the royal court in Paris in 1528. He began reconstruction work on the Louvre, and built the Tuileries palace for Cathérine de Médicis.

However, before these projects could be completed, war again intervened, this time **civil war** between Catholics and Protestants. It was sparked off by the massacre of some three thousand protestants on August 25, 1572, St Bartholomew's Day. The Protestants had gathered in Paris for the wedding of Henri III's daughter, Marguerite, to Henri, the Protestant king of Navarre. They were massacred at the instigation of the Catholic Guise family. When, through his marriage, Henri of Navarre became heir to the French throne in 1584, the Guises drove his father-in-law, Henri III, out of Paris. Forced into alliance, the two Henris laid siege to the city. Five years later, Henri III having been assassinated in the meantime, Henri of Navarre entered the city as king **Henri IV**. "Paris is worth a Mass", he is reputed to have said to justify renouncing his Protestantism in order to soothe Catholic susceptibilities.

The Paris he inherited was not a very salubrious place. No domestic building had been permitted beyond the limits of Philippe-Auguste's twelfth-century walls, and the population had doubled to around 400,000, causing an acute housing shortage and a terrible strain on the rudimentary water supply and drainage system. It is said that the first workmen who went to clean out the city's cesspools in 1633 fell dead from the fumes.

Planning and expansion

The first systematic attempts at **planning** were introduced by Henri IV at the beginning of the seventeenth century: regulating street lines and uniformity of façade, and laying out the first geometric squares. The **place des Vosges** dates from this period, as does the **Pont Neuf**. Grandiose public buildings from this period perfectly symbolise the bureaucratic, centralized power of the newly self-confident state.

Louis XIV is responsible for the construction of the **boulevards** from the Madeleine to the Bastille, the places Vendôme and Victoire, the Porte St-Martin and St-Denis gateways, the Invalides, Observatoire and the Cour Carrée of the Louvre – not to mention the vast palace at **Versailles**, which Louis made the home of his court in 1671. The aristocratic *hôtels* or mansions of the Marais were also erected during this period, to be superseded early in the eighteenth century by the Faubourg St-Germain as the fashionable quarter of the rich and powerful.

The underside of all this bricks-and-mortar self-aggrandizement was the general neglect of the living conditions of the ordinary citizenry of Paris. The centre of the city remained a densely packed and insanitary warren of medieval lanes and tenements. And it was only in the years immediately preceding the 1789 Revolution that any attempt was made to clean it up. A further source of pestilential infection was removed with the emptying of the overcrowded 800-year-old cemeteries into the catacombs.

In 1786, Paris received its penultimate ring of fortifications, the so-called wall of the Fermiers Généraux, with 57 *barrières* or toll gates (one of which survives in the middle of place Stalingrad), where a tax was levied on all goods entering the city.

The 1789 Revolution

The immediate cause of the **Revolution** of 1789 was a campaign by the clergy and nobility to protect their status – especially their exemption from taxation – from erosion by the royal government. The revolutionary movement, however, was quickly taken over by the middle classes, essentially the provincial bourgeoisie, relatively well off but politically underprivileged. They comprised the majority of the representatives of the **Third Estate**, the "order" that encompassed the whole of French society after the clergy, who formed the First Estate, and the nobility who formed the Second. It was the middle classes who took the initiative in setting up the **National Assembly** on June 17, 1789. The majority would probably have been content with constitutional reforms that checked monarchical power, as on the English model. But their power depended largely on their ability to wield the threat of a Parisian popular uprising.

Although the effects of the Revolution were felt all over France, it was in Paris that the most profound changes took place. Being as it were on the spot, the people of Paris couldn't avoid being caught up in the Revolution. They formed the revolutionary shock troops, the driving force at the crucial stages of the Revolution. Parisians marched on Versailles and forced the king to return to Paris with them. They stormed and destroyed the Bastille prison on July 14, 1789. They occupied the Hôtel de Ville, set up an insurrectionary Commune and captured the Tuileries palace on August 10, 1792. They invaded the Convention in May

1793 and secured the arrest of the more conservative Girondin faction of deputies.

Where the bourgeois deputies of the Convention were concerned principally with political reform, the poorest people, the *sans-culottes* – literally, the people without breeches – expressed their demands in economic terms: price controls, regulation of the city's food supplies, and so on. In so doing they foreshadowed the rise of the working-class and socialist movements of the nineteenth century.

Napoleon – and the barricades

Napoleon's chief legacy to France was a very centralized, authoritarian and efficient **bureaucracy** that put Paris in firm control of the rest of the country. For the rest of the nineteenth century after his demise, France was left to fight out, literally in the streets, the contradictions and unfinished business left behind by the Revolution of 1789.

On the one hand, there was a tussle between the class that had risen to wealth and power as a direct result of the destruction of the monarchy and the old order, and the survivors of the old order, who sought to make a comeback in the 1820s under the restored monarchy of **Louis XVIII** and **Charles X**. This conflict was finally resolved in favour of the new bourgeoisie. When Charles X refused to accept the result of the 1830 National Assembly elections, Adolphe Thiers – who was to become the veteran conservative politician of the nineteenth century – led the opposition in revolt. Barricades were erected in Paris and there followed three days of bitter street fighting, known as **les trois glorieuses**, in which 1800 people were killed (they are commemorated by the column on place de la Bastille). The outcome was the election of **Louis-Philippe** as constitutional monarch, and the introduction of a few liberalizing reforms, most either cosmetic or serving merely to consolidate the power of the wealthiest stratum of the population. Radical republican and working-class interests remained completely unrepresented.

The other, and more important, major political conflict was the extended struggle between this enfranchised and privileged bourgeoisie and the heirs of the 1789 *sans-culottes*, whose political consciousness had been awakened by the Revolution but whose demands remained unsatisfied. These were the people who died on the barricades of July to hoist the bourgeoisie firmly into the saddle.

As their demands continued to go unheeded, so their radicalism increased, exacerbated by deteriorating living and working conditions in the large towns, especially Paris, as the Industrial Revolution got underway. There were, for example, twenty thousand deaths from cholera in Paris in 1832, and 65 percent of the population in 1848 were too poor to be liable for tax. Eruptions of discontent invariably occurred in the capital, with insurrections in 1832 and 1834. In the absence of organized parties, opposition centred on newspapers and clandestine or informal political clubs in the tradition of 1789.

In the 1840s, the publication of the first socialist works such as Louis Blanc's *Organization of Labour* and Proudhon's *What is Property?* gave an additional spur to the impatience of the opposition. When the lid blew off the pot in **1848** and the **Second Republic** was proclaimed in Paris, it looked for a time as if working-class demands might be at least partly met. The provisional government included Louis Blanc and a Parisian manual worker. But in the face of demands for the control of industry, the setting up of co-operatives and so on, backed by agitation in the streets, the more conservative Republicans lost their nerve. The nation returned a spanking reactionary majority in the April elections.

Revolution began to appear the only possible defence for the radical left. On June 23, 1848, **working-class Paris** –

Poissonnière, Temple, St-Antoine, the Marais, Quartier Latin, Montmartre – rose in **revolt**. Men, women and children fought side by side against fifty thousand troops. In three days of fighting, nine hundred soldiers were killed. No-one knows how many of the *insurgés* – the insurgents – died. Fifteen thousand people were arrested and four thousand sentenced to prison terms.

Despite the shock and devastation of civil war in the streets of the capital, the ruling classes failed to heed the warning in the events of June 1848. Far from redressing the injustices which had provoked them, they proceeded to exacerbate them. The Republic was brought to an end in a coup d'état by **Louis Napoleon**, who within twelve months had himself crowned Emperor Napoleon III.

Expansion and the changing face of the city

There followed a period of **foreign acquisitions** on every continent and of **laissez-faire capitalism** at home, both of which greatly increased the economic wealth of France, then lagging far behind Britain in the industrialization stakes. Foreign trade trebled, a huge expansion of the rail network was carried out, investment banks were set up, and so forth. The rewards, however, were very unevenly distributed, and the regime relied unashamedly on repressive measures to hold the underdogs in check.

The response was entirely predictable. Opposition became steadily more organized and determined. In 1864, under the influence of Karl Marx in London, a French branch of the International was established in Paris and the youthful trade union movement gathered its forces in a federation. In 1869, the far from socialist Gambetta, briefly deputy for Belleville, declared, "Our generation's mission is to complete the French Revolution."

During these nearly twenty years of the Second Empire, **Baron Haussmann**, appointed Prefect of the Seine department with responsibility for Paris by Napoleon III, undertook the total transformation of the city. In love with the straight line and grand vista, he drove 135km of broad new streets through the cramped quarters of the medieval city, linking the interior and exterior boulevards, and creating north–south, east–west cross-routes. His taste dictated the uniform grey stone façades, mansard roofs and six to seven storeys that are still the architectural hallmark of the Paris street today.

The scale of demolition entailed by such massive redevelopment brought the direst social consequences. The city boundaries were extended to the 1840 fortifications where the boulevard périphérique now runs. The prosperous classes moved into the new western arrondissements, leaving the decaying older properties to the poor. These were divided and subdivided into ever smaller units as landlords sought to maximize their rents. Migrant workers from the provinces, sucked into the city to supply the vast labour requirements, crammed into the old villages of Belleville and Ménilmontant. Cholera and TB were rife, sanitation non-existent, and refuse was thrown into the streets.

Far from being concerned with Parisians' welfare, Haussmann's scheme was at least in part designed to keep the workers under control. Barracks were located at strategic points like the place du Château-d'Eau, now République, controlling the turbulent eastern districts, and the broad boulevards were intended to facilitate troop movements and artillery fire. A section of the Canal St-Martin north of the Bastille was covered over for the same reason.

The Siege of Paris and the Commune

In September 1870, Napoleon III surrendered to Bismarck at the border town of Sedan, less than two months after France had declared war on the well-prepared and superior forces of the **Prussian** state. The humiliation was enough for a Republican government to be instantly proclaimed in Paris. The Prussians advanced and by September 19 were laying **siege** to the capital. Gambetta was flown out by hot-air balloon to rally the provincial troops, but the country was defeated and liaison with Paris almost impossible. Further balloon messengers ended up in Norway or the Atlantic; the few attempts at military sorties from Paris turned into yet more blundering failures. At the same time, the peculiar conditions of a city besieged gave a greater freedom to collective discussion and dissent.

The government's half-hearted defence of the city – more afraid of revolution within than of the Prussians – angered Parisians, who clamoured for the creation of a 1789-style Commune. The Prussians meanwhile were demanding a proper government to negotiate with. In January 1871, those in power agreed to hold elections for a new national assembly with the authority to surrender officially to the Prussians. A large monarchist majority, with Thiers at its head, was returned.

On March 1, Prussian troops marched down the Champs-Élysées and garrisoned the city for three days while the populace remained behind closed doors in silent protest. On March 18, amid growing resentment from all classes of Parisians, Thiers' attempt to take possession of the National Guard's artillery in Montmartre set the barrel alight. The Commune was proclaimed from the Hôtel de Ville and Paris was promptly subjected to a second siege by Thiers' government, which had fled to Versailles, followed by all the remaining Parisian bourgeoisie.

The **Commune** lasted 72 days – a festival of the oppressed, Lenin called it. Socialist in inspiration, it had no time to implement lasting reforms. Wholly occupied with defence against Thiers' army, it succumbed finally on May 28, 1871, after a week of street-by-street fighting, in which three thousand Parisians died on the barricades and another twenty to twenty-five thousand men, women and children were killed in random revenge shootings by government troops. Thiers could declare with satisfaction – or so he thought – "Socialism is finished for a long time."

The Belle Époque

Physical recovery was remarkably quick. Within six or seven years few signs of the fighting remained. Visitors remarked admiringly on the teeming streets, the expensive shops and energetic nightlife. Charles Garnier's Opéra was opened in 1875. Aptly described as the "triumph of moulded pastry", it was a suitable image of the frivolity and materialism of the so-called naughty Eighties and Nineties. In 1889, the **Eiffel Tower** stole the show at the great Exposition. For the 1900 repeat, the **Métropolitain** (métro) – or Nécropolitain, as it was dubbed by one wit – was unveiled.

The lasting social consequence of the Commune was the confirmation of the them-and-us divide between bourgeoisie and working class. Any stance other than a revolutionary one after the Commune appeared not only feeble, but also a betrayal of the dead. In the years up to World War I, none of the contradictions had been resolved and the parties began to polarize. The trade union movement unified in 1895 to form the **Confédération Générale du Travail** (CGT), and in 1905 Jean Jaurès and Jules Guesde founded the **Parti Socialiste** (also known as the SFIO). On the extreme right, fascism began to make its ugly appearance with Maurras' proto-Brownshirt organization, the Camelots du Roi, which inaugurated another French tradition – of violence and thuggery on the far Right.

Yet despite – or maybe in some way because of – these tensions and contradictions, Paris provided the supremely inspiring environment for a concentration of **artists and** writers – the so-called **Bohemians**, both French and foreign – such as Western culture had rarely seen before. Impressionism, Fauvism and Cubism were all born in Paris in this period, while French poets like Apollinaire, Laforgue, Max Jacob, Blaise Cendrars and André Breton were preparing the way for Surrealism, concrete poetry and symbolism. Film, too, saw its first developments. After World War I, Paris remained the world's art centre, with an injection of foreign blood and a shift of venue from Montmartre to Montparnasse.

As **Depression** deepened in the 1930s and Nazi power across the Rhine became more menacing, fascist thuggery and anti-parliamentary activity increased in France, culminating in a pitched battle outside the Chamber of Deputies in February 1934. The effect of this fascist activism was to unite the Left, including the Communists, led by the Stalinist Maurice Thorez, in the **Popular Front**, who went on to win the 1936 elections with a handsome majority in the Chamber.

The German Occupation

During the **occupation of Paris** in World War II, the Germans found some sections of Parisian society, as well as the minions of the Vichy government, only too happy to hobnob with them. For four years the city suffered fascist rule with curfews, German garrisons and a Gestapo HQ. Parisian Jews were forced to wear the star of David and in 1942 were rounded up – by other Frenchmen – and shipped off to Auschwitz (see p.23).

The **Resistance** was very active in the city, gathering people of all political persuasions into its ranks, but with Communists and Socialists, especially of East European Jewish origin, well to the fore. The job of torturing them when they fell into Nazi hands – often as a result of betrayals – was left to their fellow citizens in the fascist militia.

Those who were condemned to death – rather than the concentration camps – were shot against the wall below the old fort of Mont Valérien above St-Cloud.

As Allied forces drew near to the city in 1944, the FFI (armed Resistance units), determined to play their part in driving the Germans out, called their troops onto the streets – some said, in a Leftist attempt to seize political power. To their credit, the Paris police also joined in, holding their Île de la Cité HQ for three days against German attacks. Liberation finally came on August 25, 1944.

Postwar Paris – one more try at revolution

Postwar Paris has remained no stranger to **political battles** in its streets. Violent demonstrations accompanied the Communist withdrawal from the coalition government in 1947. In the 1950s, the Left took to the streets again in protest against the colonial wars in Indochina and Algeria. And, in 1961, in one of the most shameful episodes in modern French history, some two hundred Algerians were killed by the police during a civil rights demonstration.

This "**secret massacre**", which remained covered by a veil of total official silence until the 1990s, took place during the Algerian war. It began with a peaceful demonstration against a curfew on North Africans imposed by de Gaulle's government in an attempt to inhibit FLN resistance activity in the French capital. Whether the police were acting on higher orders or merely on the authority of their own commanders is not clear, but, according to hundreds of eyewitness accounts, including some from horrified policemen, the police opened fire on the protesters, clubbing people and throwing them into the Seine to drown. For weeks afterwards the French media remained silent, in part through censorship, in part perhaps unable to comprehend that such events had happened in their own capital.

The state attempted censorship again during the events of
May 1968, though with rather less success. Throughout
this extraordinary month, a radical, libertarian, Leftist
movement spread from the Paris universities to factories
across the country, producing a general strike by nine million workers. This general dissatisfaction with society, big
business and institutionalized oppression sparked a growing
Women's Movement and political interest in civil rights.

Elections were called in June to return the Right to
power. The occupied buildings emptied and the barricades
in the Latin Quarter came down. For those who thought
they were experiencing the Revolution, the defeat was cat-
astrophic. But French institutions and French society did
change, shaken and loosened by the events of May 1968.
Most importantly, it opened up the debate of a new road to
socialism, one in which no old models would give all the
answers.

The Mitterrand era, 1981–95

The **Socialists'** first government after 23 years in opposition included four Communist ministers: an alliance reflected in the government commitments to expanded state control of industry, reduction of the hours in the working
week, high taxation for the rich, support for liberation
struggles around the world, and a public spending programme to raise the living standards of the least well-off. By
1984, however, the government had done a complete volte-
face, with Laurent Fabius presiding over a cabinet of cen-
trist to conservative "Socialist" ministers, clinging desper-
ately to power.

The government's commitments had come to little.
Attempts to bring private education under state control
were defeated by mass protests in the streets; ministers were
implicated in cover-ups and corruption; and unemployment continued to rise. Any idea of peaceful and pro-eco-

logical intent was dashed, as far as international opinion was concerned, by the French Secret Service's murder of a Greenpeace photographer on the Rainbow Warrior in New Zealand.

There were sporadic achievements – in labour laws and women's rights, notably – but no cohesive and consistent Socialist line. The Socialists' 1986 election slogan was "Help – the Right is coming back", a bizarrely self-fulfilling tactic. The right-wing **Jacques Chirac** became Prime Minister (and continued as Mayor of Paris).

Throughout 1987, the chances of François Mitterrand winning the presidential election in 1988 seemed very slim. But Chirac's economic policies of privatization and monetary control failed to deliver the goods. Millions of first-time investors in "popular capitalism" lost all their money on Black Monday. Terrorists planted bombs in Paris and took French hostages in Lebanon. Unemployment steadily rose and Chirac made the fatal mistake of flirting with the extreme Right, particularly Le Pen. **Mitterrand**, the grand old man of politics, with decades of experience, played off all the groupings of the Right in an all-but-flawless campaign, and won a second mandate.

His party, however, failed to win an absolute majority in the parliamentary elections soon afterwards. The austerity measures of Mitterrand's new prime minister, **Michel Rocard**, upset traditional Socialist supporters in the public-service sector, with nurses, civil servants, teachers and the like quick to take industrial action. Though Chirac's programmes were halted, they were not reversed.

In 1991, Mitterrand sacked Michel Rocard and appointed **Édith Cresson** as Prime Minister. Initially the French were happy to have their first woman prime minister, but she soon began to turn a few heads with her comments about special charters for illegal immigrants, her dismissal of the stock exchange as a waste of time, and attacks on her own ministers, not to mention her description of the Japanese as yellow ants and British males as homosexual.

Cresson's worst move was to propose a tax on everyone's insurance contributions to pay for compensation to haemophiliacs infected with HIV. The knowing use of infected blood in transfusions in 1985 became one of the biggest scandals of the Socialist regime.

Pierre Bérégovoy succeeded Cresson in 1992. Universally known as Béré, and mocked for his bumbling persona, he survived strikes by farmers, dockers, car workers and nurses, various scandals involving the Socialists, and the Maastricht referendum. But then a private loan was revealed from one Roger-Patrice Pelat, a friend of Mitterrand's, accused of insider dealing. Mitterrand distanced himself from his prime minister, who then shot himself, on May 1, two months after losing the elections, leaving no note of explanation.

The new prime minister, **Edouard Balladur**, a fresh and fatherly face from the Right, started off with a lot of popular support. But a series of U-turns after demonstrations by Air France workers, teachers, farmers, fishermen and school pupils, and the state's rescue of the Crédit Lyonnais bank after spectacular losses, wiped away his successes.

Meanwhile Mitterrand tottered on to the end of his presidential term, looking less and less like the nation's favourite uncle. Two months after Bérégovoy's suicide, Réné Bousquet, who was head of police in the Vichy government and due to stand trial for supervising the rounding up of Jews in 1942, was murdered. He was a friend of Mitterrand's and thought to have known shady secrets about the president.

François Mitterrand's presidency came to an end in April 1995 when he died following a battle with cancer. The last years of his presidency saw him becoming ill and aged, his reputation tarnished and his party's popularity reduced to an all-time low. But on his death in January 1996, despite everything, Mitterrand was genuinely mourned as a man of culture and vision, a supreme political operator, with unwavering commitment to the European Union, and for the mark he made on the city with his "grands projets": Parc de la Villette (inherited from Giscard), the Louvre Pyramid, the Grande Arche de la Défense, the Institut du Monde Arabe, the Opéra Bastille and the new Bibliothèque Nationale building.

Modern developments of the city

Until World War II, Paris remained pretty much as Haussmann had left it. Housing conditions showed little sign of improvement. There was even an outbreak of bubonic plague in Clignancourt in 1921. In 1925, a third of the houses still had no sewage connection. Migration to the suburbs continued, with the creation of **shantytowns** to supplement the hopelessly inadequate housing stock. After World War II, these became the exclusive territory of **Algerian** and other **North African immigrants**. In 1966, there were 89 of them, housing 40,000 immigrant workers and their families.

Only in the last thirty-odd years have the authorities begun to grapple with the housing problem, though not by expanding possibilities within Paris, but by siphoning huge numbers of people into a ring of **satellite towns** encircling the greater Paris region.

In Paris proper this same period has seen the final breaking of the mould of Haussmann's influence. Intervening architectural fashions, like Art Nouveau, Le Corbusier's International style and the Neoclassicism of the 1930s, had little more than localized cosmetic effects. It was devotion to the needs of the motorist – a cause unhesitatingly espoused by Pompidou – and the development of the high-rise tower that finally did the trick, starting with the **Tour**

Maine–Montparnasse and **La Défense**, the redevelopment of the 13e and, in the 1970s, projects like the **Pompidou Centre**, the **Front de Seine** and **Les Halles**. In recent years, new colossal public buildings in myriad conflicting styles have been inaugurated at an ever more astounding rate.

When the Les Halles flower and veg market was dismantled, a sign posted during its redevelopment lamented, "The centre of Paris will be beautiful. Luxury will be king. But we will not be here." Indeed, the city's social mix has changed more in twenty-five years than in the previous one hundred. Gentrification of the remaining working-class districts has accelerated, and the population has become essentially middle-class and white-collar.

The political present

Mitterrand's avuncular fourteen-year presidency was well calculated and a hard act to follow, but general unease demanded a change of direction.

Lionel Jospin, the uncharismatic former education minister, performed remarkably well in the election, topping the poll in the first round – in which right-wing votes were split between Balladur, Chirac, the extreme-right Le Pen and the anti-European Philippe de Villiers. In the second round run-off, Chirac stole the Left's clothes by placing **unemployment** and **social exclusion** at the top of the political agenda, and heaped promises of better times on every section of the electorate. He won, by a small margin, and was inaugurated as the new president of France in May 1995.

Chirac's presidency

Mitterrand had predicted that **Jacques Chirac** as president would become the laughing stock of the world. But it was international condemnation rather than derision that greeted the first significant act of his presidency, the decision to resume **nuclear testing** on the Pacific island of Muroroa. A typically Gaullist move, it provoked boycotts of French produce and a revival of the French peace and environmental movements.

Chirac's new prime minister, replacing Balladur who had treacherously stood against Chirac in the presidentials, was **Alain Juppé**, a clever, clinical technocrat to whom the French could not warm easily. It was down to him to square the circle of Chirac's election pledges of job creation, maintaining the value of pensions and welfare benefits and reducing the number of homeless, with tax cuts, a continuing strong franc and a reduction in the budget deficit to stay on course for monetary union.

Juppé was in trouble right from the start owing to allegations of corruption concerning his luxury flat in Paris. A summer of bomb attacks by Islamic fundamentalists diminished public confidence in the government as guardians of law and order. By October, Juppé had broken all records for prime ministerial unpopularity.

But that was nothing compared to the **1995 winter strikes**, when suddenly, and en masse, the French decided they had had enough of arrogant, elitist politicians, their false election promises and the austerity measures demanded by a free-market approach to European union. Students, teachers and nurses, workers in the transport, energy, post and telecommunications industries, bank clerks and civil servants – all took to the streets with the strong support of private sector employees struggling to get to work. Even the police showed sympathy to the strikers.

With five million people out over a period of 24 days, it was the strongest show of protest in France since May 1968. The mood this time, however, was not joyful liberation but anxiety about unemployment and social welfare, and disillusionment with politicians of all parties.

THE POLITICAL PRESENT

Amazingly, Juppé survived this "winter of discontent", abandoning some proposals, but only delaying others. In the end however, Juppé's policies did little to endear him to most French voters who gave his party their worst showing in thirty years in the first-round parliamentary elections of 1997, thus prompting him to resign.

The current Socialist government, and **Jospin** in particular, has never been so popular. The economy is strong and unemployment has gone down, albeit very little, for the first time in years. In late 1999, the government created 350,000 jobs for people under 25 in the public sector and reduced the number of hours in the working week from 39 to 35. While neither of these measures made much economic sense and were met with scepticism, and, in the case of workers happy to trim hours but not paycheques, anger, their success has lifted national spirits and eased the public's sense of despair stemming from the financially disastrous Nineties.

Contented workers evidently make for lusty spenders and the French have been fuelling their own economy through consumption and investment, particularly in stock offerings of the traditionally state-owned companies that have broken up and gone private. The government's other major priority is education, with plans for the biggest shake-up from primary school to university on the drawing-board.

The town hall scandals

The first of the **town hall scandals** broke in 1994, when it was revealed that Chirac, then mayor of Paris, was renting – at half the going rate – an apartment in the 7^e belonging to an obscure civic trust controlled by the Mairie.

Once the wall of secrecy began to crack, it wasn't long before it began to crumble. Chirac is currently under investigation for misuse of funds while mayor. His successor, Jean Tiberi, the current mayor of Paris, is also under investigation for alleged influence peddling. In addition, both men face charges of electoral fraud involving the registration of fake voters. Juppé remains under a cloud of suspicion because of his dealings in the early 1990s.

The atmosphere around city hall is so charged that in November 1999 Finance Minister Dominique Strauss-Kahn resigned, much to everyone's shock and dismay, amid accusations of forgery and stealing money from a student health insurance group, thus marking the beginning of the end of the ability of French politicians to grant themselves immunity from accountability and criminal prosecution.

In the past, politicians feathering their own nests never roused much public anger. But times have changed. People are disgusted at seeing the "elites" profiting from subsidized housing while hundreds of thousands are homeless. Even the normally obsequious right-wing press have been asking questions about the judiciary's independence. Despite Chirac's promises to uphold this independence in his election manifesto, he has kept his mouth shut throughout the affairs, and the scandal typifies the increasing gap between governors and the governed. While unemployment (around 13 percent), traffic congestion, pollution, immigration, racial tensions and quality of life remain high on the list of concerns in the 2001 mayoral elections, they are all overshadowed by that of rooting corruption out of city hall, and campaign slogans like "Emancipate Paris" are already being tossed around.

Books

An extraordinary number of **books** have been written about Paris and all things Parisian. In the selection below, publishers are detailed in the form of British publisher/American publisher. Where books are published in one country only, UK or US follows the publisher's name. The abbreviation "o/p" means "out of print".

History

Richard Cobb, *The French and their Revolution* (John Murray, UK). A selection of expert essays on the French Revolution, with a personal touch.

Alfred Cobban, *A History of Modern France* (3 vols: 1715–99, 1799–1871 and 1871–1962; Penguin/Viking). Complete and very readable account of the main political, social and economic strands in French – and inevitably Parisian – history.

Norman Hampson, *A Social History of the French Revolution* (Routledge). An analysis that concentrates on the personalities involved. Its particular interest lies in the attention it gives to the *sans-culottes*, the ordinary poor of Paris.

Christopher Hibbert, *The French Revolution* (Penguin, UK). Good, concise popular history of the period and events. *Days of the French Revolution*

(Quill, US) is a compelling account of the details, complexities, personalities, and events surrounding the French Revolution.

Alistair Horne, *How Far from Austerlitz* (Macmillan/Griffin). An excellent, modern history of Napoleon, catching him at his zenith and recounting his subsequent demise.

Colin Jones, *The Cambridge Illustrated History of France* (Cambridge UP). A political and social history of France from prehistoric times to the mid-1990s, concentrating on issues of regionalism, gender, race and class. Good illustrations and a friendly, non-academic writing style.

Lissagaray, *Paris Commune* (o/p). A highly personal and partisan account of the politics and fighting by a participant. Although Lissagaray himself is reticent about it, history has it that the last solitary Communard on the last barricade – in the rue Ramponneau in Belleville – was in fact himself.

Karl Marx, *Surveys from Exile* (Penguin); *On the Paris Commune* (Pathfinder, US). *Surveys* includes Marx's speeches and articles at the time of the 1848 Revolution and after, including an analysis, riddled with jokes, of Napoleon III's rise to power. *Paris Commune* – more rousing prose – has a history of the Commune by Engels.

Robert Rowell Palmer, *Twelve Who Ruled* (Princeton UP). Another account of the French Revolution, so readable it is almost entertaining.

Angelo Quattrocchi, *Beginning of the End: France, May 1968* (Verso Books). First-hand account of the disobedience of students that sparked the riots of factory workers and finally revolution, from the pen of an Italian journalist stationed in Paris to cover the events as they unfolded.

Paul Webster, *Pétain's Crime: The Full Story of French Collaboration in the Holocaust* (Papermac/Ivan R. Dee). The fascinating and alarming story of the Vichy regime's more than willing collaboration with the German authorities' campaign to imple-

HISTORY

347

ment the "final solution" in occupied France, and the bravery of those, especially the Communist resistance, who attempted to prevent it. A mass of hitherto unpublished evidence.

Theodore Zeldin, *A History of French Passions, 1848–1945* (2 paperback vols; Oxford UP). French history tackled by theme, such as intellect and taste – a good read.

Society, culture and politics

John Ardagh, *France Today* (Penguin). Comprehensive journalistic overview, covering food, film, education and holidays as well as politics and education. Good on detail about the urban suburbs and the shift there from the centre of Paris.

Roland Barthes, *Mythologies and Selected Writings* (both Vintage/Noonday). The first, though dated, is a classic: a brilliant description of how the ideas, prejudices and contradictions of French thought and behaviour manifest themselves, in food, wine, cars, travel guides and other cultural offerings. Barthes' piece on the Eiffel Tower doesn't appear, but it's included in the *Selected Writings*, published in the US by Noonday as *A Barthes Reader* (ed Susan Sontag).

Simone de Beauvoir, *The Second Sex* (Vintage). One of the prime texts of Western feminism, written in 1949, covering women's inferior status in history, literature, mythology, psychoanalysis, philosophy and everyday life.

Denis Belloc, *Slow Death in Paris* (Quartet, UK). A harrowing account of a heroin addict in Paris. Not recommended holiday reading, but if you want to know about the seamy underbelly of the city, this is the book.

James Campbell, *Paris Interzone* (Minerva, UK). The feuds, passions and destructive lifestyles of the Left Bank writers of 1946–60 are evoked here. The cast includes Richard Wright, James Baldwin, Samuel Beckett, Boris Vian, Alexander Trocchi, Eugene Ionesco, Sartre, de Beauvoir, Nabokov and Allan Ginsberg.

Richard Cobb, *Paris and Elsewhere* (ed David Gilmour; John Murray, UK). Selected writings by the acclaimed historian of the 1789 Revolution reveal his unique encounter with the French.

Robert Cole, *A Traveller's History of Paris* (Windrush Press/Interlink). This brief history of the city from the first Celtic settlement to today is an ideal starting point for those wishing to delve into the historical archives.

Christopher Flood and Laurence Bell (eds), *Political Ideologies in Contemporary France* (Pinter/Cassell). Beginners' guide to the current political trends in France.

Gisèle Halim, *Milk for the Orange Tree* (Quartet). Born in Tunisia, daughter of an Orthodox Jewish family, Halim ran away to Paris to become a lawyer defending women's rights, Algerian FLN fighters and all unpopular causes. A gutsy autobiographical story.

Tahar Ben Jelloun, *Racism Explained to my Daughter* (New Press). An honest and straight-forward account of the racial tensions in France as seen through the eyes of its Moroccan-born author. An international best-seller.

Peter Lennon, *Foreign Correspondents: Paris in the Sixties* (Picador/McClelland & Stewart). Irish journalist Peter Lennon went to Paris in the early 1960s unable to speak a word of French. He became a close friend of Samuel Beckett and was a witness to the May 1968 events.

François Maspero, *Roissy Express* (Blackwell/W. W. Norton & Co.) with photographs by Anaïk Frantz. A "travel book" along the RER line B from Roissy to St-Rémy-lès-Chevreuse (excluding the Paris stops). Brilliant insights into the life of the Paris suburbs, and fascinating digressions into French history and politics.

Andrea Kupfer Schneider, *Creating the Musée d'Orsay: The Politics of Culture in France* (Pennsylvania State UP). Interesting and sometimes amusing account of the strug-gles involved in transforming

SOCIETY, CULTURE AND POLITICS

349

the Gare d'Orsay into one of Paris's most visited museums. An original insight, revealing French attitudes towards such grand cultural projects.

Tyler Stovall, *Paris Noir: African Americans in the City of Light* (Marnier/Houghton Mifflin). A well-researched and vivid account of the flight of African–American artists in the 1920s from a segregated and racist America to a welcoming Paris.

Tad Szulc, *Chopin in Paris: The Life and Times of the Romantic Composer* (Da Capo). While musicologists may be disappointed by the lack of discussion of the works that made Chopin famous, others will revel in this exploration of his relationship with his friends – Balzac, Hugo, Liszt among them – and his lover, George Sand and their shared life in Paris.

William Wiser, *The Great Good Place* (o/p). An account of American expat women in Paris, from the Impressionist painter Mary Cassatt, through to writer Edith Wharton, publisher Caresse Crosby, the sad socialite novelist's wife Zelda Fitzgerald and finally the singer Josephine Baker.

Theodore Zeldin, *The French* (Harvill). A coffee-table book without the pictures, based on the author's conversations with a wide range of people, about money, sex, phobias, parents and everything else.

Art, architecture and photography

Brassaï, *Le Paris Secret des Années 30* (Gallimard, France). Extraordinary photos of the capital's nightlife in the 1930s – brothels, music halls, street cleaners, transvestites and the underworld – each one a work of art and a familiar world (now long since gone) to Brassaï and his mate, Henry Miller, who accompanied him on his nocturnal expeditions. This friendship with Miller is captured in his book *Henry Miller: the Paris Years* (Arcade; Timothy Bent, translator).

Robert Doisneau, *Three Seconds of Eternity* (Neues

Publishing Co.). The famous Kiss in front of the Hôtel de Ville takes the front cover, but there's more to Doisneau than this. A collection chosen by himself of photographs taken in France, but mainly Paris, in the 1940s and 50s. Beautifully nostalgic.

Norma Evenson, *Paris: A Century of Change, 1878–1978* (o/p). A large illustrated volume which makes the development of urban planning and the fabric of Paris an enthralling subject, mainly because the author's concern is always with people, not panoramas.

John James, *Chartres* (D. S. Brewer, UK). The story of Chartres cathedral, with insights into the medieval context, the character and attitudes of the masons, the symbolism, and the advanced mathematics of the building's geometry.

William Mahder (ed), *Paris Arts: The '80s Renaissance* (o/p), *Paris Creation: Une Renaissance* (o/p). Illustrated, magazine-style survey of French arts. The design and photos are reason enough in themselves to look it up.

Willy Ronis, *Belleville Ménilmontant* (o/p). Misty black-and-white photographs of people and streets in the two "villages" of eastern Paris in the 1940s and 50s.

Judy Rudoe, *Cartier: 1900–1939* (British Museum Press/Harry N. Abrams). Marvellous photos of the world-renowned Paris-based jeweller's creations including Art Deco necklaces, rings, bracelets and brooches, among other *objets d'art*.

Vivian Russell, *Monet's Garden* (Frances Lincoln/Stewart, Talson & Chang). An exceptional book illustrated with sumptuous colour photographs by the author, old photographs of the artist and reproductions of his paintings.

Edward Lucie-Smith, *Concise History of French Painting* (o/p). If you're after an art reference book, then this will do as well as any, though there are of course dozens of other books available on particular French artists and art movements.

Yves St-Laurent, *Forty Years of Creation* (Distributed Art

ART, ARCHITECTURE AND PHOTOGRAPHY

Publishers). Glossy pages of the best of Y-S-L's stylish fashion photography and creations.

Anthony Sutcliffe, *Paris – An Architectural History* (Yale UP). Excellent overview of Paris's changing cityscape, as dictated by fashion, social structure and political power.

Cookery

Linda Dannenberg, *Paris Bistro Cooking* (C. N. Potter). Poule au Pot and Rum Baba among other delicious French traditional dishes as cooked by some of Paris's best bistros.

Alain Ducasse, *Flavours of France* (Artisan) and *L'Atelier of Alain Ducasse: The Artistry of a Master Chef and His Protégés* (John Wiley & Sons). The charismatic culinary entrepreneur offers a tour of the gastronomy of France and some of the secrets of his successful kitchen, combining breezy prose with inspirational photos.

Nicolle Meyer & Amanda Smith, *Paris in a Basket: Markets: The Food and The*

People (Konemann). Would be little more than a glossy coffee table book if it didn't capture the sights, smells, anecdotes, and recipes of Paris's open-air markets with so much aplomb.

Patricia Wells, *Joël Robuchon – Cuisine Actuelle* (Macmillan, UK). Paris's most famous chef reveals some basic and some more advanced recipes from his restaurant.

Paris in literature

British/American

Shari Benstock, *Women of the Left Bank: Paris, 1900–1940* (Univ of Texas, US). Follows the lives and creativity of two dozen American, British and French women who moved to Paris and dared to be different.

Charles Dickens, *A Tale of Two Cities* (Penguin). Paris and London during the 1789 Revolution and before. The plot's pure Hollywood, but the streets and at least some of the social backdrop are for real.

Robert Ferguson, *Henry Miller* (o/p). Very readable biography of the old rogue and his rumbustious doings, including his long stint in Paris and affair with Anaïs Nin.

Noel Riley Fitch, *Sylvia Beach and the Lost Generation: A history of literary Paris in the Twenties and Thirties* (W. W. Norton). Founder of the original Shakespeare & Co. bookstore and publisher of James Joyce's *Ulysses*, Beach was the lightning rod of literary Paris. The work also follows her relationship with her companion, Adrienne Monnier, the documentation of which helps to place homosexuality in a larger historical context.

Brion Gysin, *The Last Museum* (o/p). The setting is the Hôtel Bardo, the Beat hotel: the co-residents are Kerouac, Ginsberg and Burroughs. Published posthumously, this is 1960s Paris in its most manic mode.

Ernest Hemingway, *A Moveable Feast* (Arrow/Touchstone). Hemingway's American-in-Paris account of life in the 1930s with Ezra Pound, F. Scott Fitzgerald, Gertrude Stein, etc. Dull, pedestrian stuff, despite its classic and best-seller status.

Jack Kerouac, *Satori in Paris* (Flamingo/Grove Press) . . . and in Brittany, too. Uniquely inconsequential Kerouac experiences.

Ian Littlewood, *Paris: A Literary Companion* (o/p). A thorough account of which literary figures went where, and what they had to say about it.

Herbert Lottman, *Colette: A Life* (Little, Brown & Co., UK). An interesting if somewhat dry account of this enigmatic Parisian writer's life.

Barry Miles, *The Beat Hotel: Ginsberg, Burroughs, and Corso in Paris, 1958–1963* (Grove Press). Follows the self-indulgent exploits of the residents of The Beat Hotel at 9 rue Git-le-Coeur on the Left Bank.

Christopher Miller, *Nationalists and Nomads: Essays on Francophone African Literature and Culture* (Chicago UP). An exploration of the intermingling

PARIS IN LITERATURE

353

issues of nationalism, colonialism and post-colonialism in Paris's ever-evolving literary landscape. Interesting topic, if somewhat overly academic prose.

Henry Miller, *Tropic of Cancer; Quiet Days in Clichy* (both Flamingo/Grove Press). Again 1930s Paris, though from a more focused angle – sex, essentially. Erratic, wild, self-obsessed writing, but with definite flights of genius.

Anaïs Nin, *The Journals 1931–1974* (7 vols) (Peter Owen/Harcourt Brace). A detailed literary narrative of French and US artists and fiction-makers from the first half of this century – not least, Nin herself – in Paris and elsewhere. The more famous *Erotica* was also written in Paris, for a local connoisseur of pornography.

George Orwell, *Down and Out in Paris and London* (Penguin/Harcourt Brace). Documentary account of breadline living in the 1930s – Orwell at his best.

Paul Rambali, *French Blues* (o/p). Movies, sex, down-and-outs, politics, fast food, bikers – a cynical, streetwise look at modern urban France.

Jean Rhys, *Quartet* (Penguin/Norton). A beautiful and evocative story of a lonely young woman's existence on the fringes of 1920s Montparnasse society.

French (in translation)

Paul Auster (ed), *The Random House Book of Twentieth Century French Poetry* (Random House). Bilingual anthology containing the major French poets of the twentieth century, most of whom were based in Paris. Includes Apollinaire, Cendrars, Aragon, Éluard and Prévert.

Honoré de Balzac, *Le Père Goriot* (Oxford UP). Cornerstone of his Comédie Humaine in which nineteenth-century Paris is the principal character.

Baudelaire's Paris, translated by Laurence Kitchen (Forest, UK). Gloom and doom by Baudelaire, Gérard de Nerval, Verlaine and Jiménez – in bilingual edition.

Calixthe Beyala, *The Little Prince of Belleville*, translated by Marjolijn De Jager (Heinemann). The tale of seven-year old Loukoum and his efforts to reconcile the hypocrisies and hard truths about his family and his adopted city. The harsh realities facing Paris's African immigrant communities are recounted with honest clarity.

André Breton, *Nadja* (Grove Press). A surrealist evocation of Paris. Fun.

Louis-Ferdinand Céline, *Death on Credit* (o/p). A landmark in twentieth-century French literature, along with his earlier *Voyage to the End of the Night*, (Calder/Cambridge UP). Céline recounts the delirium of the world as seen through the eyes of an adolescent in working-class Paris at the beginning of the twentieth century.

Blaise Cendrars, *To the End of the World* (Peter Owen/Dufour). An outrageous bawdy tale of a randy septuagenarian Parisian actress, having an affair with a deserter from the Foreign Legion.

Didier Daeninckx, *Murder in Memoriam* (Serpent's Tail). A thriller involving two murders: one of a Frenchman during the massacre of the Algerians in Paris in 1961, the other of his son twenty years later. The investigation by an honest detective lays bare dirty tricks, corruption, racism and the cover-up of the massacre.

Alexandre Dumas, *The Count of Monte Cristo* (Penguin). One hell of a good yarn, with Paris and Marseilles locations.

Gustave Flaubert, *Sentimental Education* (Oxford UP). A lively, detailed 1869 reconstruction of the life, manners, characters and politics of Parisians in the 1840s, including the 1848 Revolution.

Victor Hugo, *Les Misérables* (Penguin). A racy, eminently readable novel by the French equivalent of Dickens, about the Parisian poor and low life in the first half of the nineteenth century. Book Four contains an account of the barricade fighting during the 1832 insurrection.

PARIS IN LITERATURE

François Maspero, *Le Sourire du Chat* (translated as "Cat's Grin"; Penguin/New Amsterdam Books). Semi-autobiographical novel of the young teenager Luc in Paris during World War II, with his adored elder brother in the Resistance, his parents taken to concentration camps as Paris is liberated, and everyone else busily collaborating. An intensely moving and revealing account of the war period.

Guy de Maupassant, *Bel-Ami* (Penguin/Viking). Maupassant's chef-d'œuvre reveals the double standards of Paris during the Belle Époque with a keen observer's eye.

Daniel Pennac, *The Scapegoat and The Fairy Gunmother* (both Harvill). Finally, two of the series of four have been translated into English. Pennac has long been Paris's favourite contemporary writer, with his hilarious crime stories set among the chaos and colour of multi-ethnic Belleville.

Georges Pérec, *Life: A User's Manual* (Harvill/David R. Godine). An extraordinary literary jigsaw puzzle of life, past and present, human, animal and mineral, extracted from the residents of an imaginary apartment block in the 17e arrondissement of Paris.

Édith Piaf, *My Life* (Penguin, UK). Piaf's dramatic story told pretty much in her own words.

Marcel Proust, *Remembrance of Things Past* (Penguin). Written in and of Paris: absurdly long but bizarrely addictive.

Jean-Paul Sartre, *Roads to Freedom Trilogy* (Vintage). Metaphysics and gloom, despite the title.

Georges Simenon, *Maigret at the Crossroads* (Penguin/Harcourt Brace), or any other of the Maigret novels. Literary crime thrillers; the Montmartre and seedy criminal locations are unbeatable.

Michel Tournier, *The Golden Droplet* (Harper Collins, UK). A magical tale of a Saharan boy coming to Paris, where strange adventures, against the backdrop of immigrant life in the slums, overtake him because he never drops his desert oasis view of the world.

PARIS IN LITERATURE

Émile Zola, *Nana* (Penguin/Viking). The rise and fall of a courtesan in the decadent times of the Second Empire. Not bad on sex, but confused on sexual politics. A great story nevertheless, which brings mid-nineteenth-century Paris alive, direct, to present-day senses. Paris is also the setting for Zola's *L'Assommoir*, *L'Argent* and *Thérèse Raquin*.

PARIS IN LITERATURE

French and architectural terms: a glossary

These are either terms you'll come across in this book, or come up against on signs, maps, etc, while travelling around. For food items see p.190–193.

ABBAYE abbey

AMBULATORY covered passage around the outer edge of a choir of a church

APSE semicircular termination at the east end of a church

ARRONDISSEMENT district of the city

ASSEMBLÉE NATIONALE the French parliament

AUBERGE DE JEUNESSE (AJ) youth hostel

BAROQUE High Renaissance period of art and architecture, distinguished by extreme ornateness

BEAUX ARTS fine arts museum (and school)

CAR bus

CAROLINGIAN dynasty (and art, sculpture, etc) founded by Charlemagne, late eighth to early tenth centuries

CARREFOUR intersection

CFDT Socialist trade union

CGT Communist trade union

CHASSE, CHASSE GARDÉE hunting grounds

CHÂTEAU mansion, country house, castle

CHÂTEAU FORT castle

CHEMIN path

CHEVET end wall of a church

CIJ (Centre d'Informations Jeunesse) youth information centre

CLASSICAL architectural style incorporating Greek and Roman elements – pillars, domes, colonnades, etc – at its height

in France in the seventeenth century and revived in the nineteenth century as NEOCLASSICAL

CLERESTORY upper storey of a church, incorporating the windows

CODENE French CND

CONSIGNE luggage consignment

COURS combination of main square and main street

COUVENT convent, monastery

DÉFENSE DE . . . It is forbidden to . . .

DÉGUSTATION tasting (wine or food)

DÉPARTEMENT county (more or less)

ÉGLISE church

EN PANNE out of order

ENTRÉE entrance

FERMETURE closing period

FLAMBOYANT florid form of Gothic

FN (Front National) fascist party led by Jean-Marie Le Pen

BAROQUE–FN

359

FO Catholic trade union

FRESCO wall painting – durable through application to wet plaster

GALLO-ROMAIN period of Roman occupation of Gaul (first to fourth centuries AD)

GARE station

GARE ROUTIÈRE bus station

GARE SNCF train station

GOBELINS famous tapestry manufacturers, based in Paris; its most renowned period was during the reign of Louis XIV (seventeenth century)

GRANDE RANDONÉE (GR) long-distance footpath

HALLES covered market

HLM public housing development

HÔTEL a hotel, but also an aristocratic townhouse or mansion

HÔTEL DE VILLE town hall

JOURS FÉRIÉS public holidays

MAIRIE town hall

MARCHÉ market

MEROVINGIAN dynasty (and art, etc), ruling France and parts of Germany from the sixth to mid-eighth centuries

NARTHEX entrance hall of a church

NAVE main body of a church

PCF (Paris Communiste Français) Communist Party of France

PLACE square

PORTE gateway or door

POSTE post office

PS (Parti Socialiste) Socialist party

QUARTIER district of a town

RENAISSANCE art/architectural style developed in fifteenth-century Italy and imported to France in the early sixteenth century by François I

RETABLE altarpiece

REZ-DE-CHAUSSÉE (RC) ground floor

RN (Route Nationale) main road

ROMANESQUE early medieval architecture distinguished by squat, rounded forms and naive sculpture

RPR (Rassemblement pour la République) Gaullist party led by Philippe Seguin

SI (Syndicat d'Initiative) tourist information office; also known as OT, OTSI and Maison du Tourisme

SNCF (Société Nationale des Chemins de Fer) French railways

SOLDES sales

SORTIE exit

STUCCO plaster used to embellish ceilings, etc

TABAC bar or shop selling stamps, cigarettes, télécartes, etc

TOUR tower

TRANSEPT cross arms of a church

TYMPANUM sculpted panel above a church door

UDF centre-right party headed by François Bayrou

VAUBAN seventeenth-century military architect – his fortresses still stand all over France

VILLA a mews or a series of small residential streets, built as a unity

VOUSSOIR sculpted rings in an arch over a church door

ZONE BLEUE restricted parking zone

ZONE PIÉTONNE pedestrian zone

INDEX

INDEX

stay in touch

WALK-IN
BACKRUB

10 min.....£8.95

20 min...£15.75

rough news

Rough Guides' FREE
full-colour newsletter

News, travel issues, music reviews,
readers' letters and the latest
dispatches from authors on the road

**If you would like to receive
roughnews, please send us your
name and address:**

62-70 Shorts Gardens
London, WC2H 9AH, UK

4th Floor, 345 Hudson St,
New York NY10014, USA

newslettersubs@roughguides.co.uk

IF KNOWLEDGE IS POWER, THIS ROUGH GUIDE IS A POCKET-SIZED BATTERING RAM

Kansas City Star

£6.00
US$9.95

Written in plain English, with no hint of jargon, the Rough Guide to the Internet will make you an Internet guru in the shortest possible time. It cuts through the hype making other guides look like nerdy textbooks

ROUGH GUIDES ON THE WEB

Visit our brand new website www.roughguides.com for news about the latest books, online travel guides and updates.

AT ALL BOOKSTORES • DISTRIBUTED BY PENGUIN

around the world

Alaska ★ Algarve ★ Amsterdam ★ Andalucía ★ Antigua & Barbuda ★ Argentina ★ Auckland Restaurants ★ Australia ★ Austria ★ Bahamas ★ Bali & Lombok ★ Bangkok ★ Barbados ★ Barcelona ★ Beijing ★ Belgium & Luxembourg ★ Belize ★ Berlin ★ Big Island of Hawaii ★ Bolivia ★ Boston ★ Brazil ★ Britain ★ Brittany & Normandy ★ Bruges & Ghent ★ Brussels ★ Budapest ★ Bulgaria ★ California ★ Cambodia ★ Canada ★ Cape Town ★ The Caribbean ★ Central America ★ Chile ★ China ★ Copenhagen ★ Corsica ★ Costa Brava ★ Costa Rica ★ Crete ★ Croatia ★ Cuba ★ Cyprus ★ Czech & Slovak Republics ★ Devon & Cornwall ★ Dodecanese & East Aegean ★ Dominican Republic ★ The Dordogne & the Lot ★ Dublin ★ Ecuador ★ Edinburgh ★ Egypt ★ England ★ Europe ★ First-time Asia ★ First-time Europe ★ Florence ★ Florida ★ France ★ French Hotels & Restaurants ★ Gay & Lesbian Australia ★ Germany ★ Goa ★ Greece ★ Greek Islands ★ Guatemala ★ Hawaii ★ Holland ★ Hong Kong & Macau ★ Honolulu ★ Hungary ★ Ibiza & Formentera ★ Iceland ★ India ★ Indonesia ★ Ionian Islands ★ Ireland ★ Israel & the Palestinian Territories ★ Italy ★ Jamaica ★ Japan ★ Jerusalem ★ Jordan ★ Kenya ★ The Lake District ★ Languedoc & Roussillon ★ Laos ★ Las Vegas ★ Lisbon ★ London ★

in twenty years

also look out for our maps, phrasebooks, music guides and reference books

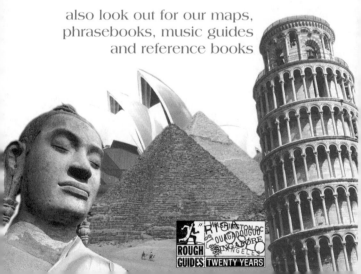

ROUGH GUIDES TWENTY YEARS

100
Essential
CDs

Eight titles,
one name

ROUGH
GUIDES

Drum 'n' bass • Hip-hop • House • Techno • Drum 'n' bass • Hip-hop • House • Techno • Drum 'n' bass •

Sorted

ROUGH
GUIDES

MUSIC ROUGH GUIDES ON CD

'Like the useful Rough Guide travel books and
television shows, these discs delve right into
the heart and soul of the region they explore'
– Rhythm Music (USA)

Available from book and record shops worldwide or order direct from
World Music Network, Unit 6, 88 Clapham Park Road, London SW4 7BX
tel: 020 7498 5252 • fax: 020 7498 5353 • email: post@worldmusic.net

Hear samples from over 50 Rough Guide CDs at
WWW.WORLDMUSIC.NET

Sandwich Jambon
sandwich Oeuf et de salade

Glace Fraise (à la Eiffel)
Le 6 Steak
Omelette Compagne
Cafe / Le Petit déjeuner à la Ashr.
Quiche Lorraine
Creme Vanille
Citron Tart au Citron
Italien - Pizze et Passe (Trughi)
        (vegetarien -
Le Petit déjeuner à la Ashr
tartine de Parisien (Jambon et Fromage)

The Eiffel Tower
Champs de Mars
le Shopping! Printemps, Gallenei
Layfette
Louvre et le Tuilleries
Musee d'Orsay
Champs Elysee + Arch de Triompe
Notre Dame x 2
Mnmatre et Sacreur Coeur
l'Ile de St louis
L'Ile de Cite
La Latine
St Germain
Place de la Concorde
Deportation
Paris Plage
La Moulin de la Galette

un ballen

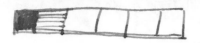

This is a very nice
pen — although me
car *gc v*

Jim's List of things to do :-
Eiffel Tower ✓
Louvre ●
                    Notre Dame.

musée d'Orsay.

Latin Quarter ✓
Montmartre - Sacaur Coeur
M

Visit us online
roughguides.com

Information on over 25,000 destinations around the world

- **Read** Rough Guides' trusted travel info
- **Share** journals, photos and travel advice with other readers
- Get exclusive Rough Guide **discounts** and travel **deals**
- Earn membership points every time you contribute to the
  Rough Guide **community** and get **free** books, flights and trips
- Browse thousands of CD reviews and artists in our **music** area

Will you have enough stories to tell your grandchildren?

©2000 Yahoo! Inc.

Yahoo! Travel

Do You Yahoo!?

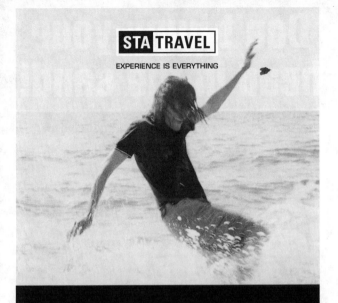

STA TRAVEL

EXPERIENCE IS EVERYTHING

300 BRANCHES WORLDWIDE

LOW COST FLIGHTS → ACCOMMODATION → INSURANCE → SKI
CAR HIRE → OVERLAND TRAVEL → ISIC/YOUTH CARDS
ROUND THE WORLD FLIGHTS → INTERNATIONAL TRAVEL HELP

For Bookings and Enquiries:
0870 160 6070

Find fares, check availability, enter competitions, book online
or find your local branch @

www.statravel.co.uk

STA TRAVEL LTD

Don't bury your head in the sand!

Take cover!

with Rough Guide Travel Insurance

**Worldwide
cover, for
Rough Guide
readers
worldwide**

UK Freefone **0800 015 09 06**
US Freefone **1 866 220 5588**
Worldwide **(+44) 1243 621 046**
Check the web at
www.roughguides.com/insurance

Insurance organized by Torribles Insurance Brokers Ltd, 21 Prince Street, Bristol, BS1 4PH, England

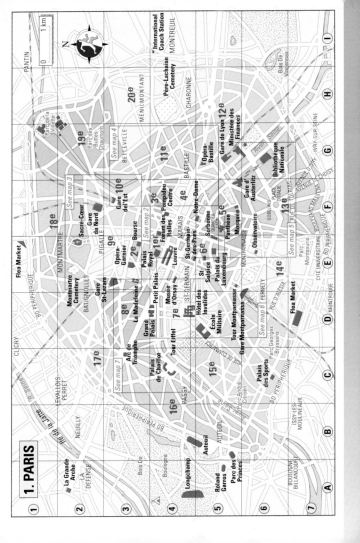

1. PARIS

LA DÉFENSE
La Grande Arche

Bois de Boulogne
Longchamp
Roland Garros
Parc des Princes

AUTEUIL

PASSY

16e

Arc de Triomphe
Palais de Chaillot
Tour Eiffel

17e

BATIGNOLLES

Montmartre Cemetery

8e
La Madeleine
Petit Palais
Grand Palais

7e
Hôtel des Invalides
Ecole Militaire

15e
Tour Montparnasse
Gare Montparnasse

Palais des Sports

Flea Market

18e
Sacré-Coeur
PIGALLE

9e
Opéra-Garnier
Gare St-Lazare

2e
Bourse
Palais Royal
Louvre
Musée d'Orsay

1er

ST-GERMAIN
St-Sulpice
Palais du Luxembourg

6e

14e

PERNETY
Flea Market

MONTROUGE

Gare du Nord

MARAIS

3e
Forum des Halles
Pompidou Centre

Notre-Dame
4e

St-Germain-des-Prés

5e
Sorbonne
Panthéon
Mosquée
Observatoire

MONTPARNASSE

GOBELINS

13e

Gare de l'Est

10e

BELLEVILLE

11e

Opéra-Bastille
BASTILLE

Gare de Lyon 12e
Ministère des Finances

Gare d'Austerlitz

Bibliothèque Nationale

19e
Parc de la Villette
Parc des Buttes-Chaumont

20e

MÉNILMONTANT

Père-Lachaise Cemetery

CHARONNE

International Coach Station
MONTREUIL

PANTIN

CLICHY
LEVALLOIS-PERRET
NEUILLY

ISSY-LES-MOULINEAUX

BOULOGNE-BILLANCOURT

N

0   1 km

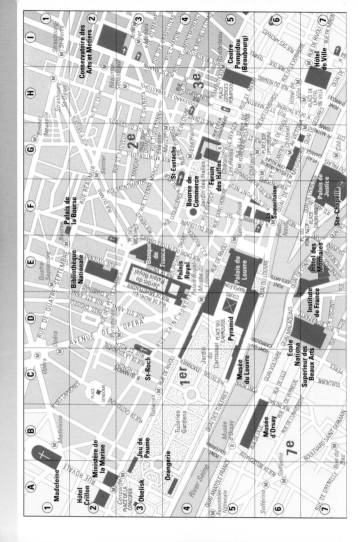

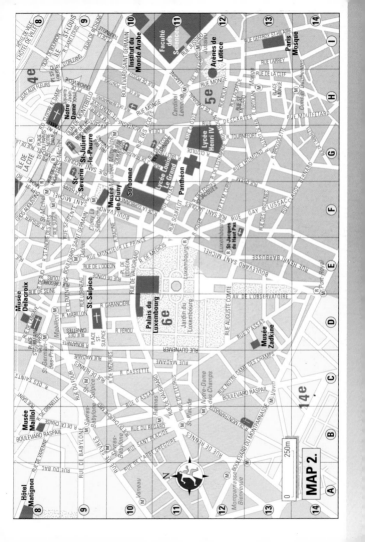

MAP 2.

0   250m

N

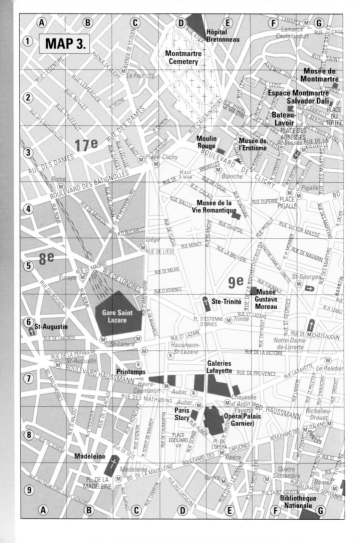

MAP 3.

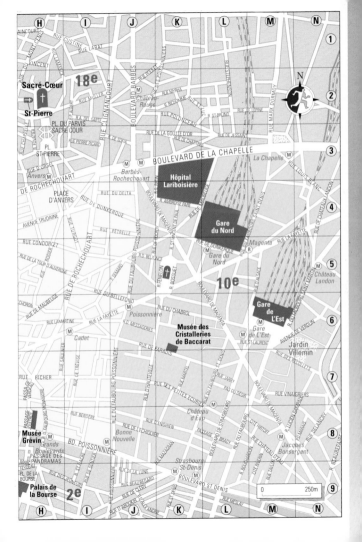

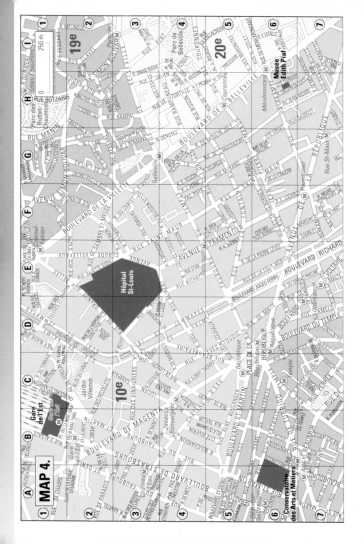

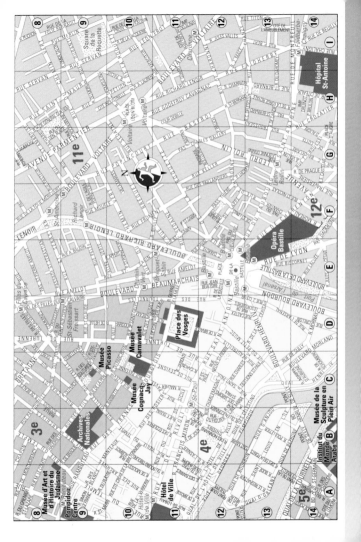

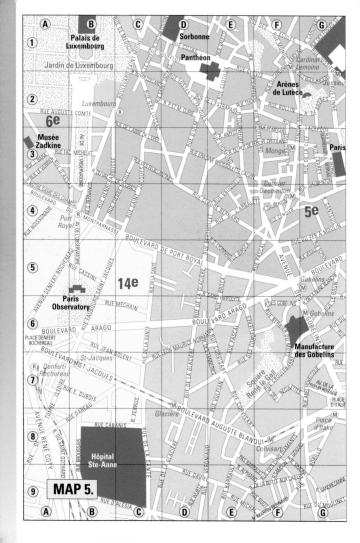

MAP 5.

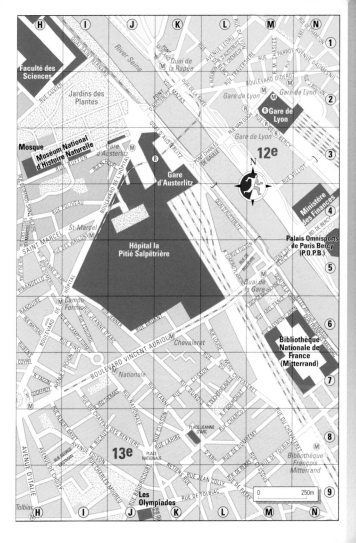

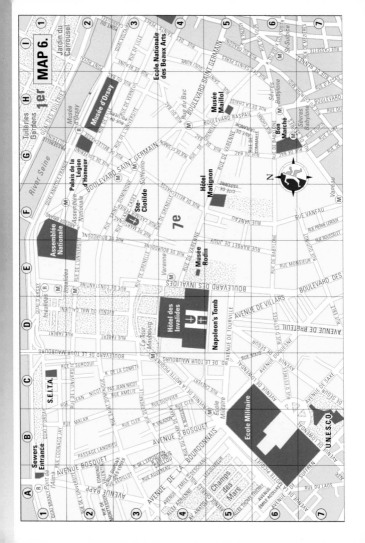

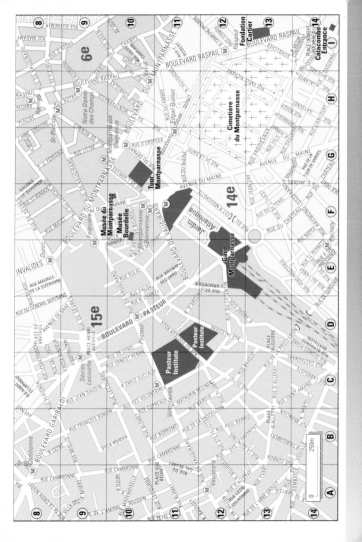

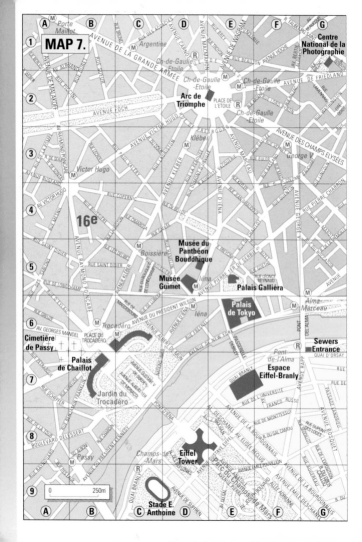

MAP 7.

16e

Porte Maillot

Argentine

AVENUE DE LA GRANDE ARMÉE

Ch-de-Gaulle -Etoile

Ch-de-Gaulle -Etoile

Arc de Triomphe

PLACE DE L'ETOILE

Ch-de-Gaulle -Etoile

Ch-de-Gaulle -Etoile

Centre National de la Photographie

AVENUE FOCH

AVENUE DE FRIEDLAND

AVENUE DES CHAMPS ELYSEES

George V

Victor Hugo

Kléber

Musée du Panthéon Bouddhique

Musée Guimet

Iéna

Boissière

Palais Galliéra

Palais de Tokyo

Iéna

Alma Marceau

Cimetière de Passy

AV. Georges Mandel

Trocadéro

PLACE DU TROCADÉRO

AVENUE DU PRÉSIDENT WILSON

Sewers Entrance

QUAI D'ORSAY

Palais de Chaillot

Pont de-l'Alma

Jardin du Trocadéro

Espace Eiffel-Branly

QUAI BRANLY

Champs-de-Mars

Passy

BOULEVARD DELESSERT

Eiffel Tower

Parc du Champs de Mars

0   250m

Stade E. Anthoine

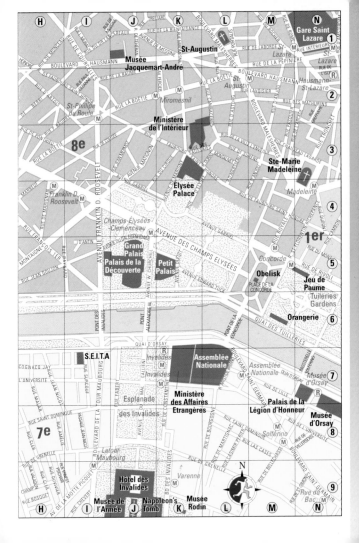

8. PARIS MÉTRO

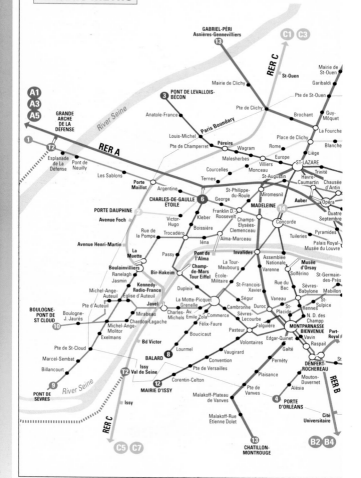